AFFIRMING DIVERGENCE
Deleuze's Reading of Leibniz

Alex Tissandier

EDINBURGH
University Press

Edinburgh University Press is one of the leading university presses in the UK. We publish academic books and journals in our selected subject areas across the humanities and social sciences, combining cutting-edge scholarship with high editorial and production values to produce academic works of lasting importance. For more information visit our website: edinburghuniversitypress.com

© Alex Tissandier, 2018

Edinburgh University Press Ltd
The Tun – Holyrood Road
12(2f) Jackson's Entry
Edinburgh EH8 8PJ

Typeset in Sabon by
Servis Filmsetting Ltd, Stockport, Cheshire

A CIP record for this book is available from the British Library

ISBN 978 1 4744 1774 7 (hardback)
ISBN 978 1 4744 1775 4 (webready PDF)
ISBN 978 1 4744 1776 1 (epub)

The right of Alex Tissandier to be identified as the author of this work has been asserted in accordance with the Copyright, Designs and Patents Act 1988, and the Copyright and Related Rights Regulations 2003 (SI No. 2498).

Contents

Acknowledgements	iv
List of Abbreviations	v
Introduction	1

Part I: *Expressionism in Philosophy: Spinoza*
1. Leibniz, Spinoza and the Anti-Cartesian Reaction — 13
2. Leibniz and Expression — 40

Part II: *Difference and Repetition* and *Logic of Sense*
3. Deleuze's Critique of Representation — 59
4. A Leibnizian World — 88

Part III: *The Fold*
5. Material Folds and the Lower Level of the Baroque House — 119
6. Spiritual Folds and the Upper Level of the Baroque House — 150

Conclusion: The New Discord	173
References	180
Index	184

Acknowledgements

This book is the result of postgraduate research at the University of Warwick. I am very grateful to have been immersed in the unique mix of Deleuzian ideas which animated the philosophy department throughout my time there. My thanks to Miguel de Beistegui, Keith Ansell-Pearson and Stephen Houlgate for making such an atmosphere possible.

My biggest thanks to my fellow researchers – especially Stephen Barrell, Benjamin Berger, Justin Laleh and Peter Wolfendale – for countless hours of intense discussion, shared confusion, and ambitious reading groups (a few of which even made it past the first chapter).

Thanks to Henry Somers-Hall and Beth Lord for their comments on the first draft, and to the staff and editors at EUP.

Dedicated to my parents for their unwavering, enthusiastic support.

List of Abbreviations

DR   Gilles Deleuze, *Difference and Repetition.*
EPS Gilles Deleuze, *Expressionism in Philosophy: Spinoza.*
LE   Gilles Deleuze, Review of Jean Hyppolite's *Logic et Existence.*
LS   Gilles Deleuze, *Logic of Sense.*
LP   Gilles Deleuze, *Le Pli.*
PPL Leibniz, *Philosophical Papers and Letters.*

Plateaus – New Directions in Deleuze Studies

'It's not a matter of bringing all sorts of things together under a single concept but rather of relating each concept to variables that explain its mutations.'
Gilles Deleuze, *Negotiations*

Series Editors
Ian Buchanan, University of Wollongong
Claire Colebrook, Penn State University

Editorial Advisory Board
Keith Ansell Pearson, Ronald Bogue, Constantin V. Boundas, Rosi Braidotti, Eugene Holland, Gregg Lambert, Dorothea Olkowski, Paul Patton, Daniel Smith, James Williams

Titles available in the series
Christian Kerslake, *Immanence and the Vertigo of Philosophy: From Kant to Deleuze*
Jean-Clet Martin, *Variations: The Philosophy of Gilles Deleuze*, translated by Constantin V. Boundas and Susan Dyrkton
Simone Bignall, *Postcolonial Agency: Critique and Constructivism*
Miguel de Beistegui, *Immanence – Deleuze and Philosophy*
Jean-Jacques Lecercle, *Badiou and Deleuze Read Literature*
Ronald Bogue, *Deleuzian Fabulation and the Scars of History*
Sean Bowden, *The Priority of Events: Deleuze's Logic of Sense*
Craig Lundy, *History and Becoming: Deleuze's Philosophy of Creativity*
Aidan Tynan, *Deleuze's Literary Clinic: Criticism and the Politics of Symptoms*
Thomas Nail, *Returning to Revolution: Deleuze, Guattari and Zapatismo*
François Zourabichvili, *Deleuze: A Philosophy of the Event* with *The Vocabulary of Deleuze* edited by Gregg Lambert and Daniel W. Smith, translated by Kieran Aarons
Frida Beckman, *Between Desire and Pleasure: A Deleuzian Theory of Sexuality*
Nadine Boljkovac, *Untimely Affects: Gilles Deleuze and an Ethics of Cinema*
Daniela Voss, *Conditions of Thought: Deleuze and Transcendental Ideas*
Daniel Barber, *Deleuze and the Naming of God: Post-Secularism and the Future of Immanence*
F. LeRon Shults, *Iconoclastic Theology: Gilles Deleuze and the Secretion of Atheism*
Janae Sholtz, *The Invention of a People: Heidegger and Deleuze on Art and the Political*
Marco Altamirano, *Time, Technology and Environment: An Essay on the Philosophy of Nature*
Sean McQueen, *Deleuze and Baudrillard: From Cyberpunk to Biopunk*
Ridvan Askin, *Narrative and Becoming*
Marc Rölli, *Gilles Deleuze's Transcendental Empiricism: From Tradition to Difference* translated by Peter Hertz-Ohmes
Guillaume Collett, *The Psychoanalysis of Sense: Deleuze and the Lacanian School*
Ryan J. Johnson, *The Deleuze-Lucretius Encounter*
Allan James Thomas, *Deleuze, Cinema and the Thought of the World*
Cheri Lynne Carr, *Deleuze's Kantian Ethos: Critique as a Way of Life*
Alex Tissandier, *Affirming Divergence: Deleuze's Reading of Leibniz*

Forthcoming volumes
Justin Litaker, *Deleuze and Guattari's Political Economy*
Nir Kedem, *A Deleuzian Critique of Queer Thought: Overcoming Sexuality*
Felice Cimatti, *Becoming-animal: Philosophy of Animality After Deleuze*, translated by Fabio Gironi

Visit the Plateaus website at edinburghuniversitypress.com/series/plat

Introduction

References to Leibniz's philosophy appear constantly throughout Deleuze's work. Despite often repeating the same themes, we find marked differences in tone, as if Deleuze is unable to arrive at a conclusive judgement. This book explores these various engagements and tries to account for these shifts in tone. Ultimately it will argue that focusing on Deleuze's interpretation of Leibniz – both his appropriations and his criticisms – helps us to understand some key moments in Deleuze's own philosophical development. A close reading, emphasising the particular context and terminology of Leibniz's work, will open a narrow point of access into some of the most difficult areas of Deleuze's philosophy. In the course of this reading, it will become clear that it is precisely Leibniz's ambiguous status for Deleuze which makes an investigation into their relationship so fruitful: by not only explaining Leibniz's positive influence, but also pinpointing the precise grounds for their eventual divergence, we hope to better articulate some of Deleuze's own philosophical priorities.

Any close reading must thus begin by taking this ambiguous status seriously.[1] There are two opposing tendencies that allow us to identify two distinct sides to Leibniz's philosophy, or indeed, the presence of two distinct 'Leibnizes', in Deleuze's readings. Leibniz, in fact, is not unused to undergoing such partitions. The first biography of Leibniz, in a eulogy by Bernard Fontenelle (the secretary of the Académie des Sciences in Paris upon Leibniz's death), likens his propensity for broad study to a charioteer expertly managing each of his horses. Fontenelle's eulogy insists that we decompose and 'make many geniuses out of one Leibniz', a maxim which has generally set the standard for later scholarship. But where traditionally the lines of Leibniz's decomposition have been drawn according to discipline (Leibniz the philosopher, Leibniz the logician, Leibniz the mathematician, and so on), in Deleuze's reading we find Leibniz split by two opposing tendencies that are not only philosophical but also theological, moral and political.

We'll briefly introduce these two tendencies or 'two Leibnizes' by looking at the first available of Deleuze's extended discussions of Leibniz. *Qu'est-ce que fonder?* (*What is Grounding?* or *What is it to Ground?*) was a lecture course given by Deleuze in 1956. It survives only in the form of student notes, and as a consequence we can't attach to it the same kind of authority as to Deleuze's published works. But its early date (twelve years before *Difference and Repetition*, thirty-two years before *The Fold*) and grand scope give us an interesting glimpse into some of Deleuze's earliest philosophical priorities. Of particular significance for us is the prominent role accorded to Leibniz. Deleuze identifies three kinds of response given by philosophers to the question 'what is it to ground?', and relies on Leibniz to represent the second kind of response (the kind which provides a *principle* as the response to problematic cases). This early discussion allows us to give a very general characterisation of Deleuze's attitude towards Leibniz, as well as of those aspects of the latter's philosophy in which he takes an interest. Again, because it was a lecture course, and because it survives only in note form, there is only so much we can convincingly reconstruct from this very early instance of 'Deleuze's Leibnizianism'. However, we can at least draw the following distinction.

On the one hand, Deleuze characterises Leibniz's philosophy as the last great attempt by theology to ground an ordered and harmonious world. We find symptoms of this in his emphasis on *sufficient reason*, as well as in his insistence that to each kind of problem there must respond a rational *principle* (it is for these principles that Leibniz is perhaps best known: the principle of non-contradiction, the principle of the identity of indiscernibles, and so on). Leibniz is thus a theological, theodical thinker: his propensity for the creation of grand principles is motivated by a desire to justify a harmonious, ordered and created world, in which a satisfying and sufficient reason can always be given in answer to Leibniz's two guiding questions: Why is there something rather than nothing? And why is there *this* rather than *that*?

On the other hand, in the same lecture, Deleuze makes passing references to Leibniz's revolutionary discoveries in mathematics, and in particular to his development of infinitesimal calculus. With this comes a new concept, that of the 'infinitely small', which threatens to resist easy incorporation into the harmonious world of sufficient reasons, and hints at the uneasy presence of another, more restless side to Leibniz's philosophy.

Throughout this book we'll see how these two contrasted images

Introduction

of Leibniz's philosophy set the pattern for how Leibniz is characterised in all of Deleuze's later works, up to and including *The Fold*. The first image presents us with Leibniz the conservative, or Leibniz the theologian, called upon by Deleuze to represent various doctrines or themes in the history of philosophy. More often than not, Deleuze is critical of these doctrines, especially when contrasting them with those of his more exciting contemporary, Spinoza. Limited to this characterisation, it is hard to see how an account of Deleuze's reading of Leibniz could produce anything more than a motley collection of ideas to which Deleuze is vaguely opposed.

But beneath the mask of Leibniz's conservatism Deleuze also discerns a second image: the blurred outline of a philosophy shot through with dynamism, whose 'dizzying creation of principles' and Baroque complexity result from the productive play of the infinitely small which lies at its ground. It is in these moments that Deleuze reveals a second, radicalised image of Leibniz, even if, ultimately, this image so often ends up obscured by the opposing tendency of Leibniz's conservatism.

These brief glimpses underneath Leibniz's conservative façade are enough, however, for Deleuze to find two important ideas: ideas which lie at the heart of 'Deleuze's Leibnizianism' and which even form a key component of his own philosophical trajectory. We can briefly introduce these two core Leibnizian ideas by turning to a second 1956 work by Deleuze: his review of Hyppolite's *Logic and Existence*.[2] In the final paragraph Deleuze asks a question which remains central to his entire subsequent philosophical project: 'Can we not construct an ontology of difference which would not have to go up to contradiction, because contradiction would be less than difference and not more? Is not contradiction itself only the phenomenal and anthropological aspect of difference?' (LE 195). For the rest of his career, one of Deleuze's central concerns is to answer this question: how to provide a concept of difference that does not reduce difference to a kind of opposition or contradiction. And it is in attempting to answer this question that Deleuze will make repeated use of Leibniz's theory of *compossibility* and *incompossibility*. This theory remains the most important influence of Leibniz's philosophy on Deleuze. Although he is referenced only once in this review, it is noteworthy that Leibniz is characterised here as someone who, in his metaphysics at least, did not go as far as contradiction, remaining instead 'with pure difference' (LE 195). The review thus already places Leibniz in opposition to Hegel, and indeed, Leibniz's theory of incompossibility is most often called upon to provide a concept of difference or of mediation that represents an alternative to Hegelian contradiction. A relation of incompossibility, Deleuze will insist again and again, is not reducible to a relation of contradiction. As we will see, however, this insistence carries with it a particular interpretation of compossibility that is not exactly self-evident in Leibniz's own philosophy.

Deleuze's reading depends upon defining compossibility and incompossibility through the relations of convergence and divergence that can be established between series of differential relations. In short, Deleuze constructs a theory of topological, transcendental structure which combines the conceptual results of Leibniz's mathematical discovery of infinitesimal analysis (infinitely small differences, the differential relations through which these differences are reciprocally determined, and the singular points that these differential relations distribute) with Leibniz's philosophical theory of compossibility. A topological understanding of compossibility (where compossibility finds its criterion in the convergence of the series of ordinary points which extend from the singular points that constitute each possible world) gives Deleuze an image of mediation which is *alogical* and *subrepresentational*.

The upshot of this is that the kinds of relation that characterise a transcendental field are not the same as the kinds of conceptual relation we find within the structure of representation. Again, then, Deleuze turns to Leibniz's original relation of compossibility precisely because it cannot be reduced to a relation of contradiction, so long as we define the former through relations of convergence and divergence between series. This is why Deleuze repeatedly opposes Leibniz to Hegel and favours the former each time.

Deleuze will turn to Leibniz again for an explanation of how individual subjects are constituted from this transcendental field, and this is the second key Leibnizian theme we find in Deleuze's work. He will develop a theory of individuals as centres of expression that envelop and actualise a particular set of the singularities distributed in a transcendental structure. In a letter to the English translator of *Expressionism in Philosophy: Spinoza*, Deleuze writes: 'What I needed was both (1) the expressive character of particular individuals, and (2) an immanence of being. Leibniz, in a way, goes even further than Spinoza on the first point' (EPS 11). In earlier discussions of Leibniz, Deleuze interprets this constitution of individuals around pre-individual singularities as proof of how, in each case, Leibniz

Introduction

begins with the inessential in order to construct essences. Later, Deleuze will emphasise how each individual monad clearly expresses a region of the world according to the singularities it envelops or the predicates it includes.

Leibniz's concepts thus make an appearance in Deleuze's description of two key elements of his own philosophy: the structure of the transcendental and the actualisation of individuals. It is clear, however, that if this is 'Leibnizianism', it is so only in a dispossessed, dislocated, form. As we'll see, much of the mathematical terminology Deleuze uses in his discussions of Leibniz's theory of compossibility is nowhere to be found in Leibniz's work. More importantly, Leibniz locates the process that establishes these relations of compossibility and incompossibility firmly in the opaque understanding of God. Deleuze instead locates the same process within his own account of a virtual transcendental field. We will look at the extent to which this represents an isolated extraction of one aspect of Leibniz's philosophy or, more radically, the construction of a new, 'neo-Leibnizian' system. While the first interpretation is often more appropriate, the second becomes more feasible by the time of *The Fold*, which is Deleuze's final, unified, account of Leibniz's philosophy.

While Deleuze's reading is closely tied to the major figures within twentieth-century French Leibniz scholarship (most notably Couturat and Gueroult), Leibniz nevertheless appears to emerge from Deleuze's reading transformed in some way. Deleuze even seems to take especially seriously those parts of Leibniz's philosophy that, in general, wider scholarship has treated with the most scepticism. Thus, where ideas such as pre-established harmony, the best possible world, or the monad 'without doors and windows' are often quietly ignored in favour of Leibniz's much more respectable discoveries in logic and mathematics, in Deleuze's hands they become the concepts which, when properly formulated, best express the essence of Leibniz's philosophy. The inevitable result of this reading is a version of Leibniz's philosophy that emphasises the tendencies to which Deleuze is most sympathetic, until it almost begins to align with his own philosophy.

In one key respect, however, Deleuze always remains distanced from Leibniz, such that there is no question that they belong to two distinct, irreconcilable philosophical epochs. Eventually, in each of Deleuze's discussions of these two themes of compossibility and the constitution of individuals, there is a point where Leibniz is left behind. There are limits on how far Deleuze can stretch Leibniz's concepts. The moment of rupture, when Deleuze is forced to turn away from Leibniz and find concepts elsewhere (most often in art, as we'll see), occurs precisely in the relation of compossibility. While compossibility finds its criterion in the topological convergence of series, incompossibility finds its criterion in the divergence of series. For Leibniz, this divergence of series marks a bifurcation into two distinct possible worlds. These worlds are disconnected from and exclude one another. But, Deleuze will argue, Leibniz treats the divergence of series as a relation of exclusion only because he is so irrevocably tied to a belief in an ordered, created universe; a universe guaranteed by a non-deceiving God who would not possibly allow incompossible events or divergent series to coexist within the same world. This is the key belief that Deleuze rejects in Leibniz, and instead affirms, repeatedly, the divergence of series – not just their coexistence, but their productive communication. As Stengers summarises: 'Again and again, in a quasi-obsessive way, Deleuze returns to the same judgement: Leibniz missed, or domesticated, the concept of series, restricting it to convergent series; he used it in order to exclude incompatibilities, that is, to save from destruction the harmonious unity of the world and the continuity of the individual' (Stengers 2009: 30).

This fundamental divergence between Deleuze and Leibniz has been framed in various ways. For Stengers, Deleuze rejects Leibniz in response to his inherent conservatism and reluctance to 'upset established sensibilities'. Smith characterises the issue in terms of the death of God: 'His Leibnizianism is a Leibnizianism minus God' (Smith 2012: 21). Duffy sees it differently, in terms of the exigencies of pure mathematics. Developments by Weierstrass and Poincaré, he points out, allowed continuity to be established between diverging series, with the result that 'the Leibnizian account of compossibility as the unity of convergent series, which relies on the exclusion of divergence, is no longer required by the mathematics' (Duffy 2010: 109). We will have cause to look at each of these views in more detail.

Nevertheless, despite this difference which lies at the heart of their relationship (their own point of divergence), Deleuze inherits from Leibniz a vision of a world of continuous, infinite series marked by singular points around which individuals are constituted. And while he criticises Leibniz for subjecting this world to conditions of convergence, the very notions of convergence and divergence become central to Deleuze's own account. Again, this tension in Deleuze's reading is a tension between two images of Leibniz: the theological, conservative thinker of sufficient reason and harmony, who always

Introduction

excludes divergence; and the radical, dynamic Leibniz, the thinker of infinitely small difference, differential relations, topology and the author behind a dizzying, baroque creation of novel concepts and principles. There are various pairs of terms we can use to describe the two poles of this tension: conservative and radical, theological and mathematical, agrarian and nomadic, Apollonian and Dionysian. They are two opposing tendencies: Leibniz is pulled towards the latter by his discoveries in mathematics and physics, but remains anchored by his firm commitment to an ordered, principled, God-governed world.

Perhaps this tension itself is even the very source of Leibniz's productivity and originality: it is only his desperation to salvage an ordered vision of the world that compels him to create a new principle each time the world confronts him with a new, problematic case. Deleuze briefly invokes this tension in a 1980 lecture on Leibniz, in a passage that neatly encapsulates Leibniz's unique and ambiguous status for Deleuze:

> Leibniz is from the great rationalist tradition. Picture Leibniz – there is something frightening there. He is the philosopher of order and, even more, of policing, in every sense of the word 'policing'. He only thinks in terms of order. But very oddly, in this taste for order, and to establish this order, he yields to the most insane concept creation that we have ever witnessed in philosophy. Disheveled concepts, the most exuberant, the most disordered, the most complex concepts, all in order to justify what is. (15/04/1980)

If we can point to one original aspect of Deleuze's reading of Leibniz, it is to unanchor him from these exigencies of order, and allow his concepts to be pushed to new limits. If for Leibniz the world is held together by rules which ensure its harmony and convergence, then for Deleuze the world is divergent and even 'broken'. Deleuze's Leibnizianism is a Leibnizianism for a discordant world, where incompossible events communicate and divergences are affirmed.

The Evolution of Deleuze's Reading of Leibniz

Which of these two images of Leibniz dominates depends upon the particular reading. In general, each of Deleuze's encounters with Leibniz suggests a gradual slide towards the second, radical characterisation of his philosophy. Along with this comes an increase in the scope of Deleuze's interest in Leibniz. With each new reading, I will argue, we find a new sympathy, and a willingness to treat Leibniz's philosophy as a unified whole. While the earliest engagements are motivated by a practical extraction of isolated Leibnizian concepts in order to be applied to particular problems, Deleuze will go on to gradually develop his own image of a unified Leibnizian philosophy, introducing more and more elements each time it appears. As a consequence, Deleuze is able to 'carry' Leibniz further and further as this system develops.

Deleuze's reading of Leibniz can be divided into three distinct periods, which correspond to the three parts of this book. Part I begins with Deleuze's minor thesis on Spinoza, *Expressionism in Philosophy: Spinoza*. Here we find a Leibniz who is a predominantly conservative thinker of sufficient reason, grounded by theological concerns. Deleuze is largely unable, or unwilling, to unleash the dynamism buried in Leibniz's philosophy, reduced as he is to an opponent of Spinoza.[3] Our discussion of this book will rely in part on the claim that we must draw a sharp distinction between the main text and the concluding chapter ('The Theory of Expression in Leibniz and Spinoza: Expressionism in Philosophy'). The marked shift in tone and emphasis between the two suggests that they written at different times. Importantly for us, Leibniz is afforded a far more central role in the conclusion than his almost incidental presence in the main text would have led us to expect.

In Part II we turn to *Difference and Repetition* and *Logic of Sense*. *Difference and Repetition* presents us with a very different image of Leibniz, introduced, alongside Hegel, as a representative of 'infinite' representation. For the first time, Deleuze draws on a more dynamic side of Leibniz's philosophy. Here, what interests Deleuze about Leibniz is his discovery, within or beneath each clear idea, of the 'restlessness' of the infinitely small. The obscure depths of the infinitely small, we'll see, harbour a kind of intoxication, giddiness and evanescence (DR 45). It is this image of the obscure, confused depths of the infinitely small that Deleuze gradually comes to treat as central to all areas of Leibniz's philosophy, and it's an image which haunts and threatens to undermine Leibniz's conservative façade.

In *Logic of Sense*, meanwhile, Deleuze turns to Leibniz for both his concept of compossibility, which provides a 'rich domain of alogical compatibilities and incompatibilities' (LS 196), and for his concept of expressive individuals. These two books thus introduce a more sympathetic tone on the part of Deleuze. The infinitely small and the theory of compossibility form the basis of a 'Leibnizian struc-

Introduction

ture' which Deleuze puts forward as an alternative to Hegelian contradiction. Nevertheless, Leibniz is still criticised for subsuming the excess of difference under a sufficient reason which 'no longer allows anything to escape' (DR 263). To this extent, Leibniz does not escape his conservative yoke. However sympathetic, there is always a point in these texts where Deleuze leaves Leibniz behind and instead finds inspiration elsewhere, citing the constraints imposed by Leibniz's own 'theological exigencies'.

Although *Difference and Repetition* and *Logic of Sense* present us with a much more sympathetic image of Leibniz than the one found in *Expressionism in Philosophy: Spinoza*, Deleuze's readings of Leibniz in all three books still share one basic characteristic: they are essentially fragmented. Deleuze extracts disparate concepts from Leibniz's philosophy and uses them like tools, often because they are representative of a particular moment in the history of philosophy, and more rarely because they coincide with his own philosophical objectives. But this always happens within the context of a larger discussion which has nothing in particular to do with Leibniz, and there is never any sense that Deleuze has an interest in Leibniz's philosophy as a unified system.

This all changes with *The Fold*, published in 1988. Here Deleuze gives a much more general, unified account of Leibniz. He regards Leibniz's philosophy, for the first time, as something more than just a collection of useful explanatory concepts to be deployed in some other context. Leibniz is promoted to the role of philosophical representative of the Baroque period itself, whose defining trait, Deleuze thinks, is a process of folding which continues indefinitely. But the themes which interested Deleuze in his earlier readings of Leibniz are not simply superseded by the much grander role he is now given. They return, without exception, in *The Fold*, but with this difference: where previously they were isolated from each other, they are now drawn together under this new concept of the 'infinite fold'. In Part III we will look at the complicated relationship between the various aspects of Leibniz's philosophy, the Baroque style and the concept of the fold.

By the time of *The Fold*, then, we find a radicalised Leibniz whose philosophy has been stretched further than ever before, but which also appears more coherent and unified. *The Fold* is Deleuze's final attempt to come to terms with Leibniz and arrive at some kind of final judgement. Eventually, it is true, even in *The Fold* he is unable to escape Leibniz's inherent conservatism, and, once again, departs from Leibniz over the issue of the exclusive nature of divergence. But, Deleuze concludes, we 'remain Leibnizian' in so far as Leibniz has finally been pinned down as a thinker of infinite folds. It is thus with this concept of the fold that we will see Leibniz at last become a figure that Deleuze can affirm without reservation.

Notes

1. Leibniz's ambiguous status for Deleuze is quickly demonstrated with two quotes. In the very last sentence of *The Fold*, published in 1988, Deleuze writes: 'We remain Leibnizian . . .'. But just a few years later, in a letter to the English translator of *Expressionism in Philosophy: Spinoza*, he remarks: 'I consider myself a Spinozist, rather than a Leibnizian . . .'. It is hardly satisfying to dismiss this ambiguity as harmless inconsistency on Deleuze's part. But it is also not enough to explain it away by pinpointing opinions which change over the course of a long career. As we will see in some detail, Deleuze's reading of Leibniz does change in key respects. But the short time separating the two quotes above is enough to demonstrate that there was never a single moment when Deleuze 'changed his mind' about Leibniz.
2. Christian Kerslake calls this review 'the only published plan, to my knowledge, in which [Deleuze] lays out the aims of his future philosophical project' (Kerslake 2002). We will return to this review in some detail in the first section of Chapter 3.
3. This book was actually published in the same year as *Difference and Repetition* (1968). We justify calling this book the 'early' reading by referring to Dosse's claim that it was 'practically finished in the late 1950s' (Dosse 2013: 118). The book itself, as we'll see, provides clear reasons for being treated as a distinct period in Deleuze's engagement with Leibniz.

PART I

Expressionism in Philosophy: Spinoza

1

Leibniz, Spinoza and the Anti-Cartesian Reaction

In the introduction I identified two general tendencies in all of Deleuze's readings of Leibniz. I characterised these as the presence of 'two Leibnizes': on the one hand, the theologically conservative Leibniz, subject to Deleuze's relentless criticism; and on the other the philosophically adventurous Leibniz, a useful source of inspiration and influence. In a very general sense, the division between the main text and the conclusion of *Expressionism in Philosophy: Spinoza* (EPS) follows this distinction: the critical tone which dominates in the main text is replaced by admiration when we arrive at the conclusion. This distinction is not clear-cut, however, and we'll often detect the more-or-less suppressed presence of both Leibnizes at each stage.

Along with their critical tone, there is one other important feature of the discussions of Leibniz we find in the main text of EPS: they are, we are forced to admit, *incidental*. Despite occasional references to an 'anti-Cartesian reaction' which unites Leibniz and Spinoza, we never get the sense that this is a central point of concern for Deleuze. It is a reading of Spinoza's philosophy through the concept of expression which motivates the text as a whole. Limited to this context, the affinities between Spinoza and Leibniz are, at best, a point of interest, and their differences are, at best, a useful point of opposition to better draw out Spinoza's originality. It is this which will change in the concluding chapter. There, it is precisely these apparently incidental affinities and oppositions between Spinoza and Leibniz that drive Deleuze's argument and become the central point of concern. The new emphasis on Leibniz will introduce, in nascent form, the Leibnizian ideas and concepts that Deleuze increasingly takes to heart in his later works.

EPS is Deleuze's most 'scholarly' book, carefully charting a comprehensive reading of Spinoza in terms of the concept of expression (and a particular perspective on that concept).[1] While we must still concede what Beistegui calls 'a degree of hermeneutic violence' in Deleuze's reading of Spinoza, the book nevertheless lacks the agile leaps between philosophers and disciplines that will characterise so many of Deleuze's later books, especially *Difference and Repetition* and *Logic of Sense* (Beistegui 2010: 28). We'll attempt a similarly careful account of Deleuze's reading of Leibniz, giving Leibniz's own texts an emphasis which will be lacking in later chapters. At the same time, however, our goal remains to clarify the gradually increasing influence of Leibnizian ideas on Deleuze's own philosophy, and not, to any significant degree, the legitimacy or fidelity of Deleuze's reading. In other words, our interest remains in what Leibniz can tell us about Deleuze, and not what Deleuze can tell us about Leibniz.

Outside a few scattered references, there are three noteworthy discussions of Leibniz in the main text of EPS. Within these discussions we'll identify two criticisms Deleuze levels against Leibniz's philosophy, the first concerning its reliance on a form of 'symbolisation', and the second its commitment to 'finality'. Ultimately, I'll argue, both of these have their roots in Leibniz's own theological and political concerns. In his later accounts of Leibniz, Deleuze will drop the first criticism, instead relying on a refined version of the second. The seeds for this decision, I will argue, can already be found here in EPS.

These three engagements with Leibniz in the main text of EPS all share roughly the same form. First, Deleuze locates a similarity between Leibniz and Spinoza in their criticism of a particular Cartesian doctrine. Second, he grounds this criticism in a shared concern for the lack of a *sufficient reason* operating in Descartes' philosophy. Third, he nominates *expression* as the concept best suited to address this lack and fulfil the requirements of sufficient reason. Finally, he shows that the way expression functions in Spinoza's philosophy is each time superior to Leibniz's own use of the concept.

This general form allows us to make some similarly general comments about Leibniz's overall role in the main text of EPS. Although we've suggested that it is the theologically conservative Leibniz who dominates in these early discussions, even under this guise he plays a complicated dual role in relation to Spinoza (and hence in relation to Deleuze himself). On the one hand he is praised as Spinoza's ally against Descartes, or as one half of what Deleuze will sometimes call the 'anti-Cartesian reaction'. Limited to this role, Deleuze is happy to oscillate between Spinozist and Leibnizian terminology, convinced that in many instances the general thrust of their arguments is the same. He even, as we will see, makes use of Leibniz's often more detailed, fleshed-out arguments on those occasions where Spinoza's own texts are lacking. But on the other hand, it is precisely Leibniz's closeness to Spinoza which inevitably exposes him to criticism. It is often only by condemning aspects of Leibniz's philosophy that Deleuze is able to articulate Spinoza's profound originality. And these criticisms will not merely or exclusively bear on the technicalities of Leibniz's arguments in each particular case, but concern fundamental beliefs or tendencies which lie at the heart of his philosophy, until they almost appear as attacks on Leibniz's very character.

1.1 Real Definitions and God's Possibility

The first instance of the pattern that will come to characterise all of Leibniz's appearances in the main text of EPS is in the fourth chapter, 'The Absolute'. This chapter is initially concerned with the inadequacy of the Cartesian concept of an infinitely perfect being for establishing the nature of God, and even for establishing God's necessary existence. By looking at this section in detail, three points will emerge. First, we'll establish that Deleuze locates the affinity between Spinoza and Leibniz in a concern for sufficient reason which grounds their criticism of Descartes. Second, we'll introduce Deleuze's first criticism of Leibniz. Finally, we'll set the stage for the subtle reinterpretation of Leibniz which takes place in the conclusion and which, I will argue in sections 1.2 and 2.1, renders Deleuze's criticism problematic, and perhaps explains why it is eventually dropped.

Descartes' ontological proof relies on identifying the nature of God with infinite perfection: God is the *ens perfectissimum,* or most perfect being. Spinoza and Leibniz both question the adequacy of this definition. Leibniz gives his criticism a precise formulation, arguing that before identifying God with infinite perfection we must first demonstrate that the idea of an infinitely perfect being is not itself contradictory. As Deleuze summarises, 'infinite perfection does not suffice to constitute the nature of God' precisely because there might perhaps be a contradiction in *ens perfectissimum,* just as there was thought to be in 'the greatest number' or 'the greatest velocity' (EPS 73). We find Leibniz's formulation of this argument in a paper written in anticipation of his meeting with Spinoza in November 1676, 'Quod ens perfectissimum existit'. By looking at this argument in some detail, a number of key ideas will emerge.

Descartes argues that the *ens perfectissimum* must necessarily exist because 'existence' is listed among the perfections contained in an infinitely perfect being. While Leibniz agrees with Descartes that 'existence is contained in the number of perfections' he finds Descartes' criteria for judging our knowledge of an infinitely perfect being inadequate: 'Descartes's reasoning about the existence of a most perfect being assumed that such a being can be conceived or is possible' (PPL 137). It is not enough, Leibniz claims, to prove the existence of God through the means of his infinite perfection without first demonstrating that the very concept of the *ens perfectissimum* is coherent or 'has reality'. This demonstration will amount to providing a real definition of an infinitely perfect being – a demonstration which must therefore go beyond Descartes' criteria of clarity and distinctness, which, Leibniz argues elsewhere, are suitable only for nominal definitions. It will be left until the next chapter to understand Leibniz's dissatisfaction with clarity and distinctness as sufficient conditions for real definitions; for now we concern ourselves only with Leibniz's attempt to correct or supplement Descartes' ontological proof by providing a real definition of God.

In his *Meditations on Knowledge, Truth and Ideas* Leibniz writes that 'We cannot safely infer from definitions until we know that they are real or that they involve no contradiction' (PPL 293); and in his *Discourse on Metaphysics* that 'as long as we only have a nominal definition, we cannot be sure of the consequences drawn from it, for if it concealed some contradiction or impossibility, we could draw conflicting conclusions' (PPL 319). A definition is real, therefore, only if it does not 'involve contradiction'. The words 'involve' and 'conceal' suggest that, if we are to demonstrate that a definition is not contradictory, it is the constituent *parts* of a definition with which we should be concerned. In a letter to Arnold Eckhard in 1677 Leibniz explains why, precisely because of the incompatibility of its parts, his favourite example of a 'most rapid motion' or 'maximum velocity' is an impossible concept: 'Whoever speaks of a maximum velocity knows what velocity is and what a maximum is, yet he cannot understand maximum velocity, for it is easy to demonstrate that this involves a contradiction' (PPL 178). The concept of 'maximum velocity' is contradictory or impossible because its constituent parts, 'maximum' and 'velocity', although readily understood in isolation, produce a contradiction when brought into relation with each other, and are thus *incompatible* when contained in the same concept. On top of this incompatibility of parts, we must also add that any concept which would include an impossible concept as one of its own constituent parts must itself therefore be impossible.

For a concept to be possible thus requires two things: first, that each of its constituent parts is compatible with every other, and second, that each of these parts is itself possible: 'We know . . . the possibility of a thing when we resolve the concept into its necessary elements or into other concepts whose possibility is known, and we know that there is nothing incompatible in them' (PPL 293). When it comes to the concept of the *ens perfectissimum*, the same two requirements apply. If we return to the letter to Eckhard, Leibniz writes: 'I hasten to the heart of the question, which is whether a most perfect being does not imply a contradiction. You have undertaken to prove this because neither Descartes nor any of the Cartesians have done it, though I have often urged them to do so' (PPL 178). Just like everything else, then, the concept of an infinitely perfect being is possible only if it does not involve contradiction; and it does not involve contradiction only if its constituent parts are each themselves possible and mutually compatible.

But what are the 'parts' of an infinitely perfect being? Leibniz treats the *ens perfectissimum* exactly as if it were the subject in which all *perfections* are included: 'There is, or can be conceived, a subject of all perfections, or a most perfect being' (PPL 169). The parts of an infinitely perfect being are thus precisely the perfections which constitute its nature as infinitely perfect. And so Leibniz's attempt to demonstrate the possibility of the *ens perfectissimum* will depend on whether these perfections, as constitutive parts, are subject to the same two criteria of possibility and mutual compatibility as the parts of other concepts. This in turn depends on the precise nature of a 'perfection'. On this, Leibniz writes: 'By a perfection I mean every simple quality which is positive and absolute or which expresses whatever it expresses without any limits' (PPL 169). Although the use of the term 'expresses' here is intriguing, it is actually the other two aspects of this definition in which we are interested: we'll see that the fact that perfections are 'simple' means they are necessarily possible, while the fact that they are 'absolute' means they are necessarily compatible with each other. With the establishment of these two features, Leibniz can demonstrate that a subject which contains all perfections does not contain a contradiction and is therefore possible. In effect, then, Leibniz thinks we must provide a real definition of God solely in terms of the nature of the perfections He includes or which constitute His nature. But what does it mean to say that God's perfections are 'simple' and 'absolute', and how do these two characteristics ensure the possibility of an infinitely perfect being?

'Simple means without parts' Leibniz tells us in section one of the *Monadology* (PPL 643), and so, in contrast to composite concepts which are conceived through the parts or terms that constitute them, perfections, as simple forms, are not reducible to parts or analysable into lower-level terms. We saw above that something 'contains contradiction' if it has parts which are incompatible with each other. Perfections, therefore, cannot contain contradiction because they do not have any parts. And because they do not contain any contradiction it follows that all perfections, as simple, are possible.

Perfections are also, we saw, absolute or 'without limits' or, in other words, without any relation to other perfections. Incompatibility can only arise between two things that relate to one another, with a shared element that is affirmed by one whilst being denied by the other. In the case of simple perfections, however, there can be no such shared element, and therefore no incompatibility. And thus even a subject which contains every perfection is at no risk of harbouring an incompatibility between its parts. Leibniz's definition of perfections as simple and absolute guarantees that, when they are contained in a single subject, the conditions for the possibility of that subject are met: each perfection is itself possible, and each is compatible with every other. Thus the subject of all perfections, the *ens perfectissimum*, is itself possible.

Deleuze briefly summarises this argument, emphasising its reliance on the two key characteristics of perfections. Regarding their simplicity, he points out that rather than containing parts, they contain or include only *themselves*, and writes that each is 'simple and irreducible, conceived in itself, *index sui*' (EPS 78). Regarding their absolute nature, which he calls their 'disparity', he writes that 'it is their very disparity that assures their compatibility (the impossibility of their contradiction), and their compatibility that assures the possibility of the Being to which they belong'. With this, Deleuze thinks, Leibniz has advanced on the nominal definition provided by Descartes towards providing a real definition or a reason for God's infinite perfection based on the nature of these simple, absolute perfections: 'For Leibniz, God is possible because infinite perfection is the *proprium* of an "absolute being" that includes in itself all "attributes", "all simple forms taken absolutely", all "natures which are susceptible of the highest degree", "all positive qualities expressing something without limitation"' (EPS 78).

It is by providing this real, as opposed to nominal, definition of God, Deleuze thinks, that Leibniz fulfils the requirement for sufficient reason that was lacking in Descartes. And in this, Spinoza and Leibniz are united: 'There is no difference between Leibniz's requirements and Spinoza's: the same call for a real definition of God, for a nature or reason of the infinitely perfect. The same subordination of the ontological proof to a real definition of God, and to the demonstration that this definition is indeed a real one' (EPS 77). And again: 'If one considers the formulations through which Leibniz himself proves the possibility of God, one does not at first sight perceive any difference between these and Spinoza's' (EPS 78).

Why, then, does Deleuze bring up Leibniz's proof for the possibility of the *ens perfectissimum* at all, if it adds nothing to what we already find in Spinoza?[2] Deleuze introduces Leibniz's argument precisely in order to simultaneously introduce his first major criticism of Leibniz, and with it his first demonstration of Spinoza's superiority. And despite the apparent affinity between Leibniz and Spinoza in proving the possibility of God, we can already detect a hint of their eventual disagreement in the quote above: it is only 'at first sight' that we do not perceive any difference between them. What happens, then, when we look more closely?

1.2 Absolutely and Relatively Simple Notions: The First Criticism of Leibniz

Deleuze locates the difference between Leibniz and Spinoza in this section of EPS in their different interpretations of the 'infinite positive forms or qualities' of God, or what above we called God's perfections. Regarding Leibniz's formulation, Deleuze makes a key claim:

> These prime possibles, 'absolutely simple notions', lie outside our knowledge: we know they are necessarily compatible, without knowing what they are. They appear anterior to, and above, any logical relation: knowledge reaches only to 'relatively simple notions' which serve as terms of our thinking, and of which the best, perhaps, one can say is that they have a symbolic relation to the prime simples. (EPS 78)

This key distinction between absolutely simple notions and relatively simple notions lies at the heart of Deleuze's first criticism of Leibniz, and will return in various forms throughout the rest of EPS. We'll see below where Deleuze locates this claim in Leibniz, but first we'll look at how Deleuze uses it to criticise Leibniz and differentiate his view from Spinoza's. Deleuze argues that by positing a clear division between the absolutely simple notions which constitute God's nature or essence and the only relatively simple notions which lie at the basis of our knowledge, Leibniz is able to leave the true nature of God suitably obscure, thereby preserving the eminence of God and the contingency of creation: 'Leibniz hereby escapes the absolute necessity which he denounces as the danger of Spinozism: he stops "metaphysical" necessity getting out from God and communicating itself to creatures.' There is a definite motivation behind this move, Deleuze thinks: 'After his meetings with Spinoza, Leibniz considers absolute necessity the enemy' (EPS 79). The way Deleuze cloaks this first departure of Leibniz from Spinoza in a language of 'dangers' and 'enemies' already suggests, I think, that beyond any philosophical incompatibility, Deleuze places the real grounds for their disagreement in Leibniz's own ideological concerns. We thus see here for the first time how Deleuze thinks Leibniz's philosophy is always constrained by certain commitments, partly theological and partly political.

An aversion to absolute necessity is indeed the basis for the criticism of Spinoza which we find in Leibniz's 1707 'Comments on Spinoza's Philosophy'. But there, the way Leibniz 'escapes the danger of absolute necessity' is very different. Leibniz writes:

> The axiom 'that without which a thing can neither be nor be conceived belongs to the essence of a thing', is to be used with regard to necessary things or species, but not with regard to individuals or contingent things, for individuals cannot distinctly be conceived. Thus, they have no necessary connection with God, but were produced freely. God was inclined towards them for a definite reason, but he was not necessitated.[3]

Here then Leibniz tries to refute Spinoza by referring to his traditional distinction between a domain of essences and a domain of existing things. The first is subject to absolute necessity, but the second is not. Leibniz's commitment to this distinction is a recurring theme in his criticisms of Spinoza. Commenting on proposition five of the *Ethics*, Leibniz writes: 'what is meant by "in the nature of things" seems obscure. Does he mean in the whole of existing things or in the region of ideas or of possible essences?' (PPL 198). At first glance this distinction between necessary essences and contingent things looks like it might coincide with Deleuze's distinction between absolutely simple notions and relatively simple notions. But as we will see in the next chapter, the two cannot be straightforwardly mapped onto each other. Why, then, does Deleuze insist on making the distinction between absolutely simple and relatively simple notions the basis for the divergence between Leibniz and Spinoza? The answer, I think, is that Deleuze wants to criticise Leibniz in a very particular way: for falling victim to the traditional notions of *eminence, analogy* and *symbolism* that Spinoza escapes: 'Could not Spinoza think, though, that in order to save creatures and creation, Leibniz was retaining all the perspectives of eminence, analogy and symbolism in general? Perhaps Leibniz only appears to advance beyond infinite perfection, only appears to arrive at a nature or reason' (EPS 79).

Escaping the concepts of eminence and analogy is in large part where Deleuze locates Spinoza's profound originality. It is this that allows him to formulate the concept of univocal expression we'll look at when we turn to the conclusion of EPS. Deleuze is thus especially concerned with showing how Leibniz, despite all his affinities with Spinoza, remains rooted in the tradition of eminence and analogy that Spinoza escapes. Leibniz's philosophy, Deleuze argues, maintains something of the mystery of God by positing the divine attributes of God as essentially unknowable. The result is that being *emanates* from God; that our own ideas have only an *analogical* relationship to the attributes of God (our ideas are only analogous to the ideas of God); and that as such they are only *signs* or *symbols* referring to something essentially transcendent. Creatures and the ideas of creatures emanate from a God who remains essentially indifferent to them. Leibniz's God, then, as opposed to Spinoza's, remains an eminent, transcendent and concealed source of expression. As such, in contrast to Spinoza's univocal concept of expression, Leibniz remains tied to the neo-Platonic model of participation, of which Beistegui writes: 'What is participated remains within itself. It is participated in so far as it produces, and produces in so far as it gives. But in order to produce or give, it need not leave or be separated from itself.'[4]

The key to understanding Deleuze's criticism is his claim that the relatively simple notions of our own understanding only have a 'symbolic relation' to the absolutely simple notions of God, and it is this symbolic relation which exposes Leibniz to the accusation that he relies on analogy and eminence. And yet, I think, we would be hard-pressed to find this view in Leibniz himself given the reference Deleuze provides. In section six of the 1679 paper 'Elements of Calculus', Leibniz does indeed speak of assigning a sign to notions whose requisites or component parts we cannot distinctly discern. In this way, he writes, 'we could at least discover all propositions by a calculation and show which ones can at least be demonstrated analytically when taken as primary for the time being, without actually being so' (PPL 236). Thus, some ideas are indeed relegated to the status of signs, but there is never a sense that this is anything other than a practical measure to make up for a temporary lack in our understanding. The example Leibniz gives illustrates this well. Euclid's geometry does not give a definition of a straight line, treating it instead as a simple, axiomatic notion. Euclid's notion of a straight line is thus something like one of the 'relatively simple notions' Deleuze claims Leibniz restricts us to. But in fact, Leibniz points out, it was treated as simple only until Archimedes was able to analyse the notion and give it an adequate definition: the least distance between two points. Thus, in this paper at least, not only is there no mention of absolutely simple notions being restricted to God, but Leibniz does not even concede the inevitability of the relative simplicity of our own notions. The implication is rather the opposite: that it is possible, at least in theory, that our relatively simple notions will one day be analysed into notions which are absolutely simple, even if such an analysis 'would scarcely be provided for mortals in many thousands of years'. We will see in the next chapter that Deleuze goes on to reference other texts which bear on this issue. But for now, it is hard to avoid the conclusion that Deleuze's criticism of Leibniz is weakened by his insistence on identifying the difference between Leibniz and Spinoza in Leibniz's reliance on eminence, analogy and symbolism, rather than on his much more obvious commitment to a division between the domain of necessary essence and the domain of contingent existence.

In this section we have seen how Spinoza and Leibniz arrive at similar solutions to the problem they identify in Descartes: a better ontological proof which demonstrates God's possibility or provides a real definition of God which reaches his absolute nature, beyond the *proprium* of infinite perfection. Eventually, however, Leibniz and Spinoza depart on the precise nature of the absolutely simple notions or attributes which constitute God's nature. The difference has its roots, Deleuze argues, in certain of Leibniz's theological commitments, which necessitate his drawing a clear line between notions as they exist in the understanding of God and the only 'relatively' simple notions that exist in our own understanding. By drawing this clear division Leibniz is forced to rely on an analogical relation between the absolutely simple notions of God and the relatively simple terms of his combinatorial logic which symbolise them.

However, we have also seen that while Deleuze is no doubt correct to emphasise the theological motivations behind Leibniz's position, he has not yet adequately demonstrated Leibniz's commitment to a division between absolutely and relatively simple notions. The complexity of Leibniz's writings on this matter in fact leave room for a different interpretation, which Deleuze himself will hint at when he reiterates this discussion in the conclusion to EPS, and which we will discuss in the next chapter.

A key question is thus whether Leibniz's theory of relatively simple notions carries with it the commitment to analogy and symbolism that Deleuze claims. Answering this question requires looking in more detail at Leibniz's understanding of ideas, and in particular at the way he introduces a notion of *adequacy* to supplement Descartes' criteria of clarity and distinctness for true ideas. Fortunately, it is in just such a discussion of adequacy that we find Deleuze's second comparison between Leibniz and Spinoza.

1.3 Adequate Ideas

The second engagement with Leibniz in EPS is closely connected to the issues above. We saw that part of Leibniz's criticism of Descartes' ontological proof was the claim that clarity and distinctness are inadequate for proving God's existence. Deleuze returns to this point in the last two pages of chapter 9, 'Inadequacy'. Clarity and distinctness, he suggests, are supplemented by an additional notion of adequacy:

> A clear and distinct idea does not in itself constitute real knowledge, any more than it contains its own ground within itself: the sufficient reason of clarity and distinctness is to be found only in adequacy, and a clear and distinct idea constitutes real knowledge only to the extent that it follows from an idea that is itself adequate. (EPS 151)

Deleuze identifies in this idea another affinity between Leibniz and Spinoza: 'We have here, once again, a point of agreement between Spinoza and Leibniz, which helps to define the anti-Cartesian reaction' (EPS 152). Once again, then, Leibniz and Spinoza are united by a criticism of Descartes which focuses on sufficient reason. But this time, Deleuze also connects it to the concept of expression:

> Descartes, in his conception of the clear and distinct, restricted himself to the representative content of ideas; he did not rise to the conception of an infinitely deeper expressive content. He didn't conceive adequacy as the necessary and sufficient reason for clarity and distinctness: didn't conceive expression, that is to say, as the basis of representation. (EPS 152)[5]

In this section we will be concerned, first, with precisely how Deleuze identifies an 'expressive content' in Leibniz's theory of ideas and, second, with how this issue informs the questions concerning Leibniz's reliance on symbolism and analogy which ended the last section.

Above, we introduced the idea that Leibniz's demonstration of the conditions of possibility of an infinitely perfect being also provides us with the conditions for a real definition of God. Indeed, Leibniz defines a real definition as one 'through which the possibility of the thing is ascertained' (PPL 293). This is in contrast to nominal definitions, which allow us to name or recognise a thing, but do not ascertain the possibility of what they define: 'I call a definition nominal when it can still be doubted that the defined concept is possible' (PPL 319). We also saw above that Leibniz criticises Descartes' ontological proof for not establishing the possibility of an infinitely perfect being. Descartes' definition of God therefore remains nominal. At the root of this criticism of Descartes lies Leibniz's dissatisfaction with clarity and distinctness as sufficient conditions for true ideas. A third criterion, Leibniz argues, must be added: adequacy. The *Meditations on Knowledge, Truth and Ideas* open with a hierarchy of types of knowledge: 'Knowledge is either obscure or clear; clear knowledge is either confused or distinct; distinct knowledge is either inadequate or adequate, and also either symbolic or intuitive. The most perfect knowledge is that which is both adequate and intuitive' (PPL 291).

A concept is clear and distinct, says Leibniz, if it allows a thing to be recognised and distinguished from other things; in other words, if it contains the 'marks' necessary for a nominal definition, which is 'nothing but the enumeration of sufficient marks'. A nominal definition thus 'contains only marks for discerning one thing from others' (PPL 293). Leibniz calls these distinguishing marks 'component marks', and it is these marks which constitute a notion, just as the absolutely simple notions or perfections constituted the notion of an infinitely perfect being. Why is an 'enumeration of sufficient marks' not sufficient to demonstrate the possibility of a concept? In other words, why does this enumeration only suffice for a nominal definition and not for a real definition? The answer is that our knowledge of these component marks, while giving us clear and distinct knowledge of what they compose, may itself not be distinct. In most cases, Leibniz tells us, our knowledge of the component marks which allow us to recognise a thing is confused. And as a result, because the distinctness of our knowledge of a concept does not extend to the parts of that concept, our knowledge of it ultimately remains inadequate. The criterion for adequate knowledge, then, is that it must render distinct not just the concept, but all components of that concept: 'When every ingredient that enters into a distinct concept is itself known distinctly, or when analysis is carried through to the end, knowledge is adequate' (PPL 292). Adequate knowledge, for Leibniz, requires analysing a concept into its parts until we arrive at distinct or *simple* parts, which themselves have no parts. This is the only way we can demonstrate with certainty that they do not harbour a hidden contradiction. This is why, in the case of the concept of an infinitely perfect being, Descartes' clear and distinct concept of infinite perfection allows us to *recognise* an 'infinitely perfect being', but remains inadequate so long as we do not have distinct knowledge of the simple perfections that serve as the requisites or 'component marks' of this concept.

Deleuze frames this criticism of Descartes in terms of his reliance on the revelations of an individual mind, rather than on a logic internal to ideas themselves. Thus, 'Descartes got no further than the form of psychological consciousness in ideas; he didn't get as far as the logical form through which an idea is explained, by which ideas are linked one to another' (EPS 152). Leibniz's model of adequation provides the logical form through which true ideas are judged through knowledge of their component parts. Leibniz himself will criticise Descartes repeatedly for ignoring this essential aspect, relying instead on some kind of qualitative criterion present in any particular clear and distinct judgement. In 'Quod ens perfectissimum existit', he writes:

> Nor does it suffice for Descartes to appeal to experience and allege that he experiences this very concept in himself, clearly and distinctly. This is not to complete the demonstration but to break it off, unless he shows a way in which others can also arrive at an experience of this kind. For whenever we inject experience into our demonstrations, we ought to show how others can produce the same experience, unless we are trying to convince them solely through our own authority. (PPL 168)

In the *Meditations*, the same point is connected to the critique of clarity and distinctness:

> [The example of most rapid motion] has shown that we do not always at once have an idea of a thing of which we are conscious of thinking. Nor is it less deceptive, I think, when men today advance the famous principle that whatever I perceive clearly and distinctly in some thing is true, or may be predicated of it. For what seems clear and distinct to men when they judge rashly is frequently obscure and confused. (PPL 293)

Leibniz's concept of adequation thus moves beyond simple representative content, and beyond a reliance on the form of a psychological consciousness. But, we are yet to see how it allows ideas to be characterised as *expressive*.

1.4 Symbolic Thinking and Relatively Simple Notions

Concerning adequate knowledge, Leibniz writes: 'Whenever our knowledge is adequate, we have *a priori* knowledge of a possibility, for if we have carried out the analysis to the end and no contradiction has appeared, the concept is obviously possible' (PPL 293). But here we must recall the basis for Deleuze's criticism of Leibniz which we discussed in the last section: that human thinking, in fact, has access only to *relatively* simple notions. These notions are not actually simple or distinct at all, but are treated as such only because we choose to ignore, for the sake of convenience, their confusion of parts. Leibniz denies us, Deleuze claims, access to the absolutely simple, truly distinct terms that constitute God's essence. But in this case, on Deleuze's reading, adequate knowledge, for Leibniz, is impossible, because we can never reach absolutely simple notions. Leibniz himself is typically reluctant to arrive at a definitive answer to this question:

> Whether men will ever be able to carry out a perfect analysis of concepts, that is, to reduce their thoughts to the *first possibles* or to irreducible concepts, or (what is the same thing) to the absolute attributes of God themselves or the first causes and the final end of things, I shall not now venture to decide. (PPL 293)

Instead, Leibniz argues, our treatment of ideas relies on replacing their real parts with signs or symbols, which we treat as simple, even if really they are just placeholders for other, equally composite concepts:

> Yet for the most part, especially in a longer analysis, we do not intuit the entire nature of the subject matter at once but make use of signs instead of things, though we usually omit the explanation of these signs in any actually present thought for the sake of brevity, knowing or believing that we have the power to do it. (PPL 293)

It is these signs which Deleuze referred to above as 'relatively' simple notions, and which were distinguished from absolutely simple notions, knowledge of which is restricted to God. But the question is whether Leibniz thinks such thinking through signs is an inevitable necessity when faced with the inferiority of our understanding in relation to the understanding of God, or whether it is an obvious convenience 'for the sake of brevity'. The first is a profound point about Leibniz's commitment to an eminent God whose true essence remains obscure. The second is a more trivial point about the necessary shortcuts in thinking caused by the finitude of human understanding.

It was the second interpretation that we were led to in our brief look at the 'Elements of Logical Calculus' in the last section, where Euclid's relatively simple axiom of the straight line was a necessary shortcut until the arrival of Archimedes' real definition. Indeed, Leibniz is critical of symbolic thinking precisely because it does not reach truly simple concepts. This is, in fact, precisely the same criticism we have already seen him level at Descartes:

> It often happens that we falsely believe ourselves to have ideas of things in our mind, when we assume wrongly that we have already explained terms which we are using. [. . .] For often we understand after a fashion each single word or remember to have understood it earlier; yet because we are content with this blind thinking and do not sufficiently press the analysis of the concepts, we overlook a contradiction which the composite concept may involve. (PPL 292)

Leibniz opposes the 'symbolic' thinking he describes here to 'intuitive' thinking. Symbolic knowledge is thus knowledge of a concept which, while distinct, leaves the composites of this concept confused, choosing instead to represent them by signs. Intuitive knowledge, by contrast, leaves nothing confused: the concept and all its components are distinct. Intuitive knowledge, then, is adequate knowledge. But again, Leibniz refuses to come to a decision on whether such knowledge is ever actually achievable: 'when [intuitive knowledge] is possible, or *insofar as* it is possible', he writes. We know what intuitive, adequate knowledge *would* be, but we don't know if we can ever reach it. Leibniz is clear on at least one thing, though: when it comes to knowledge of a 'distinct, primitive [simple] concept', only intuitive knowledge is adequate. Thus, knowledge of absolutely simple notions, if it is possible, is not knowledge based on signs or symbols.

1.5 *Expression*

What does all this mean for Deleuze's first criticism of Leibniz? When we introduced it in section 1.2 we saw that it had two components.

The first was the accusation that Leibniz leaves absolutely simple notions inaccessible to human understanding, which must rely instead on relatively simple notions. This view now finds additional support in Leibniz's obvious reluctance to admit that adequate knowledge is possible.

But the second component of Deleuze's criticism is that, as a result of this discrepancy between absolutely and relatively simple notions, the terms of our thinking are restricted to a *symbolic, analogical* relation to the notions present in the understanding of God. This, I think, is harder to defend. Leibniz is clear that signs or symbols always refer to *composite* concepts. How then, could they be symbols for the *simple* attributes of God? When it comes to simple concepts, only intuitive, adequate knowledge is sufficient, and we leave the language of signs and symbols behind. Even if such adequate knowledge is ultimately impossible, we can at least understand what the relation between absolutely simple concepts and relatively simple terms would be: absolutely simple notions serve as the requisites or components of our relatively simple notions. They may remain necessarily obscure and confused, but, in theory at least, all composite concepts can be analysed into these simple terms. And while we may not know whether any of our relatively simple notions ever are adequate, and if so which, we at least know that their adequacy is grounded in having these absolutely simple notions as components, and not through any kind of merely symbolic or analogical relation to them.

If the relation between relatively simple notions and absolutely simple notions is not one of analogy or symbolisation, then what is it? If absolutely simple notions serve as the requisites or components of all our notions, and we understand these as in some sense the cause of the notions they compose, then the relation between them is precisely one of *expression*. An effect expresses its cause, Leibniz insists, and this, then, seems to be how we find the expressive content in ideas that Deleuze believes is just as crucial to Leibniz's theory of adequacy as it is to Spinoza's. But two points must be made. The first is that if this is expression, it is so only in the limited, traditional sense that Leibniz (and Deleuze) sometimes gives it, where an effect is said to express its cause. It is not yet the 'triadic' model of expression Deleuze finds in Spinoza, but which I will argue he only finds in Leibniz much later, in the conclusion to EPS. Second, if Leibniz's ideas are expressive, they are so only by being composed of simple terms that serve as the requisites for our concepts *in the same form* as they serve as the attributes of God. If ideas are expressive, therefore, they cannot be analogical. Thus, it seems, if Leibniz's theory of adequate ideas reaches the expressive content of ideas that Deleuze credits it with, then he does so only by overcoming the reliance on analogy and symbolisation that Deleuze had earlier accused him of.

Leibniz is clear, at various points, in drawing an equivalence between absolutely simple concepts and the attributes of God. We already saw this in the quote above: 'first possibles or irreducible concepts, or (what is the same thing) the absolute attributes of God', and he makes the same point in his Paris notes of 1676: 'Any simple form whatever is an attribute of God' (PPL 160).[6] Thus, ideas become expressive or adequate precisely by attaining to the absolutely simple form of their requisites in the understanding of God, and not by symbolising them. To establish something's possibility, to provide its real definition, to possess adequate knowledge of its notion, and to provide its sufficient reason, are all processes reliant on the absolute, simple self-identities which are the attributes of God and simultaneously the requisites or components of our own composite concepts.

Leibniz is in some sense saved from facing the repercussions of this view by refusing to decide on whether adequate knowledge is ever attainable by human understanding. But he is also able to once again draw a sharp divide between the domain of logical possibility and the domain of real existence. It may well be the case that we can only prove the possibility of a thing *a priori* by reaching the absolutely simple terms which are the attributes of God, but this doesn't matter, Leibniz thinks, so long as we can also prove the possibility of a thing *a posteriori*. Thus, he writes: 'We know an idea *a posteriori* when we experience the actual existence of the thing, for what actually exists or has existed is in any case possible' (PPL 293). And this is indeed the method we usually rely on, he thinks: 'For the most part we are content to learn the reality of certain concepts by experience and then to compose other concepts from them after the pattern of nature' (PPL 293).

The problem with this, of course, is that it takes us away from the purely logical form of ideas and back into a reliance upon representational content for which Leibniz has already criticised Descartes. The representational content of ideas, which their expressive content was supposed to supplement and surpass, risks returning with an even more fundamental role, as the only thing which guarantees the possibility of the simple concepts which compose our complex concepts. Again, then, although Deleuze praises Leibniz's theory of ideas for realising their 'expressive content', this is only according to a 'weak' form of expression, this time understood as the relationship between an idea and the thing it represents. In the letter to Arnauld from which Deleuze takes this quote, Leibniz refers at various points to 'expression or representation' and 'expression or perception' (Leibniz 1967: 144).

We have thus discovered two candidates for where to locate a concept of expression functioning in Leibniz's theory of adequate knowledge. First, expression as cause, in the sense that composite ideas express their requisites as an effect expresses its cause. Second, expression as representation, in the sense that simple ideas express the thing they represent. But we have not yet discovered in Leibniz the kind of expression that Deleuze thinks is truly original: the 'triad' of expression, in which what is expressed is 'beyond real causality, beyond ideal representation', and simultaneously 'deeper than the relation of causality, deeper than the relation of representation' (EPS 335). Thus, when Deleuze writes that 'Leibniz's remark that knowledge is a species of expression could have come from Spinoza' (EPS 152), we must, I think, add this important qualification: so long as we recognise that when Leibniz talks of expression, he uses it as a synonym for either causation or representation.

In this section we've seen that Deleuze thinks there is another affinity between Leibniz and Spinoza when it comes to the 'expressive content' of ideas. This expressive content is tied up with the new idea of adequation, supplementing and providing the sufficient reason for Descartes' previous criteria of clarity and distinctness. But we've also seen that we can only find in Leibniz's theory of adequate ideas a weak form of expression understood either as a relation of causality or a relation of representation, and that even this weak form calls into question Deleuze's earlier claim that Leibniz's philosophy restricts us to symbolic, analogical knowledge of relatively simple notions.

Perhaps, though, there is a further aspect to Deleuze's symbolisation criticism, which goes beyond explicitly understanding notions as signs or symbols. Here, symbolisation returns, Deleuze claims, as an essential component of Leibniz's theory of *harmony*, and becomes a *reciprocal* relation between terms that symbolise *each other*. This new interpretation is first introduced by Deleuze in his discussion of Leibniz's criticism of Cartesian mechanism, and it is this which constitutes the third and final engagement with Leibniz in the main text of EPS.

1.6 Mechanism, Force and Essence

The third discussion of Leibniz in EPS begins with his critique of mechanism, and ends with the complex relation between metaphysical substances (or monads) and physical bodies. Looking at this discussion will introduce a new understanding of Deleuze's 'symbolisation' criticism of Leibniz: this time it refers to the harmonious relation between metaphysics and physics, rather than the unilateral symbolisation between relatively and absolutely simple notions. But it will also introduce a new, and arguably much more fundamental, criticism, based on the role of God as guarantor of this harmonious relationship. This second criticism, I will argue, grounds the first. Finally, this section will introduce a new, complex set of issues concerning Leibniz's conception of the relation between metaphysical substances and physical bodies. We have thus moved away from the realm of necessary essences and logical ideas which dominated the last two sections, and into the realm of actually existing things.

Halfway through chapter 14, 'What Can a Body Do?', Deleuze identifies another affinity between Leibniz and Spinoza: 'Their philosophies constitute two aspects of a new "naturalism"' (EPS 227). This is, once again, an aspect of their shared anti-Cartesian reaction. Descartes established a new mathematical and mechanical science, whose effect was to render nature itself 'impotent' or inert by evacuating it of any virtuality, potentiality or immanent power. The goal of the anti-Cartesian reaction, Deleuze thinks, is to 're-establish the claims of a nature endowed with forces or power' (EPS 228). Central to this will be a critique of Cartesian mechanism. But again, just as with Descartes' ontological proof and his theory of clear and distinct ideas, it is not a matter of rejecting this Cartesian doctrine outright, but of supplementing it somehow. Thus, Leibniz writes in his 'New System of the Nature and Communication of Substances', that:

> After trying to explore the principles of mechanics itself in order to account for the laws of nature which we learn from experience, I perceived that the sole consideration of *extended mass* was not enough but that it was necessary, in addition, to use the concept of *force*, which is fully intelligible, although it falls within the sphere of metaphysics. (PPL 457)

Once again, Deleuze thinks, it is the question of sufficient reason which motivates this reintroduction of the notion of force into the world of mechanical bodies. He writes: 'One thus sees that mechanism does not exclude the idea of a nature or essence of each body, but rather requires it, as the sufficient reason for a given shape or a given movement, or a given proportion of movement and rest' (EPS 228). And here, for the first time, Deleuze explicitly draws together all three of his discussions of Leibniz in the main text of EPS under this umbrella of sufficient reason: 'The anti-Cartesian reaction is, throughout, a search for sufficient reasons: a sufficient reason for infinite perfection, a sufficient reason for clarity and distinctness, and a sufficient reason, indeed, for mechanism itself' (EPS 228). We thus get the first hint that our previous discussions of Leibniz – regarding the possibility of an infinitely perfect being in section 1.1 and the adequacy of ideas in section 1.3 – may not have been as incidental as they first appeared.

How, then, does Leibniz overcome the limitations of mechanism, and provide its sufficient reason? Deleuze's account is brief, dense and complex and, I'll suggest, not without its problems. There are, he insists, three levels at work in Leibniz's account of the nature of bodies: mechanism, force and essence. On the first, mechanistic level, 'everything happens in bodies mechanically, through shape and movement' (EPS 228). However, these movements necessarily refer to forces: 'The movements themselves presuppose forces of passion and action, without which bodies would be no more distinguished than would patterns of movement. Or, if you will, mechanical laws themselves presuppose an inner nature in the bodies they govern' (EPS 229). This is the move from the level of mechanism to the level of force. The next move is from these forces themselves to a primitive force or a metaphysical essence: 'But nor does the derivative force, in its turn, contain its own reason: it is only momentary, although it links that moment to earlier and later ones. It must be referred to a law governing the series of moments, which is a sort of primitive force or individual essence' (EPS 229). These essences, Deleuze claims, are 'the source of the derivative forces attributed to bodies'. Deleuze concludes that individual essences constitute 'a genuine metaphysics of Nature, which does not enter into physics, but corresponds to such physics itself' (EPS 229, translation modified).[7]

Central to Deleuze's account of Leibniz's view of the natural world is thus this distinction between three levels: mechanism, force and essence. But the only reference Deleuze gives for this distinction is to the later sections of Leibniz's paper 'On Nature Itself' (PPL 498). And there, we struggle to find the same distinction between three levels. Deleuze insists that there is an 'inner nature' to bodies on the level of force, *prior* to the introduction of essence, and quotes the following line from section nine: 'the internal nature [of created beings] is no different from the force of acting and suffering'. But later in the same section, Leibniz is clear that this force of acting and suffering is precisely what constitutes a substance: 'everything that acts is an individual substance'. Earlier, in section eight, Leibniz writes: 'The substance of things itself consists in the force of acting and being acted upon' (PPL 502). It thus seems that, in this paper at least, Leibniz treats as equal (force and substance) what Deleuze distributes across two levels (the level of force and the level of essence).

Despite this, in the earlier sections of this paper, Leibniz *does* clearly reject Cartesian mechanism on precisely the grounds Deleuze suggests: that it ignores the internal nature or force of a thing. Why, then, does Deleuze insist on his own unnecessarily complex account? I think the answer lies in the obvious *theological* motivations behind Leibniz's arguments in those earlier sections. Deleuze is keen to identify a correspondence between Leibniz and Spinoza on this question of the inadequacy of mechanism. Thus, he will write that Spinoza's own account is 'closely analogous' to Leibniz's (EPS 229). But the result is that he must go to great lengths to give a Leibnizian account which does not rely on theological commitments, because such an account could only ever be explicitly *anti-Spinozist.* Leibniz makes clear the theological stakes by opening his account with the following question: 'In what does the nature consist which we customarily ascribe to things, whose attributes, as they are usually understood, Mr. Sturm considers to reek somewhat of paganism?' But, Leibniz argues, the true risk of 'injuring piety' comes from the view that 'matter can stand by itself and mechanism needs no intelligence or spiritual substance' (PPL 499). But far from this drawing him closer to Spinoza, Leibniz in fact extends this argument, and claims that internal force is necessary precisely because it allows us to avoid the distasteful Spinozist alternative:

> No created substance, no identical soul, would be permanent, and hence nothing would be conserved by God, but everything would reduce to certain evanescent and flowing modifications or phantasms, so to speak, of the one permanent divine substance. And, what reduces to the same thing, God would be the nature and substance of all things – a doctrine of most evil repute, which a writer who was subtle indeed but irreligious, in recent years imposed upon the world, or at least revived. (PPL 501)

It would be hard for Deleuze to draw a correspondence between Leibniz and Spinoza on this point if, as it appears from these early sections, a central part of Leibniz's account is its anti-Spinozist sentiment. Perhaps at the same time, though, we can also view this as the earliest demonstration of Deleuze's willingness to be charitable in his readings of Leibniz. Instead of framing Leibniz's rejection of mechanism purely in terms of his theologically conservative claim that it 'injures piety', he instead strives to give an alternative account which doesn't shy away from the complicated relation between metaphysical substance and physical body in Leibniz's philosophy. At the same time, Deleuze inadvertently introduces, for the first time, ideas which we'll see return, with a much more important role, in later works.

As we've seen, Deleuze's account identifies three distinct levels in Leibniz's account of nature: mechanism, force and essence. But it also contains two moments where we 'jump' from one level to the next. Thus, mechanism 'presupposes' forces, which in turn 'refer to' essences as their source. It is in these moments that we locate sufficient reason: each level refers to the one above as the source of its reason. It thus appears, at least at first glance, that there is some kind of causal relationship between the three levels. And yet we saw Deleuze conclude his account with the claim that essences constitute a metaphysics of nature which *corresponds* to a physics of bodies, but which does not *enter into* it. This isn't a causal relation, but a relation of *harmony* between two entirely autonomous domains: the metaphysical domain of essences on the one hand and the physical domain of bodies and forces on the other. But if this is the case, in what sense does force 'refer to' essences, and in what sense are essences the 'source of' forces? The danger is that if we understand the relation between the two domains as a causal relation, we undermine the autonomy of each and jeopardise Leibniz's important concept of harmony.

The solution lies in how we understand the concept of 'referral'. It involves understanding metaphysical essences as a *unifying* principle for material masses that are necessarily multiple or aggregated due to the infinitely divisible nature of matter itself. Thus, Leibniz will write:

> For if these true and real unities were dispensed with, only beings through aggregation would remain; indeed, it would follow that there would be left no true beings within bodies. For even though there are atoms of substance, namely, my monads, which lack parts, there are no atoms of mass or of minimum extension, or any last elements, since a continuum is not composed of points. (PPL 503)

Leibniz, Spinoza and the Anti-Cartesian Reaction

On this model, physics and metaphysics harmonise one another, and the same movement can at once be understood as the result of the simple internal nature or essence of a thing (its monad), and as the result of the universal interaction that makes bodies react to the 'shocks' imparted by other parts of matter, and which results from the continuous, infinitely divisible nature of matter.

Although only marginally significant here, this Leibnizian conception of the infinite divisibility of matter, and especially the continuity that corresponds to it, will become one of the most important influences of Leibniz on Deleuze. In Part II, we will use it to help characterise the 'restless' nature of the infinitely small, which will be the first component of the Leibnizian structure we find at work in *Difference and Repetition* and *Logic of Sense*. But we're not yet in a position to get to the bottom of this complex issue, and at this early stage, Deleuze himself does not make any reference to this idea of the unifying role of metaphysical substances. In fact, it seems likely that Deleuze himself had not yet fully formulated his ideas; and it is not until the first and eighth chapters of *The Fold*, twenty years later, that we get a fully developed view on this important question. Here, however, we need only address the criticism that Deleuze levels at Leibniz on the basis of this reading, and we'll see that this criticism applies however we understand the relation between these three levels.

1.7 A New Criticism of Leibniz

Following the section on Leibniz's critique of mechanism, Deleuze gives an account of Spinoza's own anti-Cartesian naturalism and then asks, once more: 'What is the real difference between Leibniz and Spinoza?' They both, he argues, posit 'singular essences' as a necessary supplement to mechanism, but with this crucial difference: 'If Leibniz recognises in things an inherent force of their own, he does so by making individual essences into so many substances. In Spinoza, on the other hand, this is done by defining particular essences as modal, and more generally, by making things themselves modes of a single substance' (EPS 232). Why is it so significant that Leibniz's essences are themselves substances rather than modes of a single substance? The nature of substances, and in particular their relation to God, means, ultimately that 'with Leibniz mechanism is referred to something deeper through the requirements of a finality that remains partly transcendent' (EPS 232, translation modified).

We can understand this finality in two ways, depending on how we understand the relation between the three levels we looked at in the last section. Deleuze's own argument seems again to rely on the language of 'referral' and sufficient reason. Mechanism refers to forces, which refer to substances or monads. What, then, do these substances themselves refer to, as the source of their own sufficient reason? The answer is God's choice of best possible world. Deleuze writes that substances are 'caught in an order of finality as the context in which they are chosen by God, or even just subject to such a choice' (EPS 232). By referring to metaphysical substances, mechanism in fact ends up relying on something transcendent, and sufficient reason thus converges each time on God and God's choice of best possible world.

Even if we understand the relation between physics and metaphysics as one of correspondence instead of referral, the result is the same: this correspondence is the result of a pre-established harmony, which again is grounded in God's choice of best possible world.[8] The point is that, whichever way we look at it, Leibniz's substances are embroiled in a transcendent, divine calculus, or in a divine choice which presides over the creation of all substances and all aggregated bodies. It is therefore here, in this discussion of mechanism, that we find a new criticism of Leibniz. And, I argue, it is this criticism which will occur again and again, in different terms, in all of Deleuze's later readings of Leibniz, including the conclusion of EPS. It boils down to the eventual dominance of Leibniz's conservative side: however radical and dynamic his philosophy may appear, there is always implicit some kind of essential reference to a theological principle of harmony, finality or divine choice, which grounds and guarantees the harmony and order of the world, while remaining completely transcendent to it.

What does this mean for Deleuze's earlier criticism of Leibniz, which was couched in terms of symbolisation and analogy? It returns here in a different form. Nature for Leibniz, Deleuze argues, is 'a Nature whose different levels are hierarchically related, harmonised and, above all, "symbolise one another". Expression is never divorced in Leibniz from a symbolisation whose principle is always finality or ultimate agreement' (EPS 232). Here, then, the idea of symbolisation returns, but with two important developments. First, it now occurs entirely on the side of 'nature': it is no longer a unilateral relation between God's infinite perfections and our own notions which symbolise them. Instead, it is a reciprocal relation in which the different levels of Leibniz's world symbolise each other. Second, and more importantly, symbolisation is now subordinated to the finality 'or ultimate agreement' which causes and governs it. It becomes a symptom of Leibniz's reliance on a transcendent God, and is therefore secondary to Deleuze's new, much more fundamental criticism of Leibniz's theology. Above we called into question Deleuze's strict closing off of absolutely simple notions in the necessarily obscured understanding of God, suggesting that, limited to the domain of logical possibilities, we at least know the requirements for the kind of adequate knowledge that would reach absolutely simple notions, even if we can never attain it. But when it comes to God's choice of the world itself, there is no longer even this commiseration. Given the infinitely, irreducibly complex nature of every possible world, any calculus which would determine the best of these worlds must be locked deeply inside the understanding of God. Not only can we never recreate this divine calculus, we cannot even begin to guess how it functions.[9] Thus the sufficient reason of the world and everything in it ultimately remains forever closed off in its transcendent creator.

In this section we've introduced the third and final connection between Leibniz and Spinoza in their critique of Cartesian mechanism. Deleuze's account of three levels in Leibniz's vision of nature has introduced the question of the relation between physics and metaphysics in Leibniz's philosophy and its place in Deleuze's reading. We have gained a sense of the important role played by individual substances or monads in relation to physical bodies, which are only 'aggregates' thanks to the infinitely divisible nature of the material world itself.

We've also established in its fullest form the true grounds for Deleuze's major criticism of Leibniz. The accusation that Leibniz relies on a 'symbolisation', which above had seemed potentially inadequate, is now better understood as a reference to a mutual relation of harmony between the various levels of his philosophy, and which is itself grounded by the harmonious principles of an ordered, law-governed world chosen and guaranteed by a transcendent God.

Finally, we've seen for the first time how Deleuze draws together all three discussions of Leibniz in the main text of EPS through the question of sufficient reason, which constitutes the core of the anti-Cartesian reaction. Having initially appeared incidental, Deleuze's discussions of Leibniz now strike us as increasingly important, a view which will be confirmed as we turn to book's concluding chapter, the entirety of which is explicitly framed in terms of the differences between Leibniz and Spinoza and their use of the concept of expression.

Notes

1. 'It was on Spinoza that I worked most seriously according to the norms of the history of philosophy' (Deleuze and Parnet 2007: 15).
2. Christian Kerslake argues that 'in seeking to characterise the coexistence of the attributes, Deleuze in fact presents Leibniz's version of the proof, silently implying that Leibniz has presented a stronger version of the Spinozist proof' (Kerslake 2009: 112). In fact, however, Deleuze *does* give a Spinozist version of the same proof, a few pages later (EPS 79), precisely in order to defend Spinoza against the accusation Leibniz levels at him in his notes on the *Ethics*: that Spinoza, like Descartes, does not demonstrate the compatibility of God's attributes (PPL 196).
3. Leibniz, 'Comments on Spinoza's Philosophy', in Leibniz 1989b.
4. Beistegui 2010: 32. For an account of precisely *why* Deleuze condemns philosophies reliant on emanation and analogy, cf. Beistegui 2010, chapter 2, section 2, as well as our own discussion of the opening of *Difference and Repetition* in Part II. Deleuze's own account of eminence, analogy and symbolism in EPS is found in chapter 3, 'Attributes and Divine Names'.
5. Cf. also EPS 153: 'All the differences between Leibniz and Spinoza take away nothing from their agreement on these fundamental principles which, above all else, constitute the anti-Cartesian reaction'; and page 154: 'In all this, Spinoza and Leibniz are fighting a common cause, a continuation of what had set them against the Cartesian ontological proof, the search for a sufficient reason singularly lacking throughout Cartesianism. Each of them, proceeding differently, discovers the expressive content of ideas, and their explicative form.'
6. See also, on this point, Loemker's note at PPL 169: 'Leibniz's argument therefore rests on his identification of the simple concepts of his combinatorial logic with the perfections of God', and also section V of his introduction, where he writes: 'For a real definition must contain in its predicate those essential concepts which serve to determine all the properties and modifications which are involved in the substance which its composite subject represents; Leibniz sometimes calls these essential determinants. These are the simple, primary essences or concepts, ultimate perfections of God, out of which concrete substances come into being, since all other qualities, essential or temporal, arise by combination from them' (PPL 25).
7. Joughin's translation of this sentence suggests that the metaphysics of Nature 'does not *merely* enter into physics', whereas in fact the key point, as we'll see, is that it does not enter into physics *at all*.

Leibniz, Spinoza and the Anti-Cartesian Reaction

8. As Gueroult writes: 'Physics and even the concept of derivative force thus leads irresistibly to the metaphysical theory of pre-established harmony' (Gueroult 1967: 203).
9. At least until, as we'll see Deleuze argue, Leibniz's own infinitesimal calculus gives us an 'approximation' of this divine process.

2

Leibniz and Expression

Titled 'The Theory of Expression in Leibniz and Spinoza', Deleuze's conclusion to *Expressionism in Philosophy: Spinoza* gives Leibniz a new, central role that was lacking in our discussions in the last chapter. While the three discussions of Leibniz we've looked at so far appeared incidental, they are now drawn together by Deleuze under a new heading: the three 'fundamental determinations' of being, knowing and acting. These correspond to God and God's nature, to adequate ideas, and to bodies imbued with force (EPS 321). At the same time, sufficient reason, a concern for which had motivated these discussions, is now itself given a clearer formulation by being distributed across these three domains. Thus, Deleuze writes, sufficient reason has three branches, the *ratio essendi* or reason for essence, the *ratio cognoscendi* or reason for knowing, and the *ratio fiendi* or *agendi* or reason for producing or acting (EPS 322).[1] It is in these three domains that Deleuze locates a crucial role for the concept of expression, which he now considers just as central to Leibniz as to Spinoza, and which constitutes the heart of their shared anti-Cartesian reaction.

Leibniz's appearances in the main text were dominated by references to his theological commitments. Here in the conclusion, by contrast, a different side of Leibniz starts to come to the fore. The Leibniz we find here is much closer to the Leibniz that Deleuze puts to work at crucial stages in *Difference and Repetition* and *Logic of Sense*. How do we explain Leibniz's sudden transformation in Deleuze's work? There are various possibilities. Although *Expressionism in Philosophy: Spinoza* was published the same year as *Difference and Repetition*, Dosse points out that it was 'practically finished in the late 1950s' (Dosse 2013: 118). It is possible, then, that the conclusion was written significantly later than the main text. And perhaps in the interval Deleuze had come to a more developed understanding and appreciation of Leibniz's philosophy.[2] On the other hand, perhaps Deleuze had always had this more radical version of Leibniz in mind, but suppressed it in the main text until it was relevant, or because he

Leibniz and Expression

wanted to emphasise Spinoza's originality. It is hard to conclusively explain the causes of this change, but it is enough for our purposes to demonstrate that the conclusion contains a new, more subtle, reading of Leibniz's philosophy which introduces, however briefly, many of the Leibnizian concepts that Deleuze continues to make use of throughout his later work.

This chapter will thus be concerned with four things. First, we'll return to two of our discussions in the last chapter in light of their new role as the 'fundamental determinations' of being and acting. We'll see that Deleuze's summary of these discussions in the conclusion introduces slight differences, showing us a new reading of Leibniz that introduces some of the key influences of Leibniz's philosophy on Deleuze.

Second, we'll turn to Deleuze's lengthy discussion of Leibniz's concept of expression. I'll argue that within this discussion there is a shift from a 'two-term' concept of expression to a triadic concept which is closer to the one Deleuze finds in Spinoza.

Third, we'll return a final time to Deleuze's criticism of Leibniz, this time understood as a criticism of his 'equivocal' concept of expression compared to Spinoza's 'univocal' concept. We'll see that ultimately all of Deleuze's criticisms of Leibniz can be reduced to an aversion to certain of Leibniz's theological commitments and motivations.

Finally, we'll look in detail at the penultimate paragraph of the conclusion to EPS which, I'll suggest, ends with a brief description of what will ultimately become Deleuze's double process of actualisation and counter-actualisation. Crucially, I'll argue that Deleuze turns to Leibniz, rather than Spinoza, in order to explain these processes.

2.1 Absolutely Simple Notions

In the conclusion, Deleuze summarises the three elements of the anti-Cartesian reaction we looked at in the main text. The first concerns the requirements for demonstrating the possibility of God as an infinitely perfect being. Here again Deleuze mentions as key to Leibniz's account the absolutely simple forms or attributes of God, through the necessary compatibility of which His nature is proved possible. At first glance this appears to be the same as the account found in chapter 4 of the main text and which we discussed in section 1.1. But while Deleuze once again references the note 'Quod ens perfectissimum existit', and the *Meditations on Knowledge, Truth and*

Ideas, this time he adds a third reference, to the *New Essays*, a book he does not reference anywhere in the main text and which reveals a potentially significant development. Deleuze refers to Leibniz's mention of 'original or distinctly knowable qualities' alongside his references to 'absolutely simple forms' and the 'attributes of God'. But, as we saw in our discussion, the criticism levelled at Leibniz in chapter 4 relied on the key claim that these absolutely simple forms were *not* distinctly knowable. The simple terms of our own logic were only relatively simple, and were thus only analogous to the actual attributes of God, and only ever symbolised them. Deleuze does not explicitly change his view, but this new reference suggests that he now agrees with the conclusion we arrived at in section 1.2: that adequate, distinct knowledge of the attributes of God is at least theoretically possible. At the same time this also implies that Deleuze has quietly dropped one aspect of his 'symbolisation' criticism of Leibniz, where our relatively simple notions unilaterally symbolise absolutely simple notions.

Jumping ahead briefly, by the time we get to *The Fold*, there is no longer any ambiguity on this point. There, Deleuze goes to great lengths to demonstrate that relatively simple notions (which he will call 'Definables') do not analogically symbolise the absolutely simple notions ('Identicals') but derive from and are composed by them: 'No doubt, in the absolute, God himself assures the passage from Identicals to Definables: he is constituted by all the primitive absolute forms, but he is also the first and last definable, from which derives all the others' (LP 61).

The idea that God's nature, essence or sufficient reason is in some sense constituted by his attributes is better understood, I think, now that we realise that these attributes are at the same time the primary terms of Leibniz's combinatorial logic. As we began to see in our discussion of adequate ideas in section 1.3, these terms are something like the 'essential determinants' that serve as the predicates of any real definition. In his Paris Notes of 1676 Leibniz calls them 'requisites' and tells us that 'A reason is the sum of requisites' (PPL 161). Thus, we find this more specific sense of God's 'reason' in the 'first possibles or irreducible concepts' which are simultaneously understood first as perfections or attributes; then as the predicates of God's real definition; and finally as the requisites which make up the concept of an infinitely perfect being.

But if these absolutely simple terms are no longer closed off in the understanding of God, we face a new question concerning their own sufficient reason or *ratio essendi*. In other words, if a concept's sufficient reason is understood as the sum of the requisites that make it up, how do we conceive of the sufficient reason of these requisites themselves, given that they are simple and without parts? For Leibniz these simple forms are essences: they stand prior to the relations of compossibility and combination which condition the rest of existence. Indeed, their only condition is that they are possible: 'Possibility is the principle of essence' (PPL 51). We've already seen that the possibility of these simple elements is guaranteed by the fact that, as simple, they contain no parts which could contradict each other. We also saw that Deleuze goes further and claims that it is not the case that in the absence of requisite parts simple elements contain nothing, but rather that they contain only themselves. They are possible, therefore, only because they do not contradict themselves. In other words, they find their reason in the fact that 'A is not non-A'. This is Leibniz's formal characterisation of the principle of non-contradiction, and it is this principle, along with the principle of identity as its counterpart, that ultimately serves as the 'sufficient reason' for the essences which constitute God's nature. There is thus a sense in which Leibniz's commitment to the principle of identity is even more foundational than his theological commitment to God's perfection. Indeed, in a note to a letter to Eckhard, Leibniz writes: 'Who would say that A is not non-A because God has decreed it?' (PPL 181).[3] This new reading thus hints at something else Deleuze will later emphasise in Leibniz. While his criticism of Leibniz's reliance on a creative God remains a constant presence, he also comes to admire his philosophy for its creative 'play of principles' – here, the principle of identity and the principle of non-contradiction. In this, we detect a recurring tension between, on the one hand, the often theological motivations that lead Leibniz to this 'dizzying creation' of principles and, on the other hand, the potential for these principles to themselves become creative, and overcome or break free from theological constraints. This tension is just one instance of the much broader tension in Deleuze's Leibnizianism between a critical stance on Leibniz's commitment to religious orthodoxy and an admiration for his creativity. But we can also see that the two are not simply opposed to one another – it is precisely Leibniz's desperation to preserve a harmonious religious order that drives his frenzied philosophical activity.

This emphasis on the role played by logical principles brings with it a re-evaluation of sufficient reason. We've already seen how Deleuze formulates this concept more rigorously in the conclusion:

while in the main text sufficient reason remains vague, motivating the anti-Cartesian reaction without any real exposition of its own status, in the conclusion Deleuze distributes it across three domains in three different forms, as the *ratio essendi*, *ratio cognoscendi* and *ratio fiendi* or *agendi*. Later, again, Deleuze will tie sufficient reason to Leibniz's creation of principles. While this first instance of sufficient reason in the form of the principle of identity is ostensibly concerned only with the proof of God's possibility, it returns in *The Fold*, whose fourth chapter (titled 'Sufficient Reason') insists on a more complex reading of this topic by identifying four Leibnizian principles, each of which serves as the sufficient reason for a particular domain. There, simple elements as absolute self-identities exist in a 'zone' in which 'noncontradiction [identity] suffices as reason' and in which, therefore, 'the principle of contradiction is a case of sufficient reason' (LP 78).

2.2 Non-causal Correspondence

After summarising the discussion of adequate ideas we looked at in section 1.2 and 1.3, Deleuze turns again to the question of material bodies, or as he now calls it the third 'fundamental determination' of acting. Here, his focus has changed significantly. In the main text, the criticism of Cartesian mechanism evolved into a discussion of the relation between metaphysics and physics, understood in a very general sense. Here, the issue for Deleuze is the more specific question of the relation between mind and body. And while Leibniz's relation of harmony between metaphysics and physics was viewed in a negative light for its necessary reference to God's choice of best possible world, it is now placed alongside Spinoza's 'parallelism' as an instance of the novel new idea of 'non-causal correspondences'. Deleuze combines this idea with a new set of terminology based on 'series', which will take on an important role in *Difference and Repetition* and especially *Logic of Sense*. Thus, each body forms a corporeal series and each mind forms a spiritual series. The progression of each of these series is explained by the operation of real causality within them. But between these two series there is no causal relation. There is nevertheless a correspondence and, Deleuze thinks, this correspondence must be explained through the concept of expression (EPS 327). Deleuze thus finds a place for Leibniz's theory of harmony without immediately condemning its reliance on a principle of finality or maximal perfection. We get the first hint that the complicated relationship between the spiritual motivations of a monad and the causal mechanism of the body which belongs to that monad can be explained in terms of a concept of expression rather than a simple reliance on God. But it's also clear that this concept of expression cannot be understood as a relation between only two terms, as it was above. In other words, the heterogeneous series of mind and body do not merely express each other. Rather, they both express some third thing, for now left mysterious as simply 'what is expressed'. Thus, Deleuze thinks, the concept of expression 'explains the possibility of distinct and heterogeneous series (expressions) expressing the same invariant (what is expressed), by establishing in each of the varying series the same concatenation of causes and effects' (EPS 327).

We must be careful to distinguish this new 'three-term' model of expression from the 'two-term' model which is much more obviously discernible in Leibniz's philosophy. The two-term expression exists between what is expressed and its expression. This is the sense in which real causality and representation were above both understood as species of expression. An effect is an expression of its cause (what is expressed), while an idea is an expression of its object. The three-term or triadic model, by contrast, distinguishes what expresses, its expressions, and what is expressed. Deleuze identifies various forms of this triad in Spinoza, the first being between substance (what expresses), attributes (expressions) and the essence of substance (what is expressed). It is not yet clear exactly how this model will be applied to Leibniz's philosophy, but we've just seen how the heterogeneous series of mind and body are both expressions of some third, deeper 'invariant' (what is expressed).

The next section will show how Deleuze's reading of Leibniz in the conclusion gradually moves from the first two-term model of expression to a three-term model. Even with this change, however, he still subjects Leibniz to the same criticisms of symbolisation and finality. It is not until the penultimate paragraph that Deleuze finally gives Leibniz's philosophy a triadic expressive character which appears equal to that of Spinoza's.

2.3 Leibniz's Expressive World

Expression is thus the concept which draws together the three fundamental determinations of being, knowing and acting, as well as the three branches of sufficient reason. And because this concept is found in Leibniz as well as Spinoza, Deleuze emphasises that 'what they have in common cannot be exaggerated' (EPS 327). Despite all Deleuze's attempts to find the concept of expression working at every stage in Spinoza's philosophy, the irony is that he thinks it is Leibniz, not Spinoza, who gives expression 'such an extension that it comes to cover everything'. And so while we find 'no explicit definition or demonstration' of expression in Spinoza, we do find many passages in Leibniz that deal with the concept explicitly. The problem, though, is that Leibniz extends the concept *too* far, until it includes even those things which Spinoza's version rejects: 'the world of signs, of similarities, of symbols and harmonies . . .' (EPS 327).

Deleuze thus turns to one of these explicit formulations of expression in Leibniz: the paper 'What is an Idea?', written, incidentally, just after his meeting with Spinoza (PPL 207). There, Leibniz defines expression as a correspondence of relations between two things: 'That is said to express a thing in which there are relations [*habitudines*] which correspond to the relations of the thing expressed.' We find a similar definition in a letter to Arnauld: 'One thing *expresses* another (in my terminology) when there exists a constant and fixed relationship between what can be said of one and the other' (Leibniz 1967: 144). Here, then, it is clear that with Leibniz we are firmly rooted in a two-term conception of expression. He gives a number of examples. Expression can be arbitrary, writes Leibniz, in the sense that a certain word or character expresses a certain idea. But it can also have a 'basis in nature', either through a similarity, such as between a geographic region and a map of the region, or through a law, such as between a circle and an ellipse which represents it, 'since any point whatever on the ellipse corresponds to some point on the circle according to a definite law' (PPL 208).

On the basis of these examples, Deleuze concludes that in Leibniz's model of expression one of the terms is always superior or dominant in relation to the other. Thus, the landscape 'enjoys the identity' which is reproduced in the map, while the circle 'involves the law' that the ellipse 'develops' (EPS 328). But Deleuze's use of the words 'involve' and 'develop' is confusing, and it is unclear how a law can be enveloped or developed. Leibniz himself claims only that there is some law which allows a correspondence to be drawn between a point on the circle and a point on the ellipse, but Deleuze seems to want to push the point further. The superior term in the relation of expression, he claims, 'concentrates in its unity' what the other 'disperses in multiplicity' (EPS 328). We thus already begin to sense that the terms of the discussion are shifting: rather than a simple relation between two terms (one of which expresses the other), this sentence opens up the possibility that there is now some third term present on both sides of the expression, concentrated into a unity on one side, and dispersed into a multiplicity on the other. In this sense, both terms would be expressions of some third term (the 'what is expressed'). What is clear, in any case, is that Deleuze's reference to 'What is an Idea?' is not enough to resolve this confusion. There is no obvious sense in which a landscape is a unity in relation to the multiplicity of a map, or a circle a unity in relation to the multiplicity of an ellipse, and indeed Leibniz makes no mention of unity or multiplicity anywhere in this paper. Instead, it is clear that once again Leibniz is using the term expression as a synonym for *representation*. It is still not clear, then, how we can draw out of Leibniz a three-term model of expression which goes beyond the two-term relation of causality or representation.

Fortunately, in a footnote Deleuze gives two other references to Leibniz on this point. Thus, in the *New Essays*, we *do* find a relation between expression on the one hand and unity and multiplicity on the other: 'Though the soul and the machine [body] have no immediate influence on each other, they mutually express each other, the soul having concentrated into a perfect unity everything that the machine has dispersed throughout its multiplicity' (Leibniz 1996: 318). We can make two points on the basis of this quote. First, the relation of expression, rather than existing between things like landscapes and maps, exists here between the mind or monad and its body. But this expressive relation is clearly not one of causation. The soul and body 'have no immediate influence' on one another. Their relation is instead one of non-causal correspondence or harmony. Second, the relation of expression is now mutual. The terms express each other, rather than one term (the expression, the map) expressing the other (the expressed, the landscape). But, within this mutual expression, one term remains superior in so far as it unifies what remains dispersed into a multiplicity in the other. In this case, the mind is superior because it is a unity in relation to all the myriad parts of its body. It is thus on the basis of a distinction between unity and multiplicity or One and Many that Deleuze distinguishes a superior and inferior term in Leibniz's model of expression.

What does this mean for the ambiguity between a two-term and three-term model of expression? Deleuze's next sentence settles the issue: 'That which expresses is "endowed with true unity" in relation to its expressions; or, which comes to the same thing, the expression is a unity in relation to the multiplicity and divisibility of what is expressed' (EPS 328, translation modified). On a two-term model, the two parts of this sentence, far from 'coming to the same thing', appear instead to contradict one another. Thus, if we consider a two-term relation of expression between myself and a self-portrait I have painted, then I am simultaneously 'what expresses' and 'what is expressed'. I have expressed myself in my self-portrait, which is my expression, and I am the 'what is expressed' of that expression. But according to Deleuze's phrasing, 'that which expresses' is a unity, while 'what is expressed' is a multiplicity, and thus they cannot be the same thing. The only way out of this confusion, then, is to introduce 'what is expressed' as a *third* term, which is present in both sides of the expression.

The introduction of a three-term model is again confirmed in Deleuze's next sentence: 'But a certain area of confusion or obscurity is thus introduced into expression: the superior term, through its unity, expresses *more distinctly* what the other in its multiplicity expresses *less distinctly*' (EPS 328). Here, we distinguish two expressions, both of which express some third thing, one more distinctly than the other. We also see that Deleuze ties the distinction between unity and multiplicity to the distinction between the clear and the obscure and between the distinct and the confused. The superior term is a unity because it expresses clearly and distinctly what remains obscure and confused (or multiple) in the inferior term. But what exactly is this third term, or this 'what is expressed'?

We get our first hint in Deleuze's appropriation of an image from another of Leibniz's letters to Arnauld (Leibniz 1967: 84). A boat, he points out, is said to be the cause of the movement of the myriad parts of the water it moves through, because it has a unity which 'allows a more distinct explanation of what is happening'. We note first of all how strange this argument appears. Is the boat really the cause of the movement of the water because it is more distinct? Surely, we would want to add, the boat moves the water because it is being propelled by a sail or an engine? But perhaps this doesn't matter, because after all the boat is only *said* to be the cause of the movement of the water. Here we are forced to confront again the radical autonomy of every part of Leibniz's universe. What appears as a particular distribution of action and passion or cause and effect is, ultimately, a difference in perspective. There's no actual causal influence between the boat and the water, just as there is no causal influence between my mind and body. The monads present in the molecules of water each have their own internally unfolding, spontaneous development, utterly indifferent to influence from of all the other monads which surround them, but corresponding and conforming to this influence perfectly. This is the essence of pre-established harmony. The water, then, is just as active as the boat; we just can't adequately grasp its activity. The boat, nevertheless, is said to be the cause of the movement because it expresses more distinctly what the parts of the water express obscurely or confusedly. But again, *what is it* that they are both expressing? Here, it is simply 'what is happening'. What is expressed, then, is what is happening. For a more satisfactory answer, we must push on, and observe how Deleuze transforms this image of the boat cutting through the water into a general account of the expressive nature of monads themselves.

The movement of the water, Deleuze points out, is expressed in the movement of the boat. Here we must introduce another key feature of the model of expression Deleuze is extracting from Leibniz. The superior term or unity *requires* the inferior term or multiplicity: its unity is precisely the involving, folding or drawing together of a part of this confused multiplicity. In other words, what is clear and distinct is so only on the basis of its relation to some obscure and confused multiplicity which it subsumes. Thus, Deleuze writes, the superior term 'carves its own distinct expression out of a dim area which surrounds it on all sides and in which it is plunged' (EPS 328). We can understand this, first, in a literal sense, in terms of the boat. The boat is plunged into the water, and it unifies a part of the confused totality of the water by carving through it and expressing it clearly as part of a unified movement.

Deleuze thinks we can understand the expression of monads in precisely the same terms: 'each monad traces its distinct partial expression against the background of a confused total expression' (EPS 328). But what is the 'water' that the boat-monad carves through, and from which it draws its clear expression? Or in other words, what is the mysterious third term, the 'what is happening' or the 'what is expressed'? It is the *world* itself: each monad 'confusedly expresses the whole world, but clearly expresses only a part of it' (EPS 329). Monads express the world, but they express it twice. First, they express it as a totality, but as such they express it only confusedly and obscurely, their limited, finite nature proving inadequate to grasp the whole world clearly. But within this confused total expression the monad carves out for itself a second, smaller, clear and distinct expression, determined by the expressive relation it has to its body. This second expression is thus simultaneously a distinct expression of a small part of the whole world, and an expression which unifies the multiplicity of its own body.

If this is the 'world', though, it is so only in a new sense, revealed by Deleuze as he draws his account of Leibniz's expression together in a final key sentence: 'The world expressed by each monad is a continuum in which there are singularities, and it is around these singularities that monads take form as expressive centres' (EPS 329). Monads are plunged into this continuum of singularities, and express a part of it clearly by drawing together or enveloping a certain group of these singularities. But what really strikes us about this sentence is just how out of place it is with everything else we've looked at so far. Nowhere else in EPS, before this point, has there been any mention of singularities, or of monads as expressive centres. None of Deleuze's various discussions of Leibniz elsewhere in EPS have equipped us to make sense of this new idea.

In fact, it's part of a set of terminology which will become very familiar in Deleuze's later works. Thus, tucked away in what at first glance looks like just one more criticism of Leibniz in comparison with Spinoza, we in fact find an account that sounds strikingly 'Deleuzian'. Jumping ahead of ourselves somewhat, we can see, for instance, its similarity to the following account of the process of 'static ontological genesis' given in series 16 of *Logic of Sense*: 'A world already envelops an infinite system of singularities [. . .]. Within this world, however, individuals are constituted which select and envelop a finite number of the singularities of the system' (LS 126). And this from *Difference and Repetition*: 'We know that each one of these completed notions (monads) expresses the totality of the world: but it expresses it precisely under a certain differential relation and around certain distinctive points [singularities] which correspond to this relation' (DR 47). And, of course, it will return in an even more elaborated form in *The Fold*: 'We have seen that the world is an infinity of convergent series, prolonged into each other, around singular points. And each individual monad expresses the same world in its entirety, although it only clearly expresses a part of this world, a series or even a finite sequence' (LP 80). In all that follows we'll see just how much Deleuze takes to heart this vision of the world, and how closely he ties it to Leibniz.

Here then, Leibniz has finally been allowed to appear, however briefly, in a more radical guise. And this new Leibniz reveals to us the potential for a new understanding of individuals and of the world itself. Leibniz's 'continuum of singularities', as we'll see in Part II, returns as a crucial part of Deleuze's description of a virtual, transcendental field in *Difference and Repetition* and *Logic of Sense*. And the expressive nature of monads will become central to his account of the actualisation of individuals from this field. As we mentioned in the introduction, in his letter to the English translator of EPS Deleuze writes: 'What I needed was both (1) the expressive character of particular individuals, and (2) an immanence of being. Leibniz, in a way, goes still further than Spinoza on the first point' (EPS 11). We thus see that the expressive nature of monads is one point where Deleuze is willing to concede a superiority to Leibniz over Spinoza. But it is telling that this concession occurs only long after the book itself was written. The brief mention here is not enough to conclusively demonstrate the importance this idea will eventually have for Deleuze. It is possible therefore that Deleuze himself only recognised its importance later, as it gradually came to play a more central role in *Difference and Repetition*, *Logic of Sense* and especially *The Fold*, which was published just before Deleuze wrote the letter quoted from above.

At the same time as this new radical Leibniz appears, however, we're forced to accept for the first time the extent to which this is only possible thanks to Deleuze's own 'radical' reading. Unlike in his earlier discussions, Deleuze provides no reference for this key sentence about the 'continuum of singularities'. Whereas the theological Leibniz is easy to pin down, the radical Leibniz, which forms the heart of Deleuze's Leibnizianism, is, we are forced to admit, just as much the result of Deleuze's own creative reading.

2.4 Leibniz's Theological and Political Motivations

Deleuze's criticism of Leibniz in the conclusion to EPS relies on precisely those elements of the account above which I have argued will eventually become so influential. Here, however, he instead puts them to use in order to undermine Leibniz's concept of expression. In particular, it is the necessary reference of expressive unities to their own obscure and confused background which means, Deleuze thinks, that each of Leibniz's expressions is *equivocal* rather than *univocal*. Thus, in Leibniz, what is expressed varies according to each of its expressions. In one monad, a certain part of the world is expressed clearly, but in another monad, this part remains obscure and confused. In other words, the world, as the expressed, takes on a different form in each of the monads which express it, in contrast to Spinoza's own *univocal* expressions, which 'never imply a change of form' (EPS 332).

But the real problem, Deleuze thinks, is the reasoning behind this necessary presence of obscurity in all of Leibniz's expressions. And here at least this reasoning is strictly theological. In order to preserve the eminence of God, monads *must* express obscurely, confusedly or inadequately that which remains clear, distinct and adequate in God. This is how Leibniz avoids the pantheist 'danger' found in Spinoza's univocal expression (EPS 330). This danger, for Leibniz, is perhaps just as much political as theological. Deleuze has already hinted, earlier in EPS, at what may really lie at the heart of Leibniz's opposition to Spinoza: 'Leibniz [. . .] reveals the true reasons for his opposition. And these are in fact practical reasons, relating to the problem of evil, to providence and to religion, relating to the practical conception of the role of philosophy as a whole' (EPS 229). What Deleuze calls Leibniz's 'practical conception of the role of philosophy as a whole' is almost certainly a reference to Leibniz's adage that philosophers should not disturb or upset 'established sentiments'. It is this which Deleuze will go on to condemn in *Logic of Sense* as a 'shameful declaration' (LS 133).

Leibniz, living in the aftermath of the devastating Thirty Years' War, is constantly preoccupied by the real-world risk of intellectual disagreements. At a time when theological disputes often provided a pretext for violent conflict, it is unlikely that Leibniz considered hyperbolic his talk of the 'dangers' of certain philosophical positions. Thus, Leibniz goes to great lengths to provide the philosophical means through which theological differences between Protestant and Catholic interpretations of doctrines like the Eucharist could be resolved. We are struck by the way Leibniz's abstract philosophical style, an exemplar of pure rationalism, is sometimes abruptly brought to bear on these dated controversies of Christian dogma. At its heart is Leibniz's touching, if naive, hope that one day, 'when there are disputes among persons', instead of resorting to conflict, 'we can simply say: Let us calculate' (Leibniz 1903: 176).

It is within this context, therefore, that we should appreciate the absolute significance which Leibniz places on the idea of an *ordered, harmonious* world. It is precisely the chaotic, fractured nature of Leibniz's seventeenth-century Europe which drives his desperate creation of an increasingly elaborate, baroque philosophical system – a system which ensures that a higher order and harmony of the world, and its eventual redemption, are guaranteed. There are thus deeply rooted political and theological grounds for Leibniz's enduring reluctance to countenance certain philosophical positions, sensing in them an attack on the glory of God and the inherent order of the world, and the subsequent very real danger that such an attack implies. It is this commitment to order and harmony which, above all, Deleuze despises in Leibniz, insisting instead on the creative, but also disruptive, power of concepts. Deleuze is similarly confronted with the legacy of a devastating European war, but displays none of Leibniz's hope to save an 'ordered' world in its aftermath. Is this because, for Deleuze, the world has become incapable of redemption?

The final irony, however, is that it is Leibniz's very desperation to cling to an ordered world which drives his creative activity, and the 'play of principles' which Deleuze so admires. And if this creative activity is ultimately restrained by Leibniz through fear of controversy, an opportunity is nevertheless glimpsed: to liberate Leibniz's concepts, and Leibniz himself, from these self-imposed limitations and to embrace the consequences of this liberation. Deleuze, by rejecting the ideal of a harmonious world in a way which Leibniz never would or could, thereby allows Leibniz's own concepts to untether themselves from the constraints which motivated their creation. Deleuze's Leibnizianism is a new, radical Leibnizianism for a new, 'broken' world. This is what we begin to detect, in its clearest form yet, in the penultimate paragraph of EPS.

2.5 The Double Movement of Expression and the World as Sense

We've followed Deleuze in his constant oscillations between emphasising the affinities between Leibniz and Spinoza and insisting on their fundamental disagreements. In the penultimate paragraph of the conclusion, though, it is the affinities which are, in the end, given the final word: 'But whatever the importance of this opposition, we must return to what is common to Leibniz and Spinoza, to that use of the notion of expression which presents the whole force of their anti-Cartesian reaction' (EPS 333). This penultimate paragraph introduces two new ideas into Deleuze's account of expression. These will demonstrate how his account of expression in Leibniz and Spinoza contributes to the philosophical system he outlines in *Difference and Repetition* and *Logic of Sense*.

The first new idea is that 'expression bears within it a double movement' (EPS 333). Significantly, Deleuze turns to Leibniz, rather than to Spinoza, in order to articulate this double movement. In the first movement, we 'take what is expressed as involved, implicit, wound up, in its expression, and so retain only the couple "expresser-expression"'. Thus, in Leibniz, the world (the expressed) is involved or folded up into the monads (expressions) which express God (the expresser). In the second movement, we 'unfold, explicate, unwind expression so as to restore [*restituer*] what is expressed (leaving the couple 'expresser-expressed')'. Thus, Deleuze writes, 'monads in their evolution restore [*restituent*] their continuous background together with the singularities about which they are themselves constituted' (EPS 333, translation modified). It is through this double movement, Deleuze claims, that we can understand Leibniz's apparently contradictory claim that 'the world has no existence outside the monads that express it, while yet God brings the world, rather than the monads, into existence'. The world, as an obscure and confused 'continuum of singularities' is in some sense prior to the constitution of individual monads (and serves as the ground of their constitution). But at the same time, it only *exists* in the monads which express a portion of it clearly and distinctly. We must take seriously Deleuze's claim that this is a double movement, rather than simply two perspectives, and it is in this that we detect its similarity to Deleuze's own processes of actualisation and counter-actualisation. Thus, the process of actualisation is one in which virtual singularities are enveloped by the individuals which express or actualise them; while the process of counter-actualisation is one in which these virtual singularities are themselves 'restored'.[4] Leibniz's 'world' is for Deleuze a virtual transcendental field, which presides over the constitution of individuals but only exists 'actually' when enveloped or folded into these individuals as constituting their expression or actualisation.

The second new idea in this penultimate paragraph is that what is expressed is really nothing other than *sense*: 'What is expressed is sense: deeper than the relation of causality, deeper than the relation of representation' (EPS 335). We've seen that in Deleuze's reading of Leibniz what is expressed is the world. The same is true of Spinoza. But while in Spinoza the world is made up of modifications of God, in Leibniz it is nothing other than a 'continuum of singularities'. And if for Deleuze the world ultimately is sense, then I think it is Leibniz's model of the world that he adopts, rather than Spinoza's. This is why, by the time of *Logic of Sense*, a Leibnizian conception of singularities is at the same time a conception of 'sense-events'. Leibniz's equivocal

Leibniz and Expression

expression is criticised in EPS for its necessary reliance on an obscure and confused background, necessary to preserve God's eminence, and contrasted to Spinoza's univocal model which allows modes to express the essence of God directly and adequately. But it is this obscure and confused background which we'll see return below with a much more positive role. In contrast to the transparent, clear and distinct self-identity of God, it is from these obscure and confused depths, and from their infinite, irreducible complexity, that difference itself springs. In other words, it is in a Leibnizian conception of an always-receding obscure and confused ground that Deleuze finds the infinite depths from which the myriad of differential relations is extracted, which in turn ultimately determine the singularities which constitute the virtual transcendental field.

On the basis of Leibniz's new role in the conclusion, and in particular the two new ideas introduced in the penultimate paragraph, Leibniz's significant contribution to EPS is clear. The ambiguous note on which Deleuze chooses to end the book is a far cry from the restricted, critical image of Leibniz our reading of the main text initially suggested. Thus, Deleuze thinks, 'it is hard, in the end, to say which is more important: the differences between Leibniz and Spinoza in their evaluation of expression; or their common reliance on this concept in founding a post-Cartesian philosophy' (EPS 335). While it is unquestionably Spinoza who provides Deleuze with the insight of an immanent, univocal being which forms one of the anchors of his philosophy, we've nonetheless seen that Deleuze's engagements with Leibniz provide him with many of the key concepts through which this philosophy is expressed. In the end, then, here in the conclusion and its key penultimate paragraph, we're tempted to characterise the relationship between Spinoza and Leibniz in the same terms as are sometimes applied to God and Satan in Milton's *Paradise Lost*: Spinoza is the hero, But Leibniz gets all the best lines.

Our discussion of *Expressionism in Philosophy: Spinoza* over the last two chapters has introduced most of the elements of Leibniz's philosophy which form the core of Deleuze's reading, and which he will go on to deploy elsewhere. The most important of these is a certain conception of the world as an obscure and confused continuum: an infinite, irreducibly complex depth, from which singularities are drawn, enveloped and expressed by finite individuals. This image returns to form the heart of the Leibnizian structure which Deleuze goes on to outline in his later works.

We've also established Deleuze's major reproach against Leibniz, remaining at the heart of all subsequent criticisms: that Leibniz never stops subjecting the world to the requirements of an ordered theology. But what we haven't yet established is precisely how Deleuze appropriates these Leibnizian elements and puts them to his own positive ends. This requires the addition of several other aspects of Leibniz's philosophy which are not present in EPS. Most important among these is Deleuze's combination of Leibniz's infinitesimal calculus and his theory of incompossibility into a new theory of convergent and divergent series. This takes place in *Difference and Repetition* and *Logic of Sense*, and it is to these texts that we now turn.

Notes

1. These three 'ratios' will return in *Difference and Repetition*. There the *ratio fiendi* and *ratio agendi* will be distinguished, resulting in a fourfold root of the principle of sufficient reason, which corresponds to the four necessary characteristics of representation (identity, opposition, analogy and resemblance).
2. The appearance of new references, especially to the *New Essays on Human Understanding*, suggests that Deleuze had been working on Leibniz at some point between writing the main text and writing this conclusion.
3. It is perhaps telling that Leibniz only writes this in his own marginal notes, knowing they would not be seen by anyone else.
4. Much of our understanding of counter-actualisation, one of the hardest aspects of Deleuze's philosophy, thus depends on what is meant by this word *restituer* (something like to restore, reconstitute, re-establish or recreate). Unfortunately there is just not enough in this brief description to arrive at any coherent picture. It is a word that will return, however, in *Logic of Sense*.

PART II

Difference and Repetition and *Logic of Sense*

3

Deleuze's Critique of Representation

At the end of the last chapter we saw how Deleuze concludes *Expressionism in Philosophy: Spinoza* by briefly invoking an image of 'Leibniz's world'. This world, we learned, is 'a continuum in which there are singularities, and it is around these singularities that monads take form as expressive centres' (EPS 329). We noted how this statement hints at a much richer reading of Leibniz than the one presented throughout most of EPS. Indeed, we also observed how out of place this statement appeared, lacking as we did the resources necessary to understand this richer reading.

Looking at the quote again, we can identify two central moments in Deleuze's reading of Leibniz. First, there is the 'continuum in which there are singularities'; this is Deleuze's vision of a Leibnizian *world*. Second, there are 'monads as expressive centres'; this is Deleuze's vision of Leibnizian *subjects*. The Leibnizian world, Deleuze believes, is a kind of ideal topological structure, the nature of which was only hinted at in EPS. This structure pre-exists the individual subjects which come to express it. Deleuze often repeats Leibniz's claim that God creates the world in which Adam sins *before* he creates Adam the sinner. The world has its own structure, defined by the distribution of singularities within it, and this world is subsequently *expressed* by individuals which come to occupy a particular point of view on it. This idea ultimately culminates in Deleuze's description of monads in *The Fold* as beings-*for*-the-world.

We will use sections from *Difference and Repetition* and *Logic of Sense* in order to describe the first of these two moments: the structure of this Leibnizian world. In these books, at various points, we find Deleuze operating within a carefully constructed 'Leibnizian theatre' (LS 113). In Part III, when we turn to *The Fold*, we will see how this Leibnizian theatre comes to be expressed by individual monads.

We note already that this Leibnizian theatre suggests a new, more unified reading of Leibniz compared to the fragmented references we were faced with in EPS. But we also note that this unity is above all the result of Deleuze's own creative drawing-together of various disparate elements of Leibniz's philosophy. The theatre or world of Leibniz we find in DR and LS is an ideal space or structure. While the characteristics and behaviour of this structure are 'Leibnizian' in various more-or-less specific senses, we would be hard-pressed to find it operating in the same way in Leibniz's own philosophy. Deleuze is thus not especially concerned with providing an accurate account of Leibniz's philosophy. Instead, he uses the concepts it provides to construct key parts of his own philosophy. In what follows I'll argue that when Deleuze refers to the 'world' in Leibniz's philosophy, he has in mind exactly the same kind of transcendental structure which in *Difference and Repetition* he refers to as a 'virtual idea' and in *Logic of Sense* he refers to as a transcendental field or surface. This will become clearer as we identify the four key elements of this strange Leibnizian world, which for now we'll briefly summarise under the following headings:

1) *The continuum*. 'The extraordinary Leibnizian world puts us in the presence of an ideal continuum', Deleuze writes in 'The Method of Dramatization' (1994b: 99) (a paper which outlines the skeletal form of the whole of *Difference and Repetition*). He turns to Leibniz's law of continuity, as well as aspects of his infinitesimal calculus, to discover a space of infinite depths which is animated by the restless activity of the infinitely small. Perhaps the most important feature of this ideal continuum is that it is not populated by individual, self-identical entities. Instead, individuals are *produced* from this *pre-individual* field.

2) *Singularities or events*. The ideal continuum is not populated by individuals, but it nevertheless harbours a distribution of singular points or singularities which allow a structure to be articulated. These singularities ultimately determine how, when, where and 'in which case' individuals will be produced. In *Difference and Repetition*, Deleuze thinks he has found a theory of singular points in an obscure area of Leibniz's mathematics. In *Logic of Sense*, he turns instead to a Leibnizian theory of *events* to explain the role of these singularities in constituting individual monads.

3) *Compossibility and incompossibility*. The singularities or events which populate the continuum are either *compossible* or *incompossible* with one another. Compossible singularities can happily coexist

as part of the same world, whereas incompossible singularities necessarily exclude one another. Crucially for Deleuze, a relation of incompossibility among singularities does not involve any kind of *logical* opposition. Instead, Deleuze will claim that these relations depend on whether the series of ordinary points which extend from each singularity 'converge' or 'diverge' with one another. Where series *converge*, singularities are compossible or continuous with one another, and may exist as parts of the same world. But where series *diverge*, singularities are incompossible or discontinuous, and signal a division between two distinct possible worlds. The result is a theory of '*alogical* incompatibilities' (LS 196) which determines the structure of a world *prior* to the constitution of the individuals which come to express it. Deleuze even coins a special name for this method, 'vice-diction', in order to emphasise its difference from logical contradiction.

4) *The divine game*. Finally, it is left up to a kind of divine game in the mind of God to decide *which* of these possible worlds will be realised in order to become the real world. This is a game which takes place once-and-for-all at the origin of the world. God selects the best possible world by selecting the best distribution of singularities or events. Subsequently, and on the basis of this distribution, individual monads come to occupy every possible point of view on this world. God's decision to realise the best possible world thus becomes the *sufficient reason* or *ground* of the world; each event, and each individual, ultimately refers back to the necessarily obscure calculus of God's divine choice.

These four elements constitute the heart of Deleuze's reading of Leibniz in DR and LS. The first three indicate the extent to which Deleuze invokes this reading in order to express key aspects of his own philosophy. First, Deleuze finds in the infinite depths of Leibniz's continuum an expression of the productive priority of *difference* over *identity*. Second, by emphasising the production of monads which comes *after* God's choice of best possible world, Deleuze describes a structure which is *pre-individual*, and contains only a particular distribution of singularities or events. Third, the rules or processes which govern the various distributions of singularities are not *logical* rules which depend on relations of opposition or contradiction between individual concepts. Instead, they are *topological* processes which depend on relations of distance and continuity between singularities as pre-individual, structural entities. In the broader context of Deleuze's philosophy, the process through which this structure produces individuals is named *actualisation*. When Deleuze refers to the same process using Leibnizian terminology, it is the *constitution of monads as expressive centres*.

However, with the fourth point, the divine game, a crucial divergence emerges between Deleuze's image of Leibniz's world and his own theory of transcendental structure. Thus, although the Leibnizian structure we find in DR and LS is in many respects Deleuze's own construction, it nevertheless brings with it the theological commitments which so often restrain its more radical elements, and signal its incompatibility with Deleuze's altogether different commitments. If on the one hand Deleuze's sympathetic appropriation of Leibnizian concepts places us in a restricted context useful for understanding Deleuze's philosophy, then on the other hand his rejection or transformation of other Leibnizian concepts allows us to better articulate the originality of his own work, and its divergence from other trends in the history of philosophy. Once again, then, it is precisely Leibniz's ambiguous status for Deleuze which drives so much of our interpretation of Deleuze's reading of Leibniz, and grounds its usefulness in understanding Deleuze's own philosophy.

The divergence between Deleuze and Leibniz comes in two related areas. First we'll see that Deleuze's critique of Leibniz's divine game amounts to a critique of the grounding influence that God exerts on every aspect of the Leibnizian world. God's choice of best possible world is the sufficient reason which grounds every finite determination. Deleuze explains this reliance on God as a 'theological exigency' on Leibniz's part. As we look closer, however, we'll see that Deleuze's divergence from Leibniz is motivated by more than just an aversion to divine or transcendent influence. It is part of Deleuze's much broader 'critique of representation'.

Deleuze's central concern in the early chapters of *Difference and Repetition* is to demonstrate how the structure of representation has exerted a strong influence over the history of philosophy. In the first chapter, he details the various ways in which the concept of difference, in particular, has been pacified by its subjection to the requirements of representation. In this context, Leibniz is introduced as a thinker of 'infinite representation'. As such, he is subject to the same criticism Deleuze levels at all philosophy which assumes the structure of representation as an unquestioned starting point. Specifically, Deleuze criticises Leibniz for subjecting the movement of vice-diction, and the relations of compossibility and incompossibility which it establishes, to the restrictions of representation. The main symptom of this subjection is the 'exclusive' role that incompossibility plays for Leibniz: it marks an uncrossable boundary or discontinuity between distinct possible worlds. Every time the movement of vice-diction uncovers two incompossible or divergent singularities, it distributes them into two distinct possible worlds. And it is for this reason that such a system must posit an external, transcendent ground, which stands above these distinct worlds and chooses between them: God's divine game. By contrast, Deleuze will reject the exclusive nature of incompossibility. Instead, incompossible singularities, and the underlying divergence of series on which this incompossibility depends, coexist as part of one and the same world, and the 'affirmation' of their divergence generates productive relations of resonance and coupling. And with this comes a very different kind of 'divine game' presiding over the constitution of the world. For Deleuze this is no longer a game played by God, but by chance itself, or the eternal repetition of difference (the dice-throw). And it is not played 'once-and-for-all' at the origin of the world, but reaffirmed at every moment.

On the one hand, then, Deleuze takes three features from the Leibnizian structure he describes in DR and LS in order to formulate some of the core features of his own philosophy: a 'differential' continuum, a theory of pre-individual singularities or events, and a theory of 'alogical incompatibilities' based on the divergence of series. On the other hand, Deleuze believes that Leibniz himself failed to live up to the potential of this structure by insisting that it remain constrained by the requirements of representation; an insistence which culminates in the theory of the divine game. Are these three points of influence enough to label Deleuze's own philosophy a 'Leibnizian' philosophy? Or does the fourth point, the divine game, signal a profound distance between the two? If 'Deleuze's Leibnizianism' names the structural space he constructs from various elements of Leibniz's philosophy, then perhaps we should call 'Deleuze's neo-Leibnizianism' this same space evacuated of the presuppositions of representation and of all divine influence. Describing the process through which Deleuze replaces a Leibnizian structure with a neo-Leibnizian structure will force us to confront some of the most difficult, and foundational, aspects of Deleuze's philosophy.

What is clear, at least, is that Deleuze's critique of representation will be crucial in understanding his reading of Leibniz. Not only does it explain why Deleuze is drawn to certain themes in Leibniz's philosophy – the first three key features outlined above – it also explains why he ultimately rejects the fourth, and questions Leibniz's assumption that incompossibility or divergence must signal a complete exclusion into discontinuous possible worlds. It is thus worth introducing Deleuze's critique of representation in more detail, as it is presented in the first chapter of *Difference and Repetition*, and just before the introduction of Leibniz as a thinker of infinite representation.

First, however, we'll attempt to characterise Deleuze's critique of representation more broadly, and suggest that the real target of his critique is the apparently innocent process through which philosophy abstracts or borrows from the structure of our naive representation of the world in order to account for the nature of this structure itself. What Deleuze criticises, above all, is the assumption that the ground, or the condition, is the same as, or analogous to, the structure of the grounded or the conditioned. We find an early form of this argument in Deleuze's critique of 'anthropology' in his review of Hyppolite's *Logic and Existence*. Turning to this review now will illustrate some of Deleuze's most general philosophical concerns, and help us understand his later attraction to certain Leibnizian ideas. At the same time, it's the first place we encounter Deleuze's criticism of Hegel's concept of contradiction, which, in *Difference and Repetition*, he intends to supplant with a Leibnizian concept of *vice-diction*.

3.1 Hyppolite's *Logic and Existence*

Deleuze's 1954 review of *Logic and Existence* is the earliest piece of work he approved for republication. Despite its short length, in the course of his response to Hyppolite Deleuze presents a fundamental philosophical problem, and a sketch of his mature philosophy as its solution. This culminates in three central claims:

1) Philosophy must be ontology and, as a consequence, philosophy cannot be anthropology.
2) Philosophy must be an ontology of sense, rather than a metaphysics of essence.
3) Hegel's attempt to ground such an ontology on a logic of contradiction is inadequate.

The review is thus one of the few places where we find a brief, linear (albeit very dense) account of the problems and claims which remain a crucial motivation behind Deleuze's philosophical project in *Difference and Repetition* and *Logic of Sense*.[1]

'That philosophy must be ontology', Deleuze writes in the opening paragraph of the review, 'means first of all that it is not anthropology' (LE 191). The concept of anthropology lies at the heart of Deleuze's reading of *Logic and Existence*: it is the injunction that 'philosophy must not be anthropology' which drives Hegel beyond a metaphysics of essence and, ultimately, provides the motive for Deleuze's own rejection of Hegel. It is also, I'll argue, a precursor to the critique of representation we find in *Difference and Repetition*.

'Anthropology' is derived from the Greek *anthropos*, meaning 'man', and *logos*, whose many meanings include 'speech', 'oration', 'account' and 'reason', but which is best translated in this context as 'discourse'. Thus, anthropology, at least as the term is commonly accepted, names a 'discourse *on* man' (LE 192), in which humanity is taken as the object of a scientific, or philosophical, discourse. In this sense, anthropology is just one discourse among many. Anthropology, biology, psychology and sociology are all discourses, and each has its own particular object. Deleuze, however, uses the term anthropology in a much broader sense, to refer to the underlying structure which *all* of these discourses have in common. This underlying structure Deleuze calls the 'empirical discourse *of* man'.

The most basic characteristic of this empirical discourse of man is that 'the one who speaks and that of which one speaks are separated' (LE 192). This characteristic seems to derive naturally from that fact that we, as experiencing subjects, encounter objects that are irreducible to our experience of them. Thus, the subject of each discourse, or 'the one who speaks', reflects on, and remains separated from, its respective object ('that of which one speaks'). This basic characteristic carries with it two seemingly inevitable implications for how we think about the subject and object of an empirical discourse. First, the subject of each discourse is always man or humanity: discourse is the 'discourse of man'. Second, the object of each discourse is in some sense pre-given: we encounter objects that are external and alien to us.

We began with a limited, common-sense definition of anthropology which designated *anthropos* as the object of the *logos*, such that anthropology was a discourse *on* man. Now, however, we have made anthropos the *subject* of the logos, such that anthropology comes to name this whole empirical discourse *of* man, and its two fundamental positions: that the subject of discourse is man, and that the object of discourse is external to man. However, we should not lose sight of the initial act of 'borrowing' which gave rise to these presuppositions: the structure of discourse was in some sense abstracted or borrowed from the basic structure of our empirical or phenomenal experience. Philosophy is 'anthropological' whenever it takes this structure as its starting point. By extension, for philosophy to become ontology proper, it must forgo this illegitimate abstraction, and evacuate itself of its corresponding presuppositions. This argument is at the centre of Deleuze's critique of anthropology, and it returns to form the heart of his critique of representation, as we'll see below. Kerslake neatly sums up the point:

> Both Hegel and Deleuze are against philosophies of representation because such philosophies claim to express what should be genuinely universal within a framework that remains relative to subjective representational experience (i.e. which has only been justified anthropologically), so that the concept of expression doesn't even gain its full extension, and thought is denied its rightful access to being. (Kerslake 2002: 11)

In the second paragraph of the review, Deleuze briefly discusses three 'types' of philosophy in order to explain the conditions under which philosophy may escape these anthropological presuppositions. He begins with pre-critical philosophy, and outlines the positions and problems which result from its commitment to the structure of the 'naive' empirical discourse we introduced above. He then introduces Kantian critical philosophy, which radically rethinks the nature of the objects which a subject reflects upon. Finally, he turns to Hegelian Absolute philosophy, which, at least at first glance, appears to avoid all the pitfalls of anthropology, and thus renders ontology possible.

Deleuze refers to these three types of philosophy as distinct forms of discourse or knowledge, but also as distinct forms of consciousness: empirical consciousness, critical consciousness and Absolute consciousness. The Hegelian language and tone are explained in part by the fact that Deleuze's account loosely mirrors the one Hyppolite presents in the text itself (LE 129–48). The review is nevertheless remarkable for lacking the usual hostile tone towards Hegel that is present in Deleuze's later writing. Deleuze's rejection of the concept of contradiction at the end of the review signals a fundamental divergence from Hegel, but it comes within a broader agreement concerning the goals and conditions of an ontology of sense. Deleuze writes: 'Following Hyppolite, we recognise that philosophy, if it has a meaning, can only be an ontology and an ontology of sense'

(LE 194). Of course, we should bear in mind that really Deleuze is agreeing with Hyppolite, rather than Hegel himself, and no doubt the Hegel we find throughout this review has been diluted and modified by Hyppolite's reading, which heavily emphasises the concept of sense. Deleuze even seems keen to widen the distance between Hyppolite and Hegel, writing in the opening paragraph that while Hyppolite's book on Hegel's *Phenomenology* was a commentary, *Logic and Existence* has a 'very different' intention.

But what really interests us here is how Deleuze transitions between these three forms of philosophical discourse. In Hyppolite's text itself, empirical consciousness is pushed towards Absolute consciousness by the unsustainable contradictions which it faces at each stage. Given that Deleuze goes on to criticise precisely this movement of contradiction, it would appear inconsistent to rely on it simultaneously to drive his own argument. Indeed, Deleuze's own account suppresses the presence of contradiction as a motivating force. Instead, we are compelled to leave each stage behind, including Hegel's Absolute philosophy, after arriving at the verdict that they 'remain anthropological'. Deleuze's account is thus driven by a desire to escape anthropology, rather than through the internal unfolding of various contradictions. The same desire, expressed differently, returns to motivate much of *Difference and Repetition*. There, it will again justify a rejection of Hegel's concept of contradiction, this time in favour of Leibnizian vice-diction. Finally, it will also mark the point of divergence between Deleuze and Leibniz.

Pre-critical philosophy and empirical consciousness

What happens, then, when philosophy assumes that the structure of the 'empirical discourse of man' introduced above is the fundamental structure of reality or being itself, and presupposes it as a natural point of departure? The result is a philosophy which separates the beings which we reflect upon from our own act of reflecting upon them. The knowledge which results from our reflection upon objects is essentially different from the object itself; knowledge remains external to it, and exists solely on the side of the subject. In other words, there is a fundamental non-identity between thought and being. The processes that animate thought, and the rules that constrain its progress, concern thought and thought alone, without any relation to the wholly different processes at work in the objects, beings or things which thought may come to reflect upon. It is in this sense that 'knowledge [. . .] is a movement which is not a movement of the thing' (LE 192).

If knowledge really is something wholly distinct from its objects, and if, furthermore, its nature differs in kind from the nature of the beings which supply its content, then it must comprise a 'power of abstraction' (LE 192) which *represents* beings, or certain of their aspects, on its own terms, or according to its own structure. As a result of this representational nature of knowledge, reflection must be understood as a formal structure that we bring to bear upon an alien content. In other words, our power to reflect upon objects, or our power to entertain them in thought, necessarily depends upon a structure of conceptual rules and relations which come to mediate and shape the data of our experience. Thus, so long as philosophy is founded on the structure of empirical consciousness, thought will be inherently representational, and our knowledge of beings will be insuperably mediated.

But what does this mean for philosophy's claims to knowledge? Pre-critical philosophical enquiry aims at knowing the truth of its objects, or at knowing beings as they are 'in themselves'. However, the fact that knowledge is representational, and the fact that beings are always mediated, seems to undermine each attempt to reach knowledge of being 'in itself'. Borrowing from Hyppolite's own account for a moment: 'The empirical subject says what the thing is, white, tasty, heavy, but this attribution is *its* work' (LE 143). Pre-critical philosophy is thus thrown into problems as soon as it lays claim to any knowledge about its objects. The problem comes from the anthropological structure which it assumes: it presupposes that knowledge of an object is fundamentally different in kind from the object itself. In other words, the two are entirely heterogeneous: thought and its knowledge on one side, being and beings on the other. But then the question arises: if the two are heterogeneous, how are they able to come into contact with one another at all? In other words, how is a relation between thought and being established such that thought can claim to know the 'truth' of its object? Faced with this crisis, pre-critical philosophy retreats into one of two attitudes: dogmatism or scepticism. It either continues to assert a relation between thought and being which it is incapable of substantiating, or it denies the possibility of knowledge altogether.

In effect, Deleuze argues that pre-critical philosophy demonstrates why ontology, or a discourse on being itself, is impossible so long as this discourse has an anthropological structure. Knowledge of beings is impossible so long as this knowledge resides with a human subject which is only able to represent objects which remain external to it. As Deleuze summarises, empirical consciousness is a 'consciousness which directs itself towards pre-existing being and relegates reflection to its subjectivity' (LE 192).

CRITICAL PHILOSOPHY

With Kant, the relation between the subject and object of philosophical discourse changes radically. We've just seen that empirical consciousness, and the pre-critical philosophy which assumes the structure of this consciousness as foundational, presupposes that objects are fundamentally different in kind from the knowledge we have of them. When an aspect of the object was discovered instead to be an aspect of our *representation* of the object, we tried to ignore this aspect in the hopes that eventually we would reach the object in itself.

The revelation of Kant's critical philosophy is that the structure of our cognition, rather than obscuring the true nature of the object of knowledge, instead constitutes this object. With this, one of philosophy's anthropological presuppositions has been transformed. Objects are no longer different in kind and alien to the subject which comes to know them. The *a priori* structure of thought and knowledge is also the *a priori* structure of the object itself. In other words, there is an identity of thought and its object. Thus Kant seems to overcome the aporias of knowledge which forced pre-critical philosophy into dogmatism or scepticism. But it comes at a price: critical philosophical discourse is possible, but it can no longer claim to be *ontological*. The objects of critical philosophy are 'merely objects relative to the subject' (LE 192). In other words, they are the objects of thought, rather than of being. When faced with the insuperable divide between thought and being, critical philosophy moves the objects of knowledge over to the side of thought. But Kant thus leaves being, or the thing-in-itself, inaccessible and unknowable. However, he never denies that it *is there*, and that it remains fundamentally distinct from thought. Deleuze concludes: 'Thus in Kant, thought and the thing are identical, but what is identical to thought is only a relative thing, not the thing as being, in itself' (LE 192).

Kantian critical philosophy advances on pre-critical philosophy by demonstrating that thought and thought's object are not necessarily different in kind. It remains anthropological, however, because it continues to insist that being, or the thing-in-itself which 'occasions' thought or knowledge, itself remains external and alien to thought.

Absolute philosophy

Finally, Deleuze moves on to Hegel's philosophy. Initially, he concurs with Hyppolite that with Hegelian Absolute consciousness the insuperable divide between thought and being is dissolved. Just as critical philosophy brings objects over to the side of thought, so Absolute philosophy brings being itself. The 'genuine identity of the position and the presupposed' means that the 'external difference between reflection and being is in another view the internal difference of Being itself' (LE 192). The thing-in-itself is no longer outside of and alien to thought; both are moments within the internal unfolding of Being that Hegel traces. Deleuze's account is brief but the key point for us is that Hegelian Absolute knowledge 'eliminates the hypothesis of a knowledge whose source is alien' (LE 192). And with this goes the anthropological structure which had presupposed that thought and being were different in kind. Knowledge of the object of thought is now not only possible, but can finally be properly named ontology, or a discourse on being itself.

But there was a second characteristic of anthropology, and with it comes a second sense of the term ontology. We said above that anthropology assumes that the subject of philosophical discourse, the 'one who speaks', is man or humanity – anthropology is the discourse *of* man. But if, in Absolute discourse, the subject and object, thought and being, have become identical, then the 'one who speaks' in this discourse is no longer man, but being itself. We can therefore subject the word ontology to the same reversal as we did anthropology: ontology as the discourse *on* being is at the same time the discourse *of* or *by* being. Absolute discourse is thus being's own discourse on being. With this, Deleuze goes on to argue, philosophy not only goes from anthropology to ontology, but from a metaphysics of essence to an ontology of sense.

We can see how the assumptions of anthropology eventually lead to a metaphysics of essence. We saw that first among these assumptions is that knowledge of an object is different in kind from the object itself. As a result, pre-critical philosophy is forced to accept that more and more features of the object are only features of its *appearance* for thought, and not features of the object as it is *in itself*. It is nevertheless assumed that these features are grounded by the true *essence* of the object, which stands outside or behind its appearance for thought. Pre-critical philosophy is thus characterised as a metaphysics of essence because it strives to go beyond the appearance of an object to the essence which grounds our knowledge of it. It confines the object of knowledge, being-in-itself, to a second world, a world of essences, which transcends and grounds the world of appearances.

Philosophy escapes anthropology by rejecting this assumption that thought, knowledge and reflection reside solely on the side of the subject, distinct from being itself. Again, it rejects 'the hypothesis of a knowledge whose source is alien'. And with this rejection goes the necessity of positing a 'second' world of essences. Deleuze's reading of Hyppolite emphasises the idea that nothing transcends the world: 'There is nothing to see behind the curtain' (LE 193). Thus, philosophy becomes ontology, rather than anthropology, when it does not speak about indifferent, transcendent essence, but about the sense which is immanent to 'the one who speaks' (being itself). The external difference between thought and being has been replaced by an internal difference or self-difference within being. Deleuze concludes: 'My discourse is logical or properly philosophical when I say the sense of what I say, and when in this manner Being says itself' (LE 193).

Absolute discourse, by positing an identity of thought and being, thereby does away with the two core presuppositions of anthropology: there is no longer a difference in kind between thought and being, and the subject of philosophical discourse is no longer man, but being itself. Thus, with Absolute knowledge, ontology, both as the discourse on being and of being, is possible. However, we must not forget the broader critique of anthropology: its structure was borrowed from the structure of our empirical consciousness or phenomenal experience. It is on these grounds that Deleuze will return to accuse Hegel's Absolute knowledge of remaining anthropological, and thus of still failing to achieve philosophy's goal of becoming properly ontological.

The fundamental point of disagreement concerns the concept of difference. Being can 'say itself', or *express* itself, only because it is different from itself: 'The difference between thought and being is sublated in the absolute by the positing of the Being identical to difference which, as such, thinks itself and reflects itself in man' (LE 195). But, Deleuze points out, according to the Hegelian model, being is identical to difference only if by difference we mean *contradiction*:

'But there is a point in all this where Hyppolite shows himself to be altogether Hegelian: Being can be identical to difference only insofar as difference is carried up to the absolute, that is up to contradiction' (LE 195). Thus, according to Hyppolite, contradiction is the only form in which difference can be identical to being, or, put differently, it is only because being contradicts itself that it is able to express itself.

Deleuze, however, questions this claim that the difference internal to being must be a self-contradicting difference. He suggests that contradiction, in fact, is 'only the phenomenal and anthropological aspect of difference' (LE 195). Why should contradiction be anthropological? An ontology of sense, as we've seen, intends to avoid the two presuppositions of anthropology by making being itself the subject and object of philosophical discourse. But these two presuppositions were only symptoms of the underlying process which is the real target of Deleuze's critique: the process which illegitimately abstracts from the facts of empirical consciousness into the structure of being and thought as such. Deleuze's argument is that even the concept of contradiction itself is the result of such an illegitimate abstraction – it is appropriated from the empirical in order to explain how being can express itself. But, Deleuze insists, it is not the same thing to say that being expresses itself and to say that it contradicts itself. And so long as philosophy is limited to a conception of difference as contradiction, it will remain anthropological, and prove inadequate to a true ontology of sense. To escape this last vestige of anthropology, Deleuze believes, what is needed is 'a theory of expression where difference is expression itself, and contradiction its merely phenomenal aspect' (LE 195). It is just such a theory that Deleuze goes on to describe in *Difference and Repetition* and *Logic of Sense*.

In the first chapter of *Difference and Repetition* Deleuze describes a history of the representation of difference. At first glance it bears little resemblance to the history of anthropology we've just discussed. It is tied to a different set of proper names, and forgoes any mention of discourse or forms of consciousness. But we'll see that the critique of representation we find there is in many ways a more mature form of the critique of anthropology we've just discussed. In both cases, Hegel's philosophy is criticised on the same basis: the inadequacy of the concept of contradiction. While here in the Hyppolite review contradiction is inadequate because it 'remains anthropological', in *Difference and Repetition* it will be inadequate because it 'remains subject to the requirements of representation'. A Leibnizian

3.2 The Critique of Representation in Difference and Repetition

The first chapter of *Difference and Repetition* describes a series of moments in the long history of philosophy's representation of 'difference'. Deleuze's initial claim is that philosophy has often failed to represent adequately difference 'as such'. The causes of this failure, he thinks, lie in the nature of representation itself. Representation imposes its own requirements and conditions, which difference, in so far as it is a difference within representation, must be subordinated to and mediated by. The result is a concept of difference that has in some sense been pacified, constrained or neutralised by its inscription within the structure of representation. 'Difference is not and cannot be thought in itself, so long as it is subject to the requirements of representation' (DR 262). The central task of *Difference and Repetition* is to recover a concept of difference which is not subject to these requirements.[2]

Deleuze's account of the history of representation in this first chapter is a diagnosis of its harmful or all-too-pervasive influence, which the system developed by the rest of the book hopes to remedy. However, when it comes to Leibniz's place in this history, this reading proves to be only half of the story. While Deleuze's first discussion of Leibniz in *Difference and Repetition* ostensibly condemns him as just one more example of the subordination of difference to representation, it simultaneously introduces many of the ideas and resources which form a key part of the philosophical system Deleuze goes on to develop in chapters 4 and 5. It is thus through Leibniz that we get our first hint of how we might understand difference as *subrepresentational*. This account, however, will only make sense after introducing the origin of representation, in Plato, and its first proper formulation, in Aristotle.

Plato and the simulacrum

Deleuze identifies the origin of representation in Plato's philosophy. This discussion occurs in *Difference and Repetition* in more or less the same form at the end of chapter 1 (DR 59–63), chapter 2 (128),

theory of 'vice-diction' is introduced precisely in order to overcome this failure of contradiction, even if, ultimately, Leibniz's philosophy will be subjected to the same criticism.

and in the conclusion (264–5). It is also found in two papers, 'Plato and the Simulacrum', originally published in 1966 but rewritten for *Logic of Sense*, and 'Plato, The Greeks', in *Essays Critical and Clinical*. In these discussions, Deleuze argues that the Platonic distinction between Ideas and the things which participate in them is usually understood as a distinction between essences and appearances. But it should also be understood as a distinction between models and copies. The model serves as the basis for a selective criterion. This selective criterion is a test which allows copies, with their well-founded internal relation to the model, to be distinguished from *simulacra* or *phantasms*, which have no internal relation to the model (even though they may claim or appear to have such a relation).

For Deleuze this Platonic model is closely tied to the emerging concerns of Athenian democracy: especially concerns for *recognition* (as citizens, rulers, and so on) among groups of friendly rivals. The copy and the simulacrum are two claimants or suitors, both claiming to possess or participate in something given by the model. Thus, the philosopher and the sophist may both claim to possess truth, but truth, as the model or ground, only grants legitimacy to the claim of the philosopher. The model gives something to be possessed, but only by the claimant who has passed the grounding test. The model is like a father who gives his daughter, but only to the best suitor.

There is another distinction, however – not between model and copy, or copy and simulacrum – but between copy and copy. Copies themselves, in so far as they participate in the same model, are distinguished by the *degree* of their participation. The model as the ground thus not only selects legitimate claimants, but distributes them all in a hierarchy where they are ranked according to their level of participation. The simulacrum, which does not participate in the model at all, must be completely excluded from this hierarchy.

This Platonic desire to 'exorcise' simulacra is ultimately moral, Deleuze claims (DR 265). It is a question of distinguishing between good and bad claims, and granting recognition only to those which can be placed in an ordered relation to one another. This ordered set of relations is a hierarchy of value, allowing us to determine who sits at the top. But, Deleuze also claims, this same desire simultaneously inaugurates 'the subjection of difference' (DR 265). We can see why by looking again at the role played by the Idea or model as ground or grounding principle. The ground distinguishes copies according to their degree of participation. 'In this sense', Deleuze writes, 'the ground measures and makes the difference' (DR 62). In other words, Platonism limits us to a conception of difference which is mediated through the regulative role of Ideas. The only things which can properly be said to differ from one another are well-founded copies, and they can differ only in relation to the Idea which grounds their difference.

Plato was thus the first to constrain difference, and inscribe it entirely within the domain of intelligible relations established by the Idea. But he was also the first to establish the constitutive conditions of these relations. Deleuze identifies four, borrowing from Foucault's own analysis in *The Order of Things*. The first is the *identity* of the model which allows it to be defined. Identity is the 'essence of the Same' (DR 265). The second is the *resemblance* which the copy bears to the model. While identity is the essence of the Same, resemblance is the 'quality of the Similar'. Third, and as a result, the copy has a relation to being which is *analogous* to the model's relation to being. Finally, the copy is constituted on the basis of selecting between predicates which are *opposed* to each other. Although they are not yet enough to define a 'world of representation', these four characteristics nevertheless constitute a 'theory of Ideas which will allow the deployment of representation' (DR 265). We will therefore recognise their subsequent return as the four 'iron collars of representation' which feature prominently throughout *Difference and Repetition*. Identity, resemblance, analogy and opposition are the four central features which Deleuze claims characterise every model of representation. We'll see them below in Aristotle's finite representation, and also, ultimately, in Leibniz's own infinite representation.

It falls to Aristotle to inaugurate this 'world of representation' and establish its conditions. Aristotle does not inherit from Plato the moral anxiety over the exclusion of simulacra. He does, however, retain its two exigencies: first, the subordination of difference to the requirements of representation, and second, the four characteristics introduced above, which Aristotle develops into the requirements for what Deleuze calls 'finite representation'. With the move from Plato to Aristotle we move away from a hierarchy of value tied to politics and towards a logical space of differences.

Before moving on, however, it is worth taking note of the status of simulacra in the picture of Platonism we're left with. The process through which the ground 'makes the difference' between copies excludes simulacra completely: they bear no genuine relation to the model, and thus fail the model's selective test. The simulacrum cannot be granted a place in the ordered hierarchy of copies, because it is not grounded by a model which would serve as the principle of its measure. And yet, the simulacrum seems nevertheless to persist or insist underneath or at the limits of Platonism. And with this haunting presence comes a question: if the simulacrum is not grounded by the model or Idea, what is it grounded by? Or is it grounded at all? 'What is condemned in the figure of the simulacrum is the state of free, oceanic differences, of nomadic distributions and crowned anarchy, along with all that malice which challenges both the notion of the model and that of the copy' (DR 265). The simulacrum's threatening or challenging presence motivates its exclusion, and for Deleuze this exclusion not only defines Platonism but founds the whole subsequent subordination of difference to representation. At the same time, however, the status of the simulacrum signals for Deleuze an opportunity. Deleuze defines his own philosophical project, at various points and borrowing a phrase from Nietzsche, as a reversal or overthrowing (*renversement*) of Platonism (LS 253). But he also insists that the seeds for this reversal can be found in Platonism itself. If the exclusion of the simulacrum from Platonism signals the 'crossroads of a decision' in philosophy (DR 265), then the reversal of Platonism will require 'bringing its motivation out into the light of day' (LS 253), by returning to the figure of the simulacrum and taking seriously its problematic status.

Aristotle and finite representation

Aristotle inscribes difference within his classificatory system of genus and species. Difference is always a difference in species or a specific difference. To differentiate between two things is thus to identify their specific differences: what is specific about cats is what differentiates them from what is specific about dogs. Specific difference is an essential difference, in so far as it is the means through which we identify things, or give things a concept: being a man is what is specific about Socrates, and constitutes an essential part of his existence.

Specific difference, however, is always subsumed under the genus which contains it. Thus, cats and dogs may disagree with respect to their species, but they agree with respect to their genus (mammal). In fact, we can talk about difference, or represent difference, only if it is mediated through and subordinated by the form of a higher-level identity present in the genus. Deleuze calls this the 'happy moment', when philosophy manages to reconcile difference with the model of the concept and represent it as subordinate to the identity of this concept (DR 29). The 'monster' of difference is thus pacified. The result is 'organic' representation: a vision of static, organised dispositions within an ordered (and orderly) space of classification.

With this subordination, we note the return of the first of the four elements which make up the 'necessarily quadripartite character of representation' (DR 34). In Platonism, we called this the identity of the model or Idea (the Same); in Aristotle, it is the identity of the concept or genus. 'Specific difference [...] refers to a particular moment in which difference is merely reconciled with the concept in general' (DR 32). A second element of representation returns when we note that the genus contains specific difference within itself in the form of an opposition or contrariety: dog and cat are opposed or contrasted in the genus mammal. In Platonism opposition defined the relation between predicates which allowed copies to be constructed. Here, it is the opposition of predicates which allows species to be determined. 'It is in relation to the form of identity in the generic concept that difference goes as far as opposition, that it is pushed as far as contrariety' (DR 31). The other two characteristics of representation (analogy and resemblance) are harder to pin down, but they relate to the necessary limits of Aristotle's theory of specific difference. These limits are the reason Deleuze describes the Aristotelian conception of representation as *finite* representation. In effect, specific difference implies a 'too large' and a 'too small' of difference, above and below which 'difference tends to become simple otherness and almost to escape the identity of the concept' (DR 30).

The 'too large' of difference refers to the difference between genera themselves, or generic difference. The genus 'mammal' is itself a species in relation to a higher genus, which contains the specific differences between mammals, reptiles and so on. Eventually, however, we reach genera which are not related to each other through a specific difference contained within a higher genus. In other words, there is no 'highest' genus. Why isn't 'being' the highest genus? Because this would deprive specific differences themselves of being. The genus cannot be contained in the specific difference which differentiates it, or, in other words, the specific difference or differentiae must remain external to the genus it differentiates.[3] The genus 'animal', for instance, cannot be contained in, or predicated of, the specific difference 'rational'. If it were, then rationality would entail animality in every case: a God who is rational would also be a God who is an animal, and the statement 'man is a rational animal' would amount to 'man is an animal and an animal'. Thus, if being were a genus, it could not be predicated of the specific differences which differentiate it and must remain external to it. Deleuze writes:

> Genus is determinable by specific difference from without; and the identity of the genus in relation to the species contrasts with the impossibility for Being of forming a similar identity in relation to the genera themselves. However, it is precisely the nature of the specific differences (the fact that they *are*) which grounds that impossibility, preventing generic differences from being related to being as if to a common genus (if being were a genus, its differences would be assimilable to specific differences, but then one could no longer say that they 'are', since a genus is not in itself attributed to its differences). (DR 34)

What, then, are we to make of the highest genera, which cannot be subsumed under a highest genus, and which Aristotle calls the categories? Here, the third feature of representation returns: analogy. Being does not relate to the categories in the same way as genera refer to their species. While the genus dog is predicated in one and the same way of every species of dog, being is predicated analogously of the categories. In order to avoid making being into a genus, then, Aristotle forces us to treat being itself as *equivocal*. Doghood is univocal and has only one sense, and as a result all dogs are dogs in the same way; but being is equivocal, and things can *be* in equivocal ways. Despite this, Deleuze claims that generic difference is still subordinated to the 'quasi-identity' of a concept: 'An identical or common concept still remains, albeit in a very particular manner' (DR 33).

The 'too small' of difference arises at the other end of the process of differentiation performed by specific differences. Eventually we reach the *infima species*, or the lowest point in this process. The *infima species* is like a block to the process of specification, which prevents it from reaching the level of the individual itself. However far we continue the differentiation of species, then, and however specific our concepts become, they retain an irreducible element of generality such that the *singular* is never reached. There is an 'authentic singularity which escapes the species' (DR 43). Beyond this limit we find only *accidental* differences between singular individuals. But, precisely as accidents, they do not contain the essence of this individual; this essence remains entirely within specific difference. The lowest level of the specification, just before we reach the limit presented by the *infima species*, is characterised by the fourth feature of representation: resemblance. 'The small units, the little genera or species, are determined by a direct perception of resemblances' (DR 34).

Deleuze thus argues that Aristotle can inscribe difference within the identity of the concept only by imposing a 'maximum' and a 'minimum' of difference. With this comes the corresponding subordination of difference to the four elements of representation. The result, just as with Plato, is that a true concept of difference is missed. 'A confusion disastrous for the entire philosophy of difference: assigning a distinctive concept of difference is confused with the inscription of difference within concepts in general' (DR 32). However, just as the simulacrum continues to haunt Platonism, so too does difference persist beyond the 'arbitrary boundaries of the happy moment' (DR 34). Deleuze characterises the philosophies of Hegel and Leibniz as an attempt to incorporate this last vestige of unpacified difference, and bring it within representation. With this attempt, representation becomes infinite.

Leibniz, Hegel and infinite representation

The 'extreme forms' which persist beyond the limits of finite representation are captured, Deleuze claims, only in relation to an *infinite* representation. As soon as a concept of infinity is introduced into representation, it rediscovers these 'limits of the organised; the tumult, restlessness and passion underneath apparent calm' (DR 42). And with this, representation goes from being calm, static and organic, to being 'orgiastic'. In the conclusion, Deleuze writes that it is 'a question of causing a little of Dionysus' blood to flow in the organic veins of Apollo' (DR 262). After the 'happy moment' where difference enters into a conceptual structure with a maximum and a minimum, representation now begins to extend beyond these limits, until it 'follows and espouses determination in all its metamorphoses, from one end to the other'. Speaking in relation to Leibniz, Deleuze writes that the concept 'extends its benediction to all parts' (DR 42), while Somers-Hall summarises infinite representation as the claim that the world is conceptual 'all the way down' (Somers-Hall 2012a: 44). There are no longer determinations which are 'too small' or 'too large' for representation, because finite determinations are no longer related to a higher-level genus as their principle. Instead, they are related to a *ground*. This ground, Deleuze writes, is the 'womb in which finite determination never ceases to be born and to disappear, to be enveloped and deployed within orgiastic representation'

(DR 43). And it is the role of the infinite to serve as mediation between finite determinations and their ground.

To understand all this we must look at how Deleuze thinks infinite representation functions for Hegel and, especially, for Leibniz. For now, we need only bear one thing in mind: central to Deleuze's characterisation of infinite representation is that there is some kind of movement, process or procedure of the infinite which 'makes the difference', or produces finite determinations. Unlike finite representation, this movement will not involve subsuming differences under a higher-level genus. Instead, it will involve mediating between a finite determination and its ground in the form of the infinite.

Things are complicated, however, by the fact that we can only *represent* this infinity and its movement through the lens of finite determinations. We represent the infinite *in* the finite, but in doing so we subject it to the same conditions of representation which characterise finite determinations. Finite determinations do not disappear into the infinite, but are 'vanishing and on the point of disappearing' (DR 44), in such a way that they are engendered in the infinite while remaining finite. This subjection takes the form of a choice between representing the infinite as infinitely large or infinitely small. Deleuze is quick to point out that these are not the same as the large and the small which characterise the limits of finite representation, but rather two ways of representing the infinite within finite representation. It is this choice, Deleuze claims, which marks the difference between Hegel and Leibniz.

The movement of the infinite in Hegel, Deleuze argues, refers to the dialectical movement of contradiction itself. Just as in Aristotle, difference is determined through an opposition, but Hegel 'raises' this opposition to the level of contradiction. The result is that, whereas in organic representation the static organisation of opposed species comes from the genus under which they are subsumed, for Hegel concepts are determined by their own orgiastic self-movement, as these contradictions are resolved. Difference is made by the 'movement of contradiction as it constitutes the true pulsation of the infinite' (DR 45), and is grounded by the labour of the negative. Regardless of the accuracy of Deleuze's interpretation of Hegel, we can introduce his reading of Leibniz in terms of its opposition to this Hegelian movement of contradiction. The first opposition arises from the same theological commitment to preserving the glory of God which we looked at in the last chapter. It is in order to prevent any possible 'admixture of God and his creatures' (DR 45), Deleuze claims, that

Leibniz confines the presence of the infinite in representation to the infinitely *small*. For Leibniz, God's infinite nature, or the infinitely large, lies outside the grasp of representation, just like the absolutely simple notions which exceeded our own relatively simple notions in Part I.

Thus, in Leibniz it is the realm of the infinitely small which lies on the border between finite differences and the ground from which differences arise. There it plays a mediating role, and relates finite difference to its ground. The infinite is said of the finite, but only as a finite difference which is 'vanishing' or 'evanescent', or in other words which is 'engendered in the infinite' (DR 44) in the form of the infinitely small. It is thus a movement appropriate to the infinitely small which 'makes the difference', and grounds finite determination. However, this is a movement which will be radically different from the movement of contradiction which operates through the infinitely large. Deleuze characterises the presence of the infinitely small in Leibniz's philosophy by its restlessness. The obscure depths of the infinitely small harbour an 'intoxication, giddiness, evanescence, and even death' (DR 45). This image of the endless, swarming activity of the infinitely small is one of Leibniz's most profound influences on Deleuze. It lies at the foundation of the Leibnizian world which Deleuze describes in *Difference and Repetition*. It testifies to the presence of a radical, dynamic tendency hidden beneath Leibniz's conservative, theological mask. As Deleuze writes of Leibniz in 'The Method of Dramatization': 'The state of the world is well expressed in the image of the murmur, of the ocean, of the water mill, of the swoon or even drunkenness, which bears witness to a Dionysian ground rumbling beneath this apparently Apollonian philosophy' (Deleuze 1994b: 99).

In fact, this image was already vaguely discernible at two points in *Expressionism in Philosophy: Spinoza*. We saw the first in section 1.6, where we briefly introduced the infinite divisibility of matter, and the second in section 2.3, where we saw how the clear and distinct expression of each monad presupposes an obscure and confused background. We will return to both of these ideas below in order to help explain the nature of the infinitely small. In both books, Deleuze even locates the origin for these ideas in the same theological commitment: to maintain the modesty of God's creatures. Once again then, we get a sense of the productive interplay between the two diverging characterisations of Leibniz we find in Deleuze's writing: a strong theological commitment, which ends up motivating a creative philosophical process, in this case the discovery of a new kind of dynamism particular to the infinitely small.

VICE-DICTION

Once again, the choice between the infinitely large and the infinitely small, Deleuze claims, marks the two ways in which Hegel and Leibniz 'go beyond the organic', or beyond finite representation to an orgiastic, infinite representation. But Deleuze also frames this choice in another way, this time concerning *where* this movement beyond the organic occurs. This is a choice, he claims, between beginning with either the 'essential' or the 'inessential'. At various points Deleuze equates this difference with the distinction between the equal and the unequal, and the identical and the different. To understand what this means requires once again beginning with a brief look at Deleuze's reading of Hegel. Hegel, Deleuze argues, 'begins with the essential as a genus' (DR 45). The Aristotelian genus was divided by specific differences which placed species in opposition to each other. When opposition is raised to the infinitely large of contradiction, however, the Hegelian 'genus' divides itself and remains simultaneously genus and species, or whole and part. What contradicts the essential (the inessential, the unequal or the different) is thus contained as part of the essential: 'it contains the other essentially, it contains it in essence' (DR 46). The key point for us is that Deleuze thinks that some kind of essence is ultimately responsible for the orgiastic movement of infinite representation in Hegel's philosophy. The infinite Hegelian 'Self', as he calls it (DR 49), is the essential, the identical or the equal which 'contradicts the unequal to the extent that it possesses it in essence, and contradicts itself to the extent that it denies itself in denying the unequal' (DR 46). And it is through this self-contradiction that finite determinations unfold as moments of the infinite Self. We might wonder about the accuracy of Deleuze's hasty appraisal of Hegel's philosophy, especially given that it neglects to mention Hegel's own extensive treatment of the 'doctrine of essence' in the second part of the *Science of Logic*. Again, however, our interest is limited to how Deleuze introduces Leibniz's philosophy of the infinitely small as an alternative to this Hegelian reliance on 'the essential'.

Deleuze thinks that Leibniz begins with the inessential or the unequal, or with 'movement, inequality and difference'. In other words, he begins with the restless movement of the infinitely small. Deleuze's argument is that there is a 'procedure of the infinitely small', which in some sense corresponds to the movement of contradiction in the Hegelian dialectic, but which is 'quite different' to it. Deleuze even gives this procedure a special name: 'vice-diction' (DR 46).

It is the concept of vice-diction which animates the Leibnizian world which Deleuze constructs in *Difference and Repetition* and whose structure we are vaguely beginning to discern. We've now introduced, albeit briefly, two fundamental features of this structure: the domain of the infinitely small, and a process of vice-diction which operates in this domain and grounds the finite determinations which arise from it. Perhaps even more importantly, we've also established that this whole structure presents a Leibnizian alternative to the Hegelian movement of contradiction. And with this, we can see why the implications of vice-diction extend further than just Deleuze's reading of Leibniz. Deleuze returns to the concept in chapter 4, and uses it to characterise the structure of Ideas themselves, without any explicit reference to Leibniz. My own reading of this concept, however, will differ significantly from the few brief characterisations it has received in other Deleuze scholarship. Briefly, while some commentators present vice-diction as a kind of human-centred, almost ethical activity or method, I will argue instead that it is a metaphysical process, movement or procedure through which identity is produced from difference.

The easiest way to approach vice-diction, at least initially, is to return to its opposition to Hegelian contradiction. The first thing we have to bear in mind is that contradiction and vice-diction are in some sense playing the same role or doing the same thing. They both, Deleuze writes, 'maintain the distinction between essences' (DR 46). To distinguish between essences is to determine the finite differences between them, or to 'make the difference' between finite determinations within representation. They do this, we've seen, by relating these finite determinations to a ground, mediated through either the infinitely large or the infinitely small. However, we've also seen that Deleuze argues that contradiction takes as its starting point an essence or Self, which is enveloped by this ground and of which all other essences are determinations. By contrast, vice-diction relates finite determinations to a ground which begins with the inessential, and from which essences are produced. This is a key aspect of vice-diction, and Deleuze cites the way Leibniz 'begins with the inessential and constructs essences' as another of the ways in which Leibniz 'goes further' than Hegel (DR 264).

The best way to explain this process of producing essences which characterises vice-diction is by looking again at the relation between the essential and the inessential. On Deleuze's reading, Hegelian 'essence' also contains the inessential as part of its own essence (the 'other' within itself which gives rise to contradiction). For Leibniz, however, the inessential does not contain the essential 'in essence', but only 'with respect to properties, in cases' (DR 264). It's not yet clear what this means, but there is at least one preliminary context in which we can see how an emphasis on the inessential might lead to a distinction between essences and 'cases'. In 'The Method of Dramatization', Deleuze distinguishes between various types of philosophical question. He argues, controversially (as the questions following the paper demonstrate), that Hegel is perhaps the only philosopher to seriously rely on questions of the form 'what is x?' Hegel is able to ask 'what is' questions, Deleuze claims, precisely because the movement of contradiction is one which presupposes empty, abstract and simple essences. 'The question "What is?" prejudices the Idea as the simplicity of essence; it then becomes obligatory that the simple essence comprehends the inessential, and comprehends it in essence, thus contradicting itself' (Deleuze 1994b: 92). By contrast, the movement of vice-diction leads us to ask *in which case* essences are constituted. 'Subsuming under the case', Deleuze argues, has its own language, distinct from the language of essences. It is a language 'of properties and events', in which the question 'what is?' is replaced by the questions 'who? how? how much? where and when? in which case?' (Deleuze 1994b: 92).

The key point is that to answer these questions, Deleuze thinks, is to give an account of the *production* of essences from the inessential. 'The inessential here refers not to that which lacks importance but, on the contrary, to the most profound, to the universal matter or continuum from which the essences are finally made' (DR 47). This, then, is the major difference between contradiction and vice-diction: vice-diction is the movement through which the essential is produced from the inessential and, by extension, the equal is produced from the unequal, or the identical is produced from the different. This, I think, is also how we should understand the term vice-diction itself. If contradiction is a 'speaking against', then vice-diction is a 'speaking in place of'. And if, in Hegel, the equal contradicts the unequal, then, for Deleuze's Leibniz, the unequal or the different vice-dicts the equal or the identical in so far as it determines cases which 'speak in place of' or prepare for the essences which will eventually be constituted on their basis.

Vice-diction is thus a procedure which constructs essences from a 'universal continuum', and it is a procedure which can only be understood within a language of cases, properties and events. But at the same time, it is a procedure which Deleuze thinks he finds operating within Leibniz's philosophy. Our goal in the next chapter will thus be to reconstruct Deleuze's reading of Leibniz, and with it the Leibnizian world within which vice-diction can operate. This requires, in effect, pinpointing exactly what Deleuze thinks the 'essential' and 'inessential' refer to in Leibniz's philosophy. Our guiding claim will be the following: Deleuze's claim that vice-diction produces essences from the inessential will find its correlate in Leibniz's claim that God does not create Adam the sinner, but rather the world in which Adam sins. This implies two things. First, that when Deleuze talks about 'essences' in Leibniz's philosophy, he is really talking about *monads*. Traditionally, a distinction is made by commentators between a monad and the complete individual notion which is that monad's essence. Deleuze, however, often collapses this distinction and happily equivocates between the terms monad and essence. We'll return to the implications of this equivocation below. Second, that when Deleuze talks about the inessential, he means the world as it is structured *prior* to the constitution of essences or monads. We've already talked about this in various ways: in EPS it was briefly invoked as a 'continuum of singularities' and as an 'obscure and confused background'; at this point in *Difference and Repetition* it is a 'continuum of properties', and if we add the language of 'The Method of Dramatisation' it is also a continuum of *events*. It is the restless domain of the infinitely small, characterised by difference and inequality, which forms the obscure and confused background against which monads are constructed as centres of finite, clear expression. Monads as centres of expression envelop into a unity a small portion of the multiplicity of the world. With this last point in mind, we can begin to see why, in his letter to the translator of EPS we quoted in the last chapter, Deleuze credits Leibniz with going further than Spinoza when it comes to the expressive character of individuals. Deleuze finds in Leibniz a way of describing the *genesis* of expressive individuals.

In this section, the important aspects of Deleuze's interpretation of Leibniz have been brought out through the latter's opposition to Hegel. It is worth noting the marked difference between this discussion, in which Leibniz is opposed to Hegel, and the discussions in EPS in which Leibniz was opposed to Spinoza. While in the latter it was Leibniz's fate to never quite live up to the achievements of

Spinoza, here he is credited with 'going further' than Hegel in various key respects (DR 264). Given that Spinoza and Hegel perhaps occupy two extremes on the list of Deleuze's philosophical affections, it's not surprising that his attitude to Leibniz lies somewhere in between – 'better' than Hegel, but not as praiseworthy as Spinoza. More interesting, perhaps, is that by opposing Leibniz to Hegel, Deleuze has allowed the radical, creative and positive side of his reading of Leibniz to dominate for the first time. Thus, in the conclusion of *Difference and Repetition*, Deleuze lists all the aspects of Leibniz's philosophy he admires:

> His conception of the Idea as an ensemble of differential relations and singular points, the manner in which he begins with the inessential and constructs essences in the form of centres of envelopment around singularities, his presentiment of divergences, his procedure of vice-diction, his approximation to an inverse ratio between the distinct and the clear, all show why the ground rumbles with greater power in the case of Leibniz, why the intoxication and giddiness are less feigned in his case, why obscurity is better understood and the Dionysian shores are closer. (DR 264)

The next chapter will address these points in detail.

Notes

1. For two close studies of Deleuze's Hyppolite review, see Widder 2008 and Kerslake 2002. While both of these accounts contain valuable insights into various aspects of the review, they share the view that it is, in itself, essentially *incomplete*. Kerslake argues that it is intelligible only on the basis of Deleuze's subsequent work, while Widder suggests that it relies on arguments that are not explicitly present in the review itself. I believe, however, that a close reading of the review *does* reveal a coherent narrative, and thus that, on its own terms, the review provides a useful means of framing Deleuze's subsequent philosophical trajectory. This account is the result of many hours of reading groups with Stephen Barrell, and I am indebted to him for the initial articulation of most of its key elements.
2. Somers-Hall summarises the project of *Difference and Repetition*: 'On the one hand, Deleuze develops an extended critique of much of the philosophical tradition, arguing that seeing difference as only comprehensible on the basis of identity has led us wrongly to construe the nature of the world and the philosophical endeavour. This critique takes in a number of thinkers from Plato, Aristotle, Descartes, Leibniz and Kant, through to Heidegger and the twentieth-century phenomenological

tradition. On the other, Deleuze develops his alternative conception of philosophy both in contrast to these philosophers, and in relation to an alternative tradition of thinkers who have managed to free themselves at least partially from the structures of what he calls representation' (Somers-Hall 2012a: 2). To this we would wish only to add that Leibniz is present on *both* sides: part of Deleuze's critique of representation, while simultaneously escaping it in key respects.

3. For more on this point see Somers-Hall 2012b: 49.

4

A Leibnizian World

The end of the last chapter introduced Deleuze's concept of vice-diction – a procedure which produces individuals from a pre-individual continuum. It is in order to explain this procedure that Deleuze turns to the four connected themes in Leibniz's philosophy which we outlined at the beginning of the last chapter. Again, these are: an inessential, or pre-individual, continuum (the restless infinitely small); a distribution of singularities which are amenable only to a language of cases, properties or events; a theory of compossibility and incompossibility which determines this distribution; and a divine game which selects the best possible distribution and produces the monads which correspond to it. Taken together, these four ideas constitute the Leibnizian structure Deleuze creates in *Difference and Repetition* and *Logic of Sense*, and within which vice-diction operates. As we now look at these in more detail, we'll start to see how Deleuze pushes disparate Leibnizian themes into the service of a new radicalised or vulgarised Leibnizianism.

4.1 The Continuum

The first step in this reconstruction is to discover the 'language' of cases, properties or events which is adequate to the domain of the infinitely small, and which Deleuze insists is distinct from the language of essences. We'll introduce this language through one final opposition between Leibniz and Hegel. When writing of the presence of the infinitely large in Hegel's philosophy, Deleuze claims that 'there is no reason to expect a mathematical treatment of the theological infinitely large' (DR 45). However, this is not the case with the infinitely small, which *can* be approached mathematically. Thus, at the same time as Deleuze claims that vice-diction has its own 'language of properties or events' he also claims that it is a 'mistake to impose upon infinitesimal analysis the alternative of being either a language of essences or a convenient fiction' (DR 46). The implication, then, is that it is 'infinitesimal analysis' which provides the

A Leibnizian World

language adequate to infinitely small difference and its movement of vice-diction. The infinitely small thus 'finds its concept' (DR 46), Deleuze claims, in the form of the mathematical notation 'dx'. It is clear, then, that for Deleuze the domain of the infinitely small is intimately connected to Leibniz's discovery of infinitesimal calculus, and the notation he developed as a result. We must therefore introduce, if only in outline, the central features of this mathematical discovery, and their philosophical implications. These implications will become clear when we move from the mathematical theory of infinitesimal analysis to Leibniz's philosophical theory of infinite analysis.

Leibniz's introduction of the symbol dx into mathematics can be explained in terms of purely mathematical exigencies, especially various enduring problems relating to the measurement of curves. Mathematicians of the time were especially concerned with two problems caused by curved lines and figures, for which the traditional resources of geometry and algebra seemed inadequate. The first problem was how to determine the gradient of a curved line at a single point, and the second was how to determine the area of a figure with curved edges. Leibniz developed his infinitesimal calculus precisely to solve these problems (and to relate them to one another). However, it is also the case that these problems were given an increased urgency by Leibniz's corresponding physical commitments. Here, we are concerned with the material bodies and processes that mathematical curves and figures try to represent. We get a better sense of the importance of infinitesimal calculus by looking at how Leibniz's claim that the material world is subject to a *law of continuity* is at the same time the claim that the world itself is in some sense 'curved'. Only then will we see how infinitesimal calculus is the language or technique most suited to this curved universe.

A useful illustration of curvature in Leibniz's physics comes from the example of a body in motion. Leibniz thinks that while it is a simple matter to describe a body moving in a uniform straight line, this kind of motion only ever exists as a useful abstraction. When it comes to real bodies in real space, we find that their motion is always curved in some way. The simplest definition of curved motion is therefore in its opposition to uniform motion: curved motion is motion that is not 'in a straight line'. But what is it about real bodies, as opposed to ideal mathematical entities, that prevents their motion from being uniform? We can explain by looking at some examples of curved motion. For instance, a cannonball fired into the air, which follows a curved arc as it falls to the ground. This is the simplest kind of curved motion, but the word 'curved' doesn't only apply to smooth arcs: it applies to any movement that is not uniformly straight. When the same cannonball is rolled down a grassy hill, for instance, even though it appears to move in a fairly straight line following the greatest slope, it is constantly being knocked slightly from left to right by the rough ground. Because of these constant fluctuations in the cannonball's movement which prevent its motion from being completely uniform, this kind of motion may also be called curved. The word 'curved', when used in this way, rather than conjuring up images of smooth arcs, more properly designates any deviation from uniform movement in a perfectly straight line, however slight or chaotic. Why, then, does Leibniz maintain that the motion of bodies is always necessarily curved or non-uniform?

We said above that the motion of a body is only straight and uniform if we consider it in abstraction. There is nothing about a body taken in isolation that would cause its movement to curve. However, in reality, the motion of a body is always influenced by its surrounding environment, like the cannonball being knocked about by the rough ground. In the preface to his *New Essays On Human Understanding*, Leibniz writes: 'Abstraction is not an error as long as one knows that what one is pretending not to notice, *is there*. This is what mathematicians are doing when they ask us to consider perfect lines and uniform motions and other regular effects, although matter (i.e. the jumble of effects of the surrounding infinity) always provides some exception' (Leibniz 1996: 57). The motion of a body changes in response to the jumble of effects emanating from the matter that surrounds it. Each part of matter is open to constant influence from an environment from which it is never completely isolated or separated, and it is this which accounts for the necessarily curved or non-uniform motion of bodies. We can think of this 'jumble of effects' from the surrounding environment as a type of pressure exerted on a body. Matter is pressed on all sides by its surrounding environment, and the result is a curvilinear movement. The themes of curvature and pressure will again be central to Deleuze's reading of Leibniz's physics of material bodies in *The Fold*, and form the basis of many of the correspondences he draws between Leibniz's philosophy and Baroque art, as we'll see in the next chapter.

As long as we are talking about flying or rolling cannonballs we are describing the curved motion of an actual body in space. Here, it is easy to explain curvature in terms of the effect of the surrounding environment: the uniform motion of the cannonball rolling down the hill is interrupted by the rough ground that constantly affects its course. But, as we've seen, there is a technical mathematical definition of curvature which applies to the mathematical description of this motion, and specifically its representation as a line drawn as a graph within a system of coordinates. Just like the actual movement it represents, this line may be straight or curved. This second, mathematical sense of curvature is useful when we come to consider the properties of a body other than its position in space. It may have a continuously varying speed, or temperature, and these properties would also be represented as curves. This gives us a second sense of the significance of curvature as it applies to material bodies, which is that it suitably represents the *continuous* nature of change.

The key point is that the trajectory of a continuously varying property mapped on to a graph is not made up of tiny straight lines that only appear as a curved line when viewed 'from a distance'. Rather, it is curved at every point, or in other words, each point is subject to an instantaneous rate of change. In fact, as we will see, it is only by positing two points that are infinitesimally close to each other that a straight line can be approximated, in order for the gradient of a curve to be determined. What's important here is that curvature in this second sense always suggests some kind of *continuous* change, variation or difference. Curvature is thus closely connected to Leibniz's dearly held law of continuity, or the law that 'Nothing takes place suddenly.' Leibniz summarises: 'It is one of my great and best confirmed maxims that nature never makes leaps. I called this the law of Continuity ... There is much work for this law to do in natural science. It implies that any change from small to large, or vice versa, passes through something which is, in respect of degrees as well as of parts, in between ...' (PPL 49). The law of continuity implies that when we consider, for instance, a continuously varying temperature, the difference in temperature between any two points always contains some third point that lies in between. However close we bring the two points to each other, and however small we make their difference in temperature, a third point, and a smaller difference, always sneaks in. This idea is somewhat familiar from our discussion of the infinite divisibility of matter in section 1.6. The law of continuity implies this infinite divisibility, and Deleuze uses both to help define the restlessness of the infinitely small that characterises the 'continuum' of the world.

The mathematical problem of measuring curves, or the fact that we can always find a third point between any two points, however close, thus corresponds to Leibniz's law of continuity. And so any mathematical technique for describing these curves will at the same time be a technique for describing the structure of Leibniz's infinite, continuous universe. What's more, as the language adequate to the infinitely small, the key to this technique will be the role played by *infinitely small differences*. We mentioned above two problems that aptly illustrate the difficulty that geometry and algebra face when dealing with curves. The first was how to find the tangent to a given point on a curve, while the second was how to find the area of a figure with curved sides. Even before Leibniz's development of infinitesimal calculus, two 'infinitesimal techniques' were developed to try and tackle these problems. Looking at each of these in turn will set the stage for Leibniz's original contribution.[1]

The first problem arises from the question of how to 'square a circle', or how to construct a square with an area equal to a given circle. Archimedes discovered a technique for determining the area of a circle that involved drawing a spiral that starts from the centre of the circle and makes one complete revolution before intersecting with its edge. The limitation of Archimedes' method was that it required knowing the tangent to the spiral at the point of its intersection with the edge of the circle. This tangent would be a line that touches the spiral at only one point. Archimedes did not know how to determine this tangent line, and subsequently the question of how to find the tangent to a point on a curve became an important problem in mathematics. Its solution would require the new concept of infinitesimal difference. If we draw a straight line intersecting any two points on a curve, and then gradually move these points towards each other until they are 'infinitely close', then the straight line drawn between them will effectively be the same as the tangent line to the point where they (almost) meet. Central to this technique is that the infinitesimal distance between the two points is ignored and they are effectively treated as the same point. This method was very effective, but an obvious criticism emerged when the analytic geometry developed by Fermat and Descartes allowed curves, and the infinitely close points located on them, to be represented as equations. At one stage in these equations, the relation between two points is used to determine a tangent to the curve. But at a later stage, this relation is specified as being equal to zero, in order that the result be a tangent to a single point, rather than a line intersecting two points. Mathematics was faced with an unsatisfying ambiguity: how can the same relation at once determine a tangent, while simultaneously being equal to zero?

A Leibnizian World

The second infinitesimal technique relates to the problem of how to determine the area of a figure with curved sides. It involved the realisation that an area could be treated as equivalent to a 'stack' of line segments. Two areas are equal if every line segment in one is the same in the other. But the same kind of objection applies to this technique as to the first. Because a line has only one dimension, its area is zero: how can we add all these zero-area lines together in order to arrive at a non-zero area of the whole figure?

Both of these techniques pre-dated Leibniz. The fundamental insight of both Newton and Leibniz was that these two methods were related to one another: the method for finding tangents to curves is related to the method for finding areas bounded by curves. The first is the object of differential calculus, while the second is the object of integral calculus. A curve is differentiated in order to find the tangent or derivative of each of its points, and these derivatives are integrated in order to reconstruct the original curve. What we are interested in, however, is how Leibniz developed the notation dx in order to avoid the ambiguities present in the two infinitesimal techniques identified above; dx is the symbol of the infinitesimal: it is the infinitely small difference in x that is nevertheless not zero. This is what Berkeley disparagingly called the ghost of a departed quantity: an infinitely small quantity, any multiple of which remains smaller than any ordinary number, but which still maintains a determinate ratio with another infinitesimal. Thus, it can serve as the denominator in the differential relation dy/dx without the risk of dividing by zero that was present in the first infinitesimal technique. Similarly, when it comes to the second infinitesimal technique, instead of conceiving of the area of a curved figure as the sum of a collection of line segments, Leibniz thought of it as the sum of a collection of infinitely thin rectangles, with a width of dx.

Deleuze's real interest in Leibniz's concept of the infinitesimal dx is how it stands as one half of a differential relation with another infinitesimal. As an infinitely small difference, dx is zero in relation to x. Despite this, it is able to form a determinate ratio with another infinitesimal, in the form of a differential relation: dx/dy. Returning to our discussion of representation, the symbol dx is significant for Deleuze precisely because it escapes representation altogether.[2] In this sense, it is not just a very small quantity; it is not a quantity at all. The point, however, is that because dx and dy have a determinate relation to each other, this ratio will allow us to find, for example, the gradient to a curve at a single point. The difference in position on the x axis which dx represents is infinitely small, as is the difference in the y axis represented by dy, but the relation between these differences, and how they change in relation to one another, nevertheless allows us to determine something concrete about the nature of the curve at that point. In so far as they are only determined in relation to one another, Deleuze claims that infinitesimals are *reciprocally* determined and subject to a principle of reciprocal determination (DR 46).[3]

The reciprocal determination of differential relations will play a fundamental role in the movement of vice-diction and its production of finite determinations. It is this reciprocal determination, in effect, which will allow us to say that finite identities are produced from the endless differences of the infinitely small. But to see how this is possible, we first have to abstract these differential relations away from the curves from which they were originally derived. While above we began with the curve whose gradient we were trying to determine at each point, there is a sense in which we can reverse this perspective and begin with the differential relations as such, and take them as the first stage in the construction of a curve. But if they are not derived from an already-existing curve, where do these differential relations come from? We know that at the basis of Deleuze's vision of Leibniz's world is the 'restlessness' of the infinitely small. We are now able to see that this restlessness really refers to the 'Dionysian' activity through which infinitely small differences spontaneously and ceaselessly enter into differential relations. The domain of the infinitely small constitutes an infinite depth in which every variation of differential relation coexists. In the context of infinite representation, it is this which allows us to say that the infinitely small relates finite differences to a ground or womb from which differences arise. It is the differential relation which mediates between the infinite and the finite, between infinite difference and finite difference. Thus, in a lecture on Spinoza given in 1981, Deleuze writes: 'One comprehends that $dy/dx = z$, that is to say the relation that is independent of its terms will designate a third term and will serve in the measurement and in the determination of a third term: the tangent. In this sense I can say that the infinite relation, that is to say the relation between the infinitely small, refers to something finite' (17/02/1981). The Leibnizian 'world' that Deleuze conceives is not a world of matter, but a kind of ideal space in which these differential relations are determined and prepare for the constitution of monads. This is why Deleuze writes in 'The Method of Dramatisation' that the 'extraordinary Leibnizian world puts us in the presence of an ideal continuum' (1994b: 99).

Our question, though, is how this ideal continuum of differential relations is responsible for the production of essences or monads (the procedure of vice-diction). Answering this question requires introducing the next two key themes in Deleuze's Leibnizianism: the singularity or singular point, and the relations of compossibility that exist between these singularities. Once again, we could explain the singular point purely in terms of mathematics. As we will see below, however, there are some problems with locating the concept of the singular point in Leibniz's mathematics. Instead, we will introduce the singularity in a quite different context in Leibniz's philosophy: the analysis of concepts or notions. There, singularities will appear as *events*. It is in *Logic of Sense*, rather than *Difference and Repetition*, that Deleuze refers to Leibniz as a philosopher of the event.[4]

4.2 Infinite Analysis, Singularities and Events

As we've already suggested, Deleuze's reading of Leibniz heavily emphasises the idea that singularities or events play a crucial role in the *production* of monads or essences. Initially, however, we'll introduce them in the context of Leibniz's theory of *analysis*. We mentioned at various points in Part I how Leibniz distinguishes between a logical domain of essences and a contingent domain of existence. The distinction is useful here to demonstrate why the analysis of the concept of a monad is a very different process than the analysis of a purely logical concept.

We are already familiar with the analysis of logical concepts from our discussion of the possibility of the *ens perfectissimum* in Chapter 1. To analyse a concept is to demonstrate its *possibility*, by demonstrating that none of its constituent parts contradicts each other or itself. We saw that although often this process is difficult, there is always, at least in theory, a finite number of steps through which an analysis must progress in order to demonstrate the logical possibility of a concept and provide its real definition. As such, the analysis of logical concepts is a *finite* analysis.

What happens, however, when we try to analyse the concept of a monad, or its complete individual notion? Leibniz famously maintains that concepts extend all the way to the individual, such that each monad has its own unique concept. There is a unique concept for Adam, for Sextus and for Caesar. Monads, however, unlike logical essences, are subject to the contingent domain of existence: they are embroiled in the continuous material world with its now-familiar universal influence and infinite divisibility. Precisely in so far as it becomes equal to the monad, then, the monad's concept must also become equal to this infinite, irreducible complexity. In effect, we can see that to analyse the individual concept of a monad would require an infinite number of steps, or an *infinite* analysis. This infinite analysis must function in a very different way than finite analysis.

The analysis of logical essences demonstrated their possibility. However, given that the concept of a monad must necessarily refer to the whole world in which that monad exists, Leibniz creates a new, more restricted version of possibility adequate to monads: *compossibility*. Whereas logical possibility required demonstrating that a concept did not harbour a hidden contradiction, compossibility requires demonstrating that a monad is *compatible* or *continuous* with all the other monads in the world to which it belongs. One of Deleuze's key claims will be that the relation of incompossibility between monads is very different than the relation of contradiction between logical concepts (which we find in Hegel, for instance). This is why, In *Logic of Sense*, he calls Leibniz the 'first theoretician of alogical incompatibilities' (LS 171). Incompossible monads exclude one another, but not on the basis of any kind of conceptual opposition or contradiction. We can see, then, that a particular reading of the theory of compossibility will play an important role in Deleuze's claim that a new theory of vice-diction presents an alternative to contradiction.

Infinite analysis is thus a process which entails determining that a monad is compossible with the world in which it exists. Setting aside the question of precisely who, or what, is performing this analysis for now, we can nevertheless begin to see how this process of infinite analysis would function. We see that just as finite analysis concerned the parts of a concept, so compossibility must concern the parts of a monad. But what are these parts? We are not talking about the material parts of a monad's body, but rather the predicates which make up its concept. And Deleuze is clear that he thinks these predicates are *events*. This is why, in *Logic of Sense*, just after Deleuze describes Leibniz as the first theoretician of alogical incompatibilities, he also describes him as the 'first important theoretician of the event'. It is in the 'Sixteenth

A Leibnizian World

Series of the Static Ontological Genesis' that we find Deleuze's first discussion of Leibnizian events. The first half of this series mirrors almost exactly the process of vice-diction found in *Difference and Repetition*, as we'll see below.

What interests us here is how the relation of compossibility is grounded by the events that a monad includes. Thus, we must recognise that compossibility is really a relation between the events that monads come to include or envelop, rather than a relation between monads themselves. Crucially, this means events are capable of defining a complete possible world *independently* of the individual monads which will eventually express it. This is thus the first step in the production of individual monads, or in the production of the essential from the inessential. Our initial discussion of analysis has thus taken us to a new discussion of production: a particular distribution of pre-individual singularities or events, with their own relations of compossibility, defines a continuous possible world without any reference to the individuals which occupy that world. This is the first of the two movements of vice-diction, or the first moment of the static ontological genesis.

What is the nature of these events? Initially, we can use the term quite literally: 'to sin' is an event included in the concept of Adam, and 'to cross the Rubicon' is an event included in the concept of Caesar. The key point is that these events are not entirely disconnected. In so far as they are both events occurring in the same world, they must be compatible or compossible with each other: Caesar can only cross the Rubicon if Adam sins. And they must both be compossible with all the other events which make up that world: Caesar can only cross the Rubicon, the event which ends the Roman Republic, if Sextus rapes Lucretia, the event which founds it. Again, then, monads are compossible with each other on the basis of an underlying compossibility between the events they include. But the question remains: how is this compossibility between events established?

The answer requires recognising that although Deleuze refers to events in the form of infinitive verbs like 'to sin' and 'to cross the Rubicon', they are in fact singularities or singular points.[5] But singular points of what? Here, we must return to Deleuze's definition of the Leibnizian world as an 'ideal continuum in which there are singularities'. It is within this ideal continuum that we find a distribution of singular points. Within the infinite depths of the infinitely small, then, with its endless varieties of differential relations and curves, we discover something which allows for a structure to be articulated: the distribution of singular points or singularities. A quote from the end of Series 14 of LS suitably demonstrates the importance of singularities for Deleuze:

> But the transcendental field is no more individual than personal, and no more general than universal. Is this to say that it is a bottomless entity, with neither shape nor difference, a schizophrenic abyss? Everything contradicts such a conclusion, beginning with the surface organisation of this field. The idea of singularities, and thus of anti-generalities, which are however impersonal and pre-individual, must now serve as our hypothesis for the determination of this domain and its genetic power. (LS 99)

As singular points within an ideal continuum, the question of compossibility between events becomes a question of continuity. With this, we must introduce two new terms: *convergence* and *divergence*. These are, in effect, the underlying technical ground for establishing relations of compossibility and incompossibility. Compossible singularities converge with one another, while incompossible singularities diverge. What does this mean? Deleuze describes singularities, at various places, as the point of origin for all kinds of series of 'ordinary' (nonsingular) points. Two of these series, each extending from a different singular point, can either converge or diverge with each other. Convergence and divergence have precise mathematical definitions, but it is enough here to think of convergence as a kind of 'overlapping' or 'merging' of two series – they are prolonged into each other. Deleuze defines a continuity between singularities by this convergence of the series which extend from them. Thus, in a 1980 lecture, he will claim that 'the ultimate possible scholarly formulation of continuity is: a given singularity is prolonged into a whole series of ordinary points all the way to the neighborhood of the following singularity' (06/05/1980). This, in turn, defines compossibility. In *Logic of Sense*, Deleuze writes: 'The extraordinary notion of compossibility is thus defined as a continuum of singularities, whereby continuity has the convergence of series as its ideational criterion' (LS 111). And in *Difference and Repetition*: 'It is undoubtedly continuity which defines the compossibility of each world [. . .] That is to say: for each world a series which converges around a distinctive point is capable of being continued in all directions in other series converging around other points' (DR 48).

By turning to the question of infinite analysis, we introduced the important theory of compossibility. To analyse a monad, or to provide its real definition, requires demonstrating the compossibility

A Leibnizian World

(and not merely the possibility) of its parts, or the events which it includes. This compossibility, we now know, finds its criterion in the theory of convergent series which defines a whole network of continuous singular points. With this final point, however, we must confront a new, potentially troubling, question. With the notions of convergence and divergence, and as Simon Duffy (2010) has suitably demonstrated, Deleuze is making use of notions from fields of mathematics that came long after Leibniz. Despite this, Deleuze repeatedly uses the idea of convergence and divergence specifically in relation to Leibniz, apparently unconcerned that they derive from fields which would have been unfamiliar to him. Duffy is thus also correct that Deleuze 'retrospectively maps these developments back onto the structure of Leibniz's metaphysics' (2010: 89). Nevertheless, we must still explain the fact that these modern mathematical techniques seem to form an essential component of Deleuze's description of an ostensibly Leibnizian world. We must therefore step back and remind ourselves of the motivations behind Deleuze's particular reading of the theory of compossibility in Leibniz's philosophy. Deleuze is keen to supplement Leibniz's theory of compossibility with the theory of convergence and divergence of series for one important reason: it is necessary to explain why incompossibility is not reducible to a kind of contradiction.

Before that, however, we can provide another, more straightforward, explanation of Deleuze's references to convergence and divergence by remaining, for a moment, within the context of infinite analysis. Infinite analysis requires demonstrating that a monad is compossible with all the other monads with which it shares a world. Crucially, however, for Leibniz such an infinite analysis is impossible to undertake. Or at least, it is impossible for *us*: infinite analysis is restricted to the understanding of God. Not only that, but we cannot even begin to imagine the processes through which it functions. It is, in fact, a central part of the 'divine game' which a calculating God plays at the origin of the world. In this sense, then, it doesn't matter if a theory of convergent and divergent series would have been alien to Leibniz, because he was content to regard the whole process as alien. Deleuze suspects, however, that Leibniz's differential calculus 'gives us an artifice so that we can operate a well-founded approximation of what happens in God's understanding' (22/04/1980). Subsequent mathematical developments, therefore, like the theory of convergent and divergent series, can be treated as attempts to strengthen this artifice.

4.3 Incompossibility and Vice-diction

Deleuze turns to convergence and divergence as a means of giving a topological ground to the theory of compossibility and incompossibility. It is, we recall, a theory of 'alogical incompatibility': the compatibility or incompatibility of singularities or events is not derived from the logical relations between fully formed concepts. This is important because it allows incompossibility to simultaneously escape the requirements of the structure of representation as well as play a role in the *production* of individuals. We saw how singularities allow a structure to be articulated within a pre-individual transcendental continuum. The theory of incompossibility forms a crucial part in the articulation of this structure, by determining which particular sets of singularities are continuous with each other. But, this means incompossibility must be able to function *before* the emergence of the essences, individuals or monads which are caught up in various conceptual relations of opposition and contradiction. Thus, while the theory of the infinite analysis of monads introduced us to the importance of singularities and compossibility, we must in a sense *reverse* this theory in order to come up with an account of how these monads are themselves produced.

Infinite analysis, as we've described it, demonstrates the compossibility of a monad by demonstrating the continuity of a set of singularities, and the inclusion of these singularities within the concept of a monad. As an analysis, it is a process which 'breaks apart' already-existing concepts in order to discover their predicates: their events or singularities. However, our concern is not how monads are analysed, but how they are produced. By in some sense reversing the process of infinite analysis, we can use the same movement to describe how monads are entirely constituted by events or singularities which pre-exist them. With this reversal, infinite analysis becomes the second part of the movement of vice-diction or static ontological genesis. There, instead of demonstrating continuity between singularities, it *establishes* or *produces* this continuity. And instead of demonstrating that a monad contains certain events, it will construct the monad itself on the basis of these events.

> We see that the continuum of singularities is entirely distinct from the individuals which envelop it in variable and complementary degrees of clarity: singularities are pre-individual. If it is true that the expressed world exists only in individuals, and that it exists there only as a predicate, it subsists in an entirely different manner, as an event or a verb, in

the singularities which preside over the constitution of individuals. (LS 111)

Compossibility is thus, for Deleuze, the 'rule of a world synthesis' (LS 111). But unlike Kant's *a priori* categories, compossibility is not conceptual: it functions through the topological process of convergence which brings singular points into relation with each other. 'For what Leibniz called the "compossible" and the "incompossible" cannot be reduced to the identical and the contradictory' (LS 196). It is thus a question of priority: compossibility must be prior to contradiction because it structures a pre-individual transcendental field. This is why Deleuze goes further, and claims that contradiction itself must derive from compossibility: 'The contradiction between Adam-the-sinner and Adam-non-sinner results from the incompossibility of worlds in which Adam sins or does not sin' (LS 111). The reason why Adam-non-sinner contradicts Adam-the-sinner isn't because the two concepts can't coexist, but because the event 'to sin' diverges from the event 'to not sin' – they belong to two incompossible worlds. The contradiction between monads therefore only makes sense on the basis of a world which has already established and distributed a set of possible singularities or events, and which is therefore a world that has already accounted for the production of a certain set of individuals or essences: one world produces Adam the sinner and the other produces Adam the non-sinner. We can begin to see here why, in his review of Hyppolite, Deleuze suggested that contradiction was only the anthropological or phenomenal aspect of difference.

The importance of grounding compossibility in convergence and divergence rather than contradiction is clear: 'Convergence and divergence are entirely original relations which cover the rich domain of alogical compatibilities and incompatibilities and therefore form an essential component of the theory of sense' (LS 196). We can further demonstrate the importance of this structure by briefly looking at the project of *Logic of Sense* as a whole.[6] Following the ideas we introduced in the last chapter while discussing his review of Hyppolite, Deleuze believes a logic of sense should not be grounded in the concept (as it was in Hyppolite and Hegel). Rather, if it is possible at all, it must begin with the subrepresentational dynamism of the world itself, and show how, from it, a conceptual structure is immanently derived. Deleuze's goal is thus to construct an emergent transcendental philosophy, in which the subrepresentational movement of nature produces a transcendental field which is constituted by topological relations and processes. A topological transcendental field avoids the circularity inherent in abstracting an image of the ground from the world which is to be grounded. Or in other words it does away with the illegitimate abstractions and borrowings from the structure of representation which we saw Deleuze criticise throughout his review of Hyppolite. Thus, in a key quote from Series 15, Deleuze writes: 'We seek to determine an impersonal and pre-individual transcendental field which does not resemble the corresponding empirical fields and which nevertheless is not confused with an undifferentiated depth' (LS 102).

But this is only the first half of the story. This transcendental field then 'folds back' on its point of origin in order to produce the conceptual and empirical structure of the world of representation and experience. Rather than the transcendental logic we find in Kant, Deleuze constructs a transcendental topology that will ultimately come to ground a conceptual structure. The three distinct meanings of the French word *sens* are used by Deleuze to frame this new immanent ontology of sense, which he believes eluded Hegel: First, the subrepresentational movement of nature, which is identical to a disorganised thought (sense as chaotic 'sensation'). Second, the emergent transcendental field, in which topological relation precedes identity (sense as 'direction'). And finally, the conceptual structure of the empirical itself (sense as 'meaning').

By keeping this overall project in mind, it is clear why Deleuze is so insistent that compossibility should not be confused with contradiction. In fact, in *Difference and Repetition*, we find Deleuze making precisely the same argument:

> We can see why the notion of incompossibility in no way reduces to contradiction and does not even imply real opposition: it implies only divergence, while compossibility is only an analytic continuation which translates the originality of the process of vice-diction. In the continuum of a compossible world, differential relations and distinctive points thus determine expressive centres. (DR 48)

The 'first level of actualisation' of the static ontological genesis in *Logic of Sense* is thus made up of the same two movements as vice-diction in *Difference and Repetition*. First, it establishes continuity between a set of singularities, establishing an ideal continuum and 'defining compossibility as the rule of a world synthesis' (LS 111). Second, it defines monads as centres of expression on the basis of these singularities.

A Leibnizian World

In chapter 4 of *Difference and Repetition*, however, vice-diction returns, with one crucial difference: this time there is no mention of Leibniz at all. Deleuze uses the word to describe the process through which *virtual Ideas* are determined or structured. These virtual Ideas therefore share a similar structure to what above we have been calling Leibniz's 'world': an ideal continuum populated by singular points. The first movement of vice-diction, we saw, established relations of continuity between these singular points. Now, as Deleuze returns to vice-diction, we find precisely the same movement. He employs a new set of mathematical terms ('auxiliaries and adjunctions'), and does not mention the theory of compossibility. But from all that we've established so far it is clear that the process is the same:

> It is vice-diction which engenders cases, on the basis of auxiliaries and adjunctions. It presides over the distribution of distinctive points within the Idea; it decides the manner in which a series must be continued, from one singular point among regular points up to which other; it determines whether the series obtained within the Idea are convergent or divergent. (DR 190)

Vice-diction is a kind of non-conceptual mediation which relates singular points to one another, and here again, its most important feature for Deleuze is its difference from contradiction: 'the procedure capable of following and describing multiplicities and themes, the procedure of vice-diction, is more important than that of contradiction, which purports to determine essences and preserve their simplicity' (DR 189). Vice-diction functions independently of already-determined individual essences, and provides the condition for their production. Thus: 'The problem of thought is tied not to essences but to the evaluation of what is important and what is not, to the distribution of singular and regular, distinctive and ordinary points, which takes place entirely within the inessential or within the description of a multiplicity, in relation to the ideal events which constitute the conditions of a "problem"' (DR 189).

But this is only the first movement of vice-diction – the traversal or description of an ideal continuum with a corresponding distribution of singular points. The second movement, as we saw above, involves the envelopment of this ideal continuum within the individual monads which come to express it. But again, Deleuze's return to vice-diction in chapter 4, independently of Leibniz, also contains this second movement: 'Vice-diction has two procedures which intervene both in the determination of the conditions of the problem and in the correlative genesis of cases of solution: these are, in the first case, the specification of adjunct fields and, in the second, the condensation of singularities' (DR 189). From what we've already established, it's clear that these two procedures of vice-diction have their correlates in the Leibnizian structure we've described in this chapter. The 'specification of adjunct fields' corresponds to the condition of continuity which determines a complete possible world; while the 'condensation of singularities' corresponds to the envelopment of singularities within an expressive individual.[7]

A picture has slowly emerged, in which vice-diction traverses an ideal continuum, and determines relations of convergence or divergence between singular points. Singular points that converge are compossible, and may be enveloped within a single individual, presiding, therefore, over the generation of a world. But is there any reason to expect the restlessness of the infinitely small to spontaneously produce an ordered distribution of convergent singularities? This would be to refer genesis to a single, harmonious act of creation, and to imbue the restlessness of the small with an inherent order. This is justifiable, perhaps, if we confine the process to the divine understanding of Leibniz's God. For Deleuze, however, the ideal continuum is characterized only by its abundance of relations, and its ceaseless creativity. Condensation is the accretion, or ossification, of an excessive, otherwise untamed, activity. This restlessness produces a whole variety of differential relations, and ensures that a whole series of possible singular points are distributed at once. What happens, then, when instead of a harmonious convergence of series, we are faced with an excess of overwhelming divergences? The differing answers to this question will mark the fundamental difference between the Leibnizian world and Deleuze's neo-Leibnizian world – their own point of divergence.

4.4 Deleuze's Critique of Leibniz

Central to Deleuze's account, as we've seen, is his claim that Leibniz's 'world' pre-exists the individual monads which eventually come to occupy and express it. The world is nothing other than a particular distribution of compossible singularities or events. His account has so far remained traditionally Leibnizian, however, in so far as this distribution is just one of many possible distributions, each of which constitutes a complete *possible world*. According to this view, the divergence of singularities must necessarily signal a bifurcation into

A Leibnizian World

two distinct possible worlds. Thus Leibniz, Deleuze thinks, only ever made an 'exclusive' use of incompossibility: it is the criterion which ensures that each world contains only events which are continuous, convergent and compossible with one another, which in turn ensures that each world remains ordered and harmonious. Discontinuous, divergent and incompossible events exclude one another – their coexistence too offensive to ordered thought to bear contemplation. Deleuze writes: 'Leibniz makes use of this rule of incompossibility in order to exclude events from one another. He made a negative use of divergence of disjunction – one of exclusion' (LS 197). It is this exclusive nature of divergence or incompossibility that Deleuze repeatedly criticises in Leibniz. Thus, at the same time as Deleuze praises Leibniz for employing 'the method of vice-diction with such genius', he laments the fact that Leibniz 'subordinated it to illegitimate conditions of convergence'. And crucially, the grounds for this subordination lie in the requirements of representation. Leibniz's theory of convergence and divergence indicates for Deleuze 'the presence of a continuing pressure on the part of the requirements of representation' (DR 279).

The critique of representation provides the general basis for all of Deleuze's critical statements about Leibniz's philosophy in *Difference and Repetition*. It explains, Deleuze thinks, Leibniz's commitment to the principle of identity, which in turn explains the exclusive role of divergence. In *Logic of Sense*, however, we find Deleuze's criticisms framed differently. Here, he is concerned with the necessary presence of God as a transcendent ground for the coherence of the world. Thus, the question of *which* distribution of singularities will be realised reduces to the more traditional question of God's choice of best possible world. We'll begin to understand how these two criticisms relate to each other by looking at Deleuze's critique of the concept of possibility itself.

THE POSSIBLE AND THE VIRTUAL IN *LOGIC OF SENSE*

Deleuze discusses the concept of possibility in some detail in the tenth Series of *Logic of Sense*, 'The Ideal Game'. Similar themes are also found in the fifth chapter of his 1962 book *Bergsonism*. A simple example, like rolling a dice, illustrates the ways in which Deleuze believes thinking is constrained by its reliance on possibility. When considering a future event, we try to conceive of every possible outcome. In this case, we conceive of six possibilities corresponding to the six faces of the dice. These possibilities constitute the elements of a logical set, and we can establish the probability of a certain outcome by dividing certainty (1) among all the elements of this set: 1/6 in the case of the fair dice. This account has several key features.

First, when the considered event comes to pass (when the dice is rolled) the outcome is understood as the *realisation* of a possibility which was already contained within the set of all possible outcomes. There is a relationship of *resemblance* between this possibility and the real outcome: the movement of realisation is understood as adding existence or reality to a possibility in such a way that it 'passes into the real' (Deleuze 1988a: 96). We recall that resemblance was one of the four features of representation which Deleuze identifies in *Difference and Repetition* and which we looked at above. For instance, Platonic copies *resemble* the ideal forms they participate in. Here, the situation is slightly different: a real event or state of the world resembles the *possible* state that pre-exists it.

This relationship of resemblance thus requires that the total set of possible outcomes is completely delineated *prior* to the realisation of one of its elements, and this is the second key feature of Deleuze's account of possibility: 'we give ourselves a real that is ready-made, preformed, pre-existent to itself . . . Everything is already *completely given*: all of the real is in the pseudo-actuality of the possible' (Deleuze 1988a: 98). Because of this antecedence, the set of possibilities as a whole is unaffected by which one of its elements is realised. In other words, the possible is indifferent to its own realisation. Finally, then, there is nothing about a possibility or a set of possibilities which allows us to determine which will in fact be realised. Instead, we must look *outside* the set in order to discover some external criterion or set of conditions on the basis of which a possibility is selected and realised. This selection can at the same time be viewed as a *limitation* which prevents every possibility from being realised at once: 'every possibility is not realised, realisation involves a limitation by which some possibilities are supposed to be repulsed or thwarted, while others pass into the real' (Deleuze 1988a: 96).

This final point amounts to the claim that there must be a *reason* why a particular possibility is realised. Thus, the question of possibility is closely connected to the question of sufficient reason. Within the context of our discussion of Leibniz, the task is to provide a reason why one singularity or event would be realised rather than some other. For instance, why, in the region of the world which Adam comes to envelop, do we find the event 'to sin', rather than the event 'to not sin'? For Leibniz, of course, with his law of continuity and commitment to the universal influence which extends between every event of the world, the answer will inevitably refer to all the other events with which 'to sin' is continuous, convergent and compossible. In effect, then, for Leibniz, each distinct set of possible events collapses into a single set which encompasses every possible state of the entire world. Each element of this set is a complete possible world, and a single moment of selection establishes once-and-for-all which distribution of singularities is realised. Even at this point, however, there is nothing internal to this all-encompassing set of possible worlds which determines which world is realised in order to become the real world. An external criterion is still required – something which stands outside the domain in which sufficient reason applies, or outside the world itself. Thus, for Leibniz, sufficient reason will inevitably refer back to God's free choice between internally compossible and complete possible worlds.

Relying on a particular understanding of possibility thus seems to commit a Leibnizian system to two important views. First, there is only a single point of selection or determination: not just a selection of a particular possibility but of an entire possible world. The events which define the world are selected once-and-for-all at its origin. Second, it relies on God as a being with a special ontological status in three senses: God is a being that necessarily stands outside the domain in which sufficient reasons are intelligible; the sufficient reason of every other being is only intelligible in so far as it contains a reference to God; and God has an intellect capable of grasping every possible distribution, and selecting the best possible for eventual realisation.

The real cause of these two views is the model of possibility: in particular, a certain idea of *closure*. There is a closed set of possible worlds which God chooses between, and each possible world is itself closed. The closure of possible worlds stems from the condition of convergence we looked at above. It's a theory of careful, orderly, agrarian distributions and enclosures. Deleuze's rejection of the condition of convergence will thus also entail a rejection of a world genesis based on the realisation of a possibility. The distribution of singularities does not rely on a single moment of selection, and it also does not rely on a transcendent agent which grounds this selection. One of the key differences between a purely Leibnizian model and Deleuze's own model is thus the mechanism behind this distribution of singularities. On the Leibnizian model it is governed by God's choice of best possible world, and occurs at the origin of the world. Deleuze's alternative turns this distribution into an on-going, nomadic process.

Affirming divergence

We know by now that the notions of convergence and divergence only come into play with the series of ordinary points which extend from each singular point. Convergence functions as a criterion of selection: a world is constituted on the condition that the series extending from singularities converge. A world envelops a system of singularities which have been selected through convergence. Where they don't converge we get a second possible world. Convergence is only determined with the prolongation or *actualisation* of singularities: technically it is the series of ordinary points extending from a singular point that are said to converge or diverge with each other, rather than the singular points themselves. Since it is this convergence of series which determines the compossibility of each possible world, it follows that God chooses between already-formed possible worlds, or worlds whose singularities have already been prolonged and extended into each other and therefore fully actualised. Just like the initial distribution of singularities, the subsequent actualisation of singularities has already occurred in the understanding of God prior to the realisation of the best possible world. In other words, Leibniz's model entirely precludes individuals from having any kind of 'virtual' aspect: an individual's potential is distributed across completely disconnected possible worlds, and all the individuals contained in each particular world are completely actualised at its origin.

In *Logic of Sense*, just as in *Difference and Repetition*, Deleuze makes two related claims: first, that this criterion of convergence is what defines compossibility, and second, that the relation of compossibility is therefore not reducible to a relation of contradiction. The key consequence of the first claim is that compossibility does not just describe a static series of relations, but describes a dynamic and genetic process. Given that the convergence of series is simultaneously the actualisation of individuals, there is no structural compossibility prior to this actualisation. Again, this is why above we saw that Leibniz's possible worlds are devoid of any virtuality: they are structured according to their compossibility and as such must already be fully actual. In a reversal of Deleuze's favourite Proustian formulation, they are possible without being virtual, or actual without being real.

By contrast, the key moment in Deleuze's modification of the

A Leibnizian World

Leibnizian model is his insistence on a *communication* or *resonance* between divergent series. This idea is incoherent so long as we understand divergence as a relation between series belonging to incompossible worlds, and instead requires us to consider the virtual structure of a single world whose singularities have not yet been fully actualised. Communication between divergent series lies at the heart of Deleuze's 'neo-Leibnizianism': it is dependent on a Leibnizian topological structure but remains inconceivable to Leibniz himself thanks to the restrictions of his own thought. Deleuze argues that the assumption that divergent singularities exclude and are forever closed off from each other is justified 'only to the extent that events are already grasped under the hypothesis of a God who calculates and chooses, and from the point of view of their actualisation in distinct worlds or individuals' (LS 197). Here in *Logic of Sense*, then, we ultimately find the conservative, theological Leibniz returning to supress the creative potential of divergent events. Leibniz's divine game makes use of divergence as a rule of exclusion which distributes events into distinct possible worlds; it is the metaphysical expression of Leibniz's conservatism and longing for order.[8]

But the exclusive nature of divergence is not justified, Deleuze argues, 'if we consider the pure events and the ideal game whose principle Leibniz was unable to grasp, hindered as he was by theological exigencies'. In Deleuze's ideal game 'the divergence of series or the disjunction of members cease to be negative rules of exclusion according to which events would be incompossible or incompatible. Divergence and disjunction are, on the contrary, affirmed as such' (LS 197). When it comes to affirming divergence, it is Nietzsche that Deleuze must turn to for inspiration, and no longer Leibniz: 'Nietzsche's perspective – his perspectivism – is a much more profound art than Leibniz's point of view; for divergence is no longer a principle of exclusion, and disjunction no longer a means of separation' (LS 198). To affirm divergence means, in effect, to posit a relationship of coupling or resonance between divergent series. The entire productive result of Deleuze's break with Leibniz's own conditions of convergence is thus summarised in Deleuze's claim that 'incompossibility is now a means of communication' (LS 198).

The possible and the virtual in *Difference and Repetition*

In *Difference and Repetition* we find precisely the same argument as the one we've just seen in *Logic of Sense*: 'Ideas have the power to affirm divergence; they establish a kind of resonance between divergent series' (DR 278). This is the basis on which we distinguish between a Leibnizian procedure of vice-diction, with its necessary addition of a divine game, and Deleuze's own, neo-Leibnizian vice-diction, which relies on an ideal game or a play of events which diverge from one another: 'The procedures of vice-diction cannot, therefore, be expressed in terms of representation, even infinite: as we saw with Leibniz, they thereby lose their principal power, that of affirming divergence or decentring' (DR 191). However, Deleuze's treatment of Leibniz in these sections of *Difference and Repetition* differs from that in *Logic of Sense* in two respects. First, the ground for Leibniz's failure to grasp the productive role of divergence is no longer located solely in 'theological exigencies', but in a commitment to the requirements of representation. Second, Deleuze is willing to concede a more ambiguous status to Leibniz, arguing that he stands 'hesitant' between various opposed positions.

The tension between two opposing characterisations of Leibniz first reappears in Deleuze's discussion of the difference between the virtual and the possible. This account shares many of the features of Deleuze's account of possibility in Series 10 of *Logic of Sense*, but again, while there it was the necessary role of God as a selective principle which Deleuze criticised, here it is the underlying representational structure which possibility presupposes. Thus, Deleuze argues that the difference between the possible and the real, or the movement from the possible to the real, amounts to the simple addition of existence. The only thing possibilities lack is reality or existence: 'What difference can there be between the existent and the non-existent if the non-existent is already possible, already included in the concept and having all the characteristics that the concept confers upon it as a possibility?' (DR 211). This means that while realisation may occur in space and time, this space and time is really nothing but an indifferent milieu because existence doesn't add anything that wasn't already present in the possible. The possible, Deleuze thinks, already refers to the form of identity in the concept, and is already fully determined through the form of the concept. Thus, the possible, in so far as it is capable of being realised, already possesses the 'image of the real'. The real therefore *resembles* the possible: 'It is difficult to understand what existence adds to the concept when all it does is double like with like' (DR 212). Deleuze condemns possibility for being subordinated to the requirements of representation: the form of possibility is subject to identity in the concept, while the relation between the possible and the real is understood as one of resemblance. The genesis of the illusion of possibility has its source in the same mistaken procedure which we've seen Deleuze condemn so frequently: the possible is 'produced after the fact, as retroactively fabricated in the image of what resembles it' (DR 212). Far from being capable of fulfilling its grounding or conditioning role, the possible instead ends up an inert, abstract shadow of that which it was intended to ground. This is why Deleuze will go on to claim that Leibniz's divine game, in which God selects the best possible world for realisation, is a game which is 'indistinguishable from the practice of representation, of which it presents all the elements' (DR 283).

Leibniz's philosophy is ultimately a philosophy constrained by representation, for Deleuze, because it 'does not free itself from the principle of identity as a presupposition of representation' (DR 49). Just as in *Logic of Sense*, this presupposition of representation manifests itself in the technical definition of divergence as a rule of exclusion: 'that is why it remains subject to the condition of the convergence of series in the case of Leibniz' (DR 49). Deleuze's rejection of Leibniz can always be brought back to this single point of difference. This gives us a much better grasp of some of Deleuze's philosophical goals than if we had simply located Deleuze's critique of Leibniz in a vague distaste for conservative theology and a reliance on a transcendent divine agent. Of course, Deleuze *does* have a distaste for these things, but he is able to locate their precise influence in the technical, metaphysical role of divergence. Deleuze even goes as far as to say that this is Leibniz's *only* error:

> Leibniz's only error was to have linked difference to the negative of limitation, because he maintained the dominance of the old principle, because he linked the series to a principle of convergence, without seeing that divergence itself was an object of affirmation, or that the incompossibles belonged to the same world and were affirmed as the greatest crime and the greatest virtue of the one and only world, that of the eternal return. (DR 51)

The actualisation of the virtual is opposed to the realisation of the possible on all of these grounds. 'Actualisation breaks with resemblance as a process no less than it does with identity as a principle. Actual terms never resemble the singularities they incarnate. In this sense, actualisation or differenciation is always a genuine creation' (DR 212). And key to this process of actualisation are the relations of resonance between divergent singularities.

Leibniz is saved from a fate as nothing but a thinker of representation because, Deleuze thinks, he is a figure standing hesitant between these two movements: the topological movement of the virtual and the conceptual movement of the possible. 'Any hesitation between the virtual and the possible, the order of the Idea and the order of the concept, is disastrous, since it abolishes the reality of the virtual. There are traces of such an oscillation in the philosophy of Leibniz' (DR 212). This oscillation between the virtual and the possible encapsulates the double-sided nature of all of Deleuze's readings of Leibniz. On the one hand, we get the dynamic, Dionysian side: 'Every time Leibniz speaks of Ideas, he presents them as virtual multiplicities made of differential relations and singular points, which thought apprehends in a state close to sleep, stupor, swooning, death, amnesia, murmuring or intoxication' (DR 213). But on the other hand the conservative, Apollonian theological tendency returns and subordinates this conception of the Idea to a model of possibility: 'However, that in which Ideas are actualised is rather conceived as a possible, a realised possible.' This hesitation turns out to be the very source of Leibniz's originality and creativity: 'No one has come closer to a movement of vice-diction in the Idea, but no one has better maintained the supposed right of representation' (DR 213).

The clear and the confused

There is one more 'hesitation' in Leibniz's philosophy, Deleuze thinks, this time concerning his steps towards a theory of differential, unconscious ideas: 'No one has been better able to immerse thought in the element of difference and provide it with a differential unconscious, surround it with little glimmerings and singularities, all in order to save and reconstitute the homogeneity of a natural light à la Descartes' (DR 213). Leibniz's contribution here is framed by its opposition to Descartes, just as it was throughout *Expressionism in Philosophy: Spinoza*. Descartes' principle of the clear and distinct is the 'highest form' of the principle of representation as good sense or common sense, Deleuze thinks. The proportionality between clarity and distinctness entails that as an idea becomes clearer so it also becomes more distinct: 'Clarity-distinctness constitutes the light which renders thought possible in the common exercise of all the faculties.' With Leibniz, however, this proportionality is broken: 'Given this principle, we cannot overemphasise the importance of a remark that Leibniz constantly makes in his logic of ideas: a clear idea is in itself confused, it is confused in so far as it is clear' (DR 213). Thus, for Leibniz, clarity and distinctness are inversely proportional: the clearer an idea is, the less distinct it is. Clarity is always confused, and distinctness is always obscure. This is a theme broad enough for Deleuze to identity various examples across Leibniz's philosophy. Thus, while here it is introduced in the context of a logic of ideas, Deleuze concedes that here the true force is not yet felt by Leibniz himself: 'Without doubt, this remark may be accommodated within the Cartesian logic, and taken to mean simply that a clear idea is confused because it is not yet clear enough in all its parts. Moreover, is this not how Leibniz himself finally tends to interpret it?' (DR 213). But it returns in full force in his model of minute perceptions:

> Despite the complexity and ambiguity of [Leibniz's] texts, it does indeed seem at times that the expressed (the continuum of differential relations or the unconscious virtual Idea) should be in itself distinct and obscure: for example, all the drops of water in the sea like so many genetic elements with the differential relations, the variations in these relations and the distinctive points they comprise. In addition, it seems that the expresser (the perceiving, imagining or thinking individual) should be by nature clear and confused: for example, our perception of the noise of the sea, which confusedly includes the whole and clearly expresses only certain relations or certain points by virtue of our bodies and a threshold of consciousness they determine. (DR 253)

The individual drops of water are distinct but we perceive them only obscurely, while the clear perception of the sea is a confusion of all these individual drops. But this quote is also useful for pointing out what almost seems like a reluctance on Deleuze's part to credit Leibniz with such a view. It is only despite the 'complexity and ambiguity' of Leibniz's texts, and only 'at times', that it *seems* as if Leibniz breaks the connection between clarity and distinctness. By contrast, when Deleuze returns to this question in *The Fold*, where it will play a crucial role, there is no such reluctance: when it comes to both perceptions and ideas, distinctness is necessarily obscure, and clarity is necessarily confused.

The question of clarity and distinctness is especially important for the question of the 'region of clear expression' which defines a monad. Given the model we've outlined in this chapter, we know that Deleuze's reading of Leibniz makes a central point of the fact that monads are defined or produced by the singularities or events which they envelop and eventually express. This is the second moment within the process of vice-diction or static ontological genesis, and follows the initial distribution of singularities themselves. Even in *Difference and Repetition* and *Logic of Sense*, it is already clear that Deleuze conceives this as a theory of *envelopment*. But it is not until twenty years later that we find a fully developed account of this theory. We now therefore turn to *The Fold* in order to explain why a theory of individuals as 'centres of expression' forms another central part of Deleuze's reading of Leibniz. As part of this process, we will have to find correlates for the central features of Deleuze's Leibnizian structure which we've reconstructed in this chapter. As we'll see, each returns modified in some sense by the concept of the fold. But we'll also see that *The Fold*, as a text and as a concept, is not enough to liberate Leibniz's philosophy from its constraints (whether theological or representational) and that in fact, precisely the same criticisms will return and come to a head in this final engagement.

Notes

1. For much of the following section I rely on the history of calculus found in Zill and Wright 2009: xxvi–xxvii. For other accounts of calculus as it relates to Deleuze's philosophy see Somers-Hall (2012b) and Duffy (2006a, 2006b, 2010).
2. As Somers-Hall writes: 'What draws Deleuze to the calculus is the fact that it can be understood to operate according to entities that simply cannot be represented – that is, that simply cannot be incorporated into judgements' (2012b: 5).
3. Again, as Somers-Hall writes 'What is important about the calculus is that it presents an account of how undetermined elements can become determinate through entering into reciprocal relations' (2012b: 142).
4. Much has been made of Deleuze's use of concepts from mathematics that came after Leibniz. For instance, DeLanda (2002) insists that a theory of singularities can only be understood in terms of René Thom's catastrophe theory; while Durie (2006) thinks that convergence must be understood in terms of the mathematical theory of Taylor series. However, the fact that we are also able to describe the process of 'actualisation' or individualisation as a kind of reversed Leibnizian infinite analysis demonstrates, I think, the independence of Deleuze's philosophy from any particular mathematical apparatus.
5. For a different reading of the correspondence between singular points and singular events, see Bowden 2011. Bowden allows for an additional category, 'ordinary events', which are distinct from 'singular events', rather than assuming all events singular in so far as they correspond to a singular point.
6. I am indebted to conversations with Stephen Barrell for the main features

A Leibnizian World

of this account. See his forthcoming *The Form and Function of Deleuze's Engagement with Psychoanalysis in The Logic of Sense*.

7. This account of vice-diction conflicts with that of James Williams, for whom vice-diction is a kind of ethical operation on the side of human subjects: 'The concept of vice-diction is Deleuze's answer to the question of how to live with the way virtual Ideas and, therefore, pure differences condition our actions. This leads to answers to the question of how to act' (Williams 2003: 168). But, we've seen that vice-diction is a metaphysical procedure or movement, rather than a peculiarly human activity. Thus, Deleuze writes: 'There is an objectivity on the part of adjunction and condensation, and an objectivity of conditions, which implies that Ideas no more than Problems do not exist only in our heads but occur here and there in the production of an actual historical world' (DR 189).

8. Stengers makes a similar point when she writes of Leibniz's refusal to acknowledge the 'depths': 'Leibniz is a central figure in Deleuze's *Logic of Sense*. He appears as the creator of concepts Deleuze clearly loves, but he is also the one who exhibits the danger specific to what Deleuze calls a surface thought: not a thought that remains at the surface of things, but a thought that is creating this surface, refusing both the height, the high point from which things can be judged, and the depths, which subvert and destroy any order' (Stengers 2009: 30).

PART III
The Fold

5

Material Folds and the Lower Level of the Baroque House

The Leibnizian structure we discovered in *Difference and Repetition* and *Logic of Sense* returns in *The Fold*. Although its central elements remain the same, there are some key differences. Here, for the first time, Deleuze is careful to introduce each element of his reading of Leibniz in a particular order. In the lecture series on Leibniz that Deleuze gave in 1986, at around the same time *The Fold* was written, Deleuze calls this a 'non-philosophical reading' of a philosopher, and insists it must accompany any philosophical understanding of Leibniz. This non-philosophical reading relies on a kind of intuitive deduction of the impetus behind Leibniz's creation of certain concepts: 'all sorts of sensible intuitions that you must allow to be born within you; extremely rudimentary sensible intuitions, but by the same token, extremely lively' (16/12/1986). Thus, for example, we will see that when Deleuze initially asks 'why are things folded?', the intuitive answer he relies on to advance his account is 'in order to be put inside something'. It is only on this basis that we move from the folded nature of predicates or events to their 'inclusion' in subjects or individual notions. Regardless of how we interpret the legitimacy of this method, it at least demonstrates the extent to which *The Fold* presents Leibniz's philosophy, for the first time, as a unified whole, all of whose elements are connected.[1]

The Fold starts with a discussion of curvature in Leibniz's conception of matter. Deleuze draws on Wölfflin's analysis of Renaissance and Baroque architecture to characterise the propensity for curved forms with fuzzy edges and the neglect of sharp edges – a propensity that finds its correlate both in the contemporary mathematical problem of curved lines and figures and in Leibniz's own philosophical conception of infinitely divisible matter. We discover, however, that Leibniz's infinitely divisible, continuous matter ends up referring to centres of unity that exist outside of the material domain. Deleuze's non-philosophical progression thus moves us to a different domain, where metaphysical unities or souls exist. It is here that Deleuze's Leibnizian structure returns in familiar form. Once again,

Deleuze describes a process through which singular points (this time themselves understood as points of inflection or folds) are enveloped by monads that come to occupy certain points of view. Deleuze describes the clear region of the world that these monads express in terms of Baroque painting, whose characteristic chiaroscuro style allows clear forms to emerge from an obscured dark background. We also see here Deleuze's most explicit attempt to equate the Leibnizian monad with the singular complete notion. The singularities enfolded in a monad are simultaneously the predicates which are included in the monad's complete notion. What we 'see' in the monad, Deleuze thinks, we 'read' in the monad's notion.

In *The Fold* we find Deleuze's own characterisation of the two images of Leibniz we have traced through his work. Any 'portrait of Leibniz', he will write in chapter 3, is marked by the tension between an 'open façade' and a 'closed interiority', especially when it comes to the ways in which he presents his philosophy. But even in *The Fold*, Deleuze cannot free Leibniz from the theological constraints of his time and thought. However far he is pushed, we return again and again to the same point: Leibniz cannot be brought to 'affirm divergence' in the way Deleuze insists is necessary.

5.1 The Baroque

We mustn't forget the other word that accompanies Leibniz in the subtitle of *The Fold: Leibniz and the Baroque*. Throughout the book, Deleuze refers to Baroque architecture, sculpture, painting and music. Pinpointing the intention behind Deleuze's references to the Baroque forces us to make some fairly bold claims about the intentions of the book as a whole, and especially how the Baroque stands in relation to Leibniz's philosophy. It is tempting, given our focus, to interpret all of Deleuze's references to Baroque art as nothing more than a useful set of analogies and images that allow us to better understand Leibniz's philosophy. We could argue that the various discussions of Baroque architecture, sculpture, painting and music give us a fresh, alternative viewpoint on complex Leibnizian concepts, and that these viewpoints help us visualise Leibniz's elaborate philosophical system and add some colour to what would otherwise be a fairly dry, technical text.

But perhaps the Baroque signifies something much more important for Deleuze. It might signify a particular context within which Leibniz's philosophy should be situated, where it can be labelled 'Baroque philosophy' and placed alongside Baroque architecture,

Material Folds

music, even a Baroque mathematics, and so on. If this is the case, then the discussions of Baroque art still help us understand Leibniz's philosophy, but only in so far as they describe 'Baroque traits' which are common to all these various disciplines. Leibniz's philosophy thus becomes one expression among many of the traits that define the Baroque.

The difference between these two possible interpretations of Baroque art in *The Fold* boils down to a decision over which word in the subtitle should take priority: does the significance of the Baroque stem solely from its affinity with the images conjured up by a Leibnizian universe, or does Leibniz's significance stem from his role as philosophical ambassador for the Baroque, understood as some kind of historical event, or perhaps even a Baroque 'plane of immanence'? Although it runs counter to our emphasis on Leibniz, I would argue that the second interpretation is correct: it is Leibniz who falls under the umbrella of the Baroque, and not vice versa. I think this is clear from the very first page, where Deleuze writes that the 'trait of the Baroque' is the infinite fold, or the infinite process of folding. Thus – and before we even broach the question of how Deleuze is using the term 'fold' – it is clear that the Baroque, by itself, has a defining trait, and it is through this common trait that we justify the analogies which Deleuze draws between Baroque art, philosophy and mathematics. The key point, then, is that the infinite fold is not just a concept we can extract from Leibniz's philosophy, it is the very trait which allows Leibniz's philosophy to express the Baroque world, and for Leibniz to be considered the Baroque philosopher *par excellence*.

For our present purposes then, in order to justify the relevance of *The Fold* it suffices only to point out that Deleuze's passages on the Baroque always shed some light on Leibniz, whichever way we view the relationship between the two: whether because they are deliberately constructed as analogies, or because they share key traits, these passages always correspond to some area or theme within Leibniz's philosophy. Manola Antonioli points out how *The Fold* presents a complex relationship between the Baroque and Leibniz's philosophy:

> Even if this book seems like a return to the preceding monographs, it presents in reality a much more complex structure of internal folding: an implication of the thought of Leibniz in the thought of the Baroque, and an implication and complication of fundamental concepts of Deleuze in the thought of the fold of Leibniz and of the Baroque. (Antonioli 1999: 109)

None of this should take away from Leibniz's singular importance, however. However wide Deleuze's analyses may spread, in so far as *The Fold* remains a book of philosophy, Leibniz's central role is assured. This is especially clear when we consider the question of defining the Baroque more precisely. Deleuze suggests that commentators on the Baroque often display a kind of doubt about the 'consistency' of the concept. They worry that it is too broad a term, and threatens to takes on an arbitrary extension: a label applied so liberally that it becomes meaningless. In response to this fear, different strategies can be employed. We could restrict the Baroque to a single domain, like architecture, or to narrower and narrower periods and places. We could even simply deny that the Baroque is a meaningful concept at all, and claim that the Baroque has never really existed. But to deny the existence of the Baroque is not the same as, for instance, denying the existence of unicorns. In the case of the unicorn, the concept is at least available: we know what a unicorn *would* be; we simply deny that anything exists in the world which matches this concept. In the case of the Baroque, however, the question is precisely whether we can adequately determine the concept itself. To render the Baroque inexistent we can simply refuse to provide a concept for what the Baroque would be. But the challenge is precisely to invent a concept of the Baroque that makes it exist, or that provides its reason for existing.

For Deleuze, the criterion or the 'operatory concept' of the Baroque is the fold. It is this concept which allows us to extend the Baroque beyond its historical limits while giving it a precise condition. In other words, particular figures from various points in history are labelled 'Baroque' if and only if their work includes folding in some way. This is why Deleuze can insist, for example, that Mallarmé is a Baroque poet, and Hantaï is a Baroque painter. There is a Baroque line or lineage throughout history, Deleuze claims, recognisable thanks to the concept of the fold, and which unites architects, painters, musicians, poets and philosophers. But does Deleuze's own criterion fall prey to the very criticism he has just levelled at previous attempts? Does defining the Baroque in terms of folding leave us with far too broad a concept? Surely we could find 'folds' pretty much everywhere, in every period and discipline? Deleuze recognises the danger: 'which period and which style would ignore the fold as a trait of painting or of sculpture?' (LP 47). There are already Roman folds, Oriental folds, etc. Key for Deleuze is that the Baroque is identified specifically with the *infinite* fold, the fold that 'goes to infinity', and which thereby attains a kind of 'unlimited freedom'.

We'll look more at what Deleuze means by the infinite fold below. What matters here is that by identifying certain 'Baroque traits' such as the infinite fold, Deleuze is able to draw analogies between various artistic disciplines. The idea that particular disciplines refer to more general traits that define the Baroque period isn't new. Bukofzer shows in his *Music in the Baroque era* that: 'The renaissance artist saw in music a self-contained autonomous art, subject only to its own laws. The baroque artist saw in music a heteronomous art, subordinated to words and serving only as musical means to a dramatic end that transcended music' (Bukofzer 2008: 8). Similarly, Wölfflin writes in *Renaissance and Baroque*: 'what we are discussing is a general approach to form which embraces all the arts, including music, and which implies a more fundamental common source' (Wölfflin 1964: 36). What interests us is that by drawing on these general Baroque traits Deleuze is also able to draw analogies between artistic disciplines and Leibniz's own philosophy and mathematics. In the final chapter, for instance, Deleuze writes there is a 'clear analogy' between the concepts of harmony found in Baroque music and Leibniz's philosophy (LP 179).

While Wölfflin is largely concerned with architecture, his identification of more general Baroque traits is particularly influential on Deleuze. Wölfflin pinpoints, within the 200-year Baroque period, a gradual change or tendency within its 'general approach to form'. The early Baroque style is 'heavy, massive, restrained and solemn'. Gradually, the 'pressure' of this early period begins to lift, and we find a 'lighter and gayer' style, culminating with the 'playful dissolution of all structural elements' in the Rococo style (Wölfflin 1964: 16). This movement from heaviness to lightness is like an elevation, or perhaps an overflowing, and it is a theme that will return again and again throughout *The Fold*. We find it not only in chapter 1, where Deleuze addresses Wölfflin's architectural theory directly, but also in chapter 9, where he characterises Baroque art through the tendency for its matter to extend or overflow its frame. But Deleuze also insists that this tendency is not limited to art. In Leibniz's philosophy, for instance, we'll see how the unfolding of organisms is a kind of overflowing, while souls are 'elevated' to the status of reasonable spirits. I would like to go even further, and suggest that just as Wölfflin identified a gradual process of elevation within the Baroque style, there is a corresponding elevation throughout the structure of *The Fold* itself.

We see this first in the areas of Leibniz's philosophy Deleuze turns his attention to, and second in their corresponding artistic analogies. The first chapter is concerned with Leibniz's theory of matter, and thus it is in the weighty, heavy masses of architecture that Deleuze finds inspiration. Then, as we move to a discussion of the 'weightless' soul or monad in chapters 2 and 3, we turn to painting and sculpture. In chapters 5 and 6, which address souls that have been elevated to a 'reasonable' status, Deleuze draws heavily on literature, and in the final chapter he discusses music as an analogy for Leibniz's theory of harmony. In the most general terms, *The Fold* displays a tendency to move from material heaviness towards spiritual weightlessness.

5.2 Folding and the Baroque House

We find this theme again in one of the most enduring images of *The Fold*: the metaphor of the Baroque house. The most important feature of the Baroque house is that it has two floors or levels: above we find weightless souls, while below we find heavy, material masses. This distinction between these two levels or floors is crucial for Deleuze: the two floors of the Baroque house are also the two levels of the Baroque conception of the world. The lower level of the Baroque house is made up of crowded, communal areas. There is no privacy, and everything communicates. It is on this lower level that we find weighty, material masses. Deleuze uses the image of the communal area to hint at the continuous and open nature of matter: the parts of matter are not 'closed off' from one another, and each is open to the influence of every other part. By contrast, the upper level of the Baroque house contains completely private rooms, which do not communicate or interact with each other or with the outside world. These private chambers are the monads that, we are constantly reminded, 'have no doors or windows'. The upper, spiritual level of the Baroque house is where we find absolute individuality in the form of monads or souls. It is hard to imagine two more opposed domains: the openness, exteriority and continuity of material bodies below, and the closure, interiority and individuality of spiritual monads above. The two levels of the Baroque house seem irredeemably detached from one another. They are, to use the terminology familiar to Leibniz's period, *really distinct*.

And yet there is a third, more elusive, current within Leibniz's philosophy which hints at a reconciliation or even a blurring between these two levels, and this is where the concept of folding becomes

Material Folds

crucial. The essence of folding is present in Deleuze's repeated references to a favourite thesis of Leibniz: real distinction does not imply separability, which means that two things, including the two levels of the Baroque house, can be really distinct from one another and yet remain inseparable.[2] It is as if the two levels of the Baroque house are distinguished only while simultaneously being folded over or into each other in such a way that they become inseparable. In the same way, we'll see that an organic body is distinct, yet also inseparable, from the monad that unifies it.

In addition to the fold that passes between the upper and lower level of the Baroque house, there are operations of folding on each level itself, specific to that level. On the lower level there is a fold which amasses the parts of matter into inorganic aggregates, while a second fold organises (the same) parts into organic bodies. Meanwhile, on the upper level, a monad's perception has nothing to do with a view onto an outside, but with an unfolding or drawing out of something already folded within the obscure darkness of its own interiority. Deleuze devotes the first chapter of *The Fold* to the lower level of the Baroque house, or to the types of folding found in material bodies. The second chapter deals with the type of folding found in souls on the upper level. It is not until chapter 3 that we begin to see how there is a process of folding which passes between these two levels themselves.

These then are the three central aspects of the Baroque house, and by extension, the Baroque world: two really distinct levels, folded into a single world. They are also indicative of the three central areas of Leibniz's philosophy which Deleuze thinks are pivotal. Leibniz provides a conception of a continuous, infinitely divisible matter on the one hand, and a conception of absolute individuality, in the form of closed monads, on the other. But he also provides, or at least hints at, a third concept, the fold, as the defining concept of the Baroque itself, through which the two levels of the Baroque world begin to resonate, are brought into a correspondence and perhaps even a communication. This is why, in the final chapter, Deleuze is able to write that 'the world of Leibniz has no trouble in reconciling full continuity in extension with the most comprehensive and tightest individuality' (LP 169).

Chapter 1 of *The Fold* is concerned with the 'lower' level of the Baroque house and with the material bodies found there. Among these material bodies Deleuze identifies two types of fold, or two distinct operations of folding. The first of these corresponds to inorganic aggregates, while the second corresponds to living organisms. In order to pinpoint the difference between 'inorganic folds' and 'organic folds' (as we will call them), Deleuze thus devotes much of his attention to the difference between inorganic aggregates and living organisms. This is an unusual place to begin a treatment of Leibniz's philosophy, and sheds some additional light on the intent behind *The Fold* as a whole. If *The Fold* were a conventional account of Leibniz's philosophy we would expect it to begin with an introduction of its more well-known aspects: his theory of analytic truth, his understanding of predication, the theory of monads, and so on. The difference between inorganic aggregates and living organisms seems to be a secondary question: it might be addressed, but only after these more properly philosophical issues have been settled. And even Deleuze's own earlier reading of Leibniz, in *Expressionism in Philosophy: Spinoza*, followed this approach: as we saw in Chapter 1, while the nature of matter and organisms was eventually discussed, it was interesting only in so far as it was informed by the great metaphysical 'principles of reason', an understanding of which remained Deleuze's real concern. The way *The Fold* plunges headfirst into the intricacies of matter and living organisms is therefore surprising. But it is surprising only so long as we treat this strictly as a book about Leibniz. As I have argued above, *The Fold* does not just introduce the concept of folding in order to explain Leibniz's philosophy, but places Leibniz's philosophy alongside other expressions of the 'infinite fold' as the concept which defines the Baroque. As we struggle to understand the nature of folding in all of its various aspects, it is perhaps the inorganic and the organic fold which are the easiest to grasp. And so, if we accept that an account of folding is one of Deleuze's central goals for the book as a whole, then a discussion of inorganic matter and living organisms, as the domains in which the inorganic and the organic fold operate, whilst apparently unorthodox, instead becomes the most logical starting point. The choice of topics contained in this first chapter is thus guided by Deleuze's overall plan to develop an account of folding, and it should not imply that Deleuze believes that these topics play any kind of grounding role in Leibniz's philosophy.

5.3 Baroque Architecture and the Inorganic Fold

Deleuze identifies three important characteristics within Leibniz's theory of inorganic matter. But he does not turn to Leibniz directly in order to introduce these characteristics. Instead, we find an

Material Folds

apparently unconnected discussion of Baroque architecture. Often, throughout *The Fold*, and as we saw above, the same idea is expressed in various ways, or approached from different angles, across several disciplines. Sometimes it is only through a careful reading that the correspondence between these apparently disconnected discussions becomes clear. In this case, it is necessary to summarise the important features of Deleuze's brief foray into architectural theory in order to draw out their later relevance. The authority Deleuze turns to is Heinrich Wölfflin, the figure largely responsible for legitimising the Baroque period. Until Wölfflin's 1888 work *Renaissance und Barock*, the term had always been derogatory, indicating a noisy, redundant abundance of detail or complexity. As Wölfflin points out, the Baroque was customarily seen, not as a progression from the Renaissance, but as that 'into which the Renaissance degenerated' (Wölfflin 1964: 15). Wölfflin's work marks the point at which the term came to designate a particular stylistic category, and therefore a serious area of study. Deleuze credits Wölfflin with identifying the 'material traits' of the Baroque through his analysis of Baroque architecture. We've already established that Deleuze thinks the same Baroque characteristics apply across disciplines, and so the 'material traits' which he finds in Wölfflin must inevitably extend beyond architecture. We saw that Wölfflin himself even says as much: 'what we are discussing is a general approach to form which embraces all the arts, including music, and which implies a more fundamental common source' (1964: 36). Of course Deleuze goes further, and claims that these traits are not just limited to the arts, but extend into Baroque mathematics, science and philosophy. This means that in so far as Leibniz is the philosophical representative of the Baroque, the material traits which Deleuze finds in Wölfflin's analysis of Baroque architecture will correspond to the material traits of Leibniz's own philosophy, or in other words to certain features of Leibniz's own understanding of the nature of material bodies. Looking at the key characteristics of Baroque architecture is thus how we begin to visualise and understand Leibniz's conception of the material world: a world of masses and aggregates and, subsequently, a world of inorganic folds. With this in mind, we'll summarise the material traits which Deleuze finds in Wölfflin, and which will correspond to the characteristics of Leibniz's theory of matter.

The first key trait of Baroque architecture Deleuze picks out is its use of curved forms in place of straight edges: 'the rounding of corners and the avoidance of right angles', as well as 'the substitution of the rounded acanthus for the jagged acanthus ...' (LP 7) (the acanthus is an ornamental decoration styled after the leaves of the acanthus plant). Wölfflin writes that as part of the transition from Renaissance to Baroque architecture 'all hard and pointed shapes were blunted and softened, and everything angular became rounded' (1964: 47). This emphasis on curved lines should strike us as familiar: we already introduced the importance of curvature when we used it to characterise the non-uniform motion of bodies in the last chapter. There, 'curved lines' were connected to the *continuity* of matter which ensured, for instance, the rolling cannonball was subject to a constant, subtle influence by its environment. The same idea returns here in *The Fold*, with the addition of this new feature: the 'blurring' of edges, such that the boundary or transition between two forms is impossible to pinpoint precisely. Baroque architectural forms are curved precisely because they lack sharp boundaries. Indeed, Wölfflin goes so far as to say that 'this very antipathy to any form with a clear contour is perhaps the most basic trait of the Baroque style' (1964: 64). The transition from the discontinuous, sharp forms of the Renaissance to the continuous, curved forms of the Baroque is thus one in which 'corners were rounded off, so that the boundaries between light and dark, which had formerly been clearly defined, now formed a quivering transition' (Wölfflin 1964: 35). This last quote also hints at two additional themes: the blurring of edges occurs not just between forms, but between light and darkness; and the border isn't just blurred, it is 'quivering', suggesting, once again, a return of some kind of restlessness.

Second, Deleuze references the 'horizontal widening of the base', the 'lowering of the pediment' and the 'low and curved steps ...' which are characteristic of Baroque architecture (LP 7). All of these are symptomatic of what Wölfflin calls the Baroque's 'broad, heavy, massive forms'. A sense of weight dominates Baroque architecture to the extent that its forms are 'almost crushed by the pressure'. The resulting church and palace façades feature 'as much width as possible', pediments that are 'heavily depressed', and staircases with 'low, spreading forms' (Wölfflin 1964: 44). Wölfflin writes that 'this effect of yielding to an oppressive weight is sometimes so powerful that we imagine that the forms affected are actually suffering' (1964: 45). The second material trait of the Baroque is thus this sense of weight or pressure: Baroque forms strike us being compressed or squashed by an outside force.

The ubiquity of curvature carries with it a third aspect, which

Material Folds

Wölfflin hints at when he writes: 'The Renaissance work looks fragile, its brittle stuff terminates in sharp edges and hard angles, while the Baroque forms are full, opulent, and curled over in round and generous whorls' (1964: 35). Baroque architectural forms do not only have curved *external* edges, but the 'quivering transition' between forms in some way reaches into the interior of the form itself, which becomes animated by 'generous whorls' or vortices. Deleuze expands on this when he writes of 'the utilisation of travertine [a particularly porous form of limestone] to produce spongy, cavernous forms, or the constitution of a vortical form which is always fed by new turbulences and which ends only in the fashion of a horse's mane or the foam of a wave' (LP 7). There is thus a kind of *dynamism* or restless activity nestling within Baroque forms. This animated matter even displays a tendency 'to overflow space, in the style of a fluid' (LP 7). Wölfflin writes: 'the Baroque puts the emphasis on the material, and either omits the frame altogether or makes it seem inadequate to contain the bulging mass it encloses' (1964: 55). This tendency presents an interesting counterpoint to the sense of weight and pressure we introduced above. Caught between these two tendencies, Baroque architecture is 'crowded and massive and makes us fear that the filling will burst out of the frames' (1964: 56).

Deleuze's brief account of Wöllflin's analysis of Baroque architecture in the first chapter of *The Fold* thus gives us three 'material traits' of the Baroque, encapsulated in three terms: curvature, pressure and internal dynamism. Taken together these three ideas will also form the core of Deleuze's reading of Leibniz's theory of matter. Finally, they form the core of the first of the two types of fold that Deleuze puts to use throughout the whole of the book. Again, we are already somewhat familiar with the importance of curvature from the last chapter: we know it is connected with Leibniz's law of *continuity*, and with his discovery of the infinitesimal calculus. This idea of continuity was important, because it led us to a description of a *differential continuum*, populated by singularities, which formed an important part of the Leibnizian structure Deleuze puts to use in *Difference and Repetition* and *Logic of Sense*. In the first chapter of *The Fold*, it becomes central to the analogy Deleuze draws between Baroque architecture and a 'Baroque mathematical physics'.

Deleuze suggests that the Dutch mathematician Huygens, with whom Leibniz corresponded, is responsible for particular developments in mathematical physics which we can describe as 'Baroque' precisely because of their emphasis on curvature. Following Huygens,

Leibniz maintained that the biggest challenge facing our observation of bodies moving in space is to describe their curved, or non-uniform, motion. In Huygens' case, the development of a branch of mathematical physics 'aimed at curvature' leads to the discovery of centrifugal force. In Leibniz's case, as we've seen, it leads to the development of infinitesimal calculus. Here in *The Fold*, however, Deleuze does not immediately relate the idea of curvature to Leibniz's mathematics. Instead, we are still firmly in the domain of the material. Deleuze describes three 'fundamental notions' in Leibniz's theory of matter which will correspond to the three traits of Baroque architecture we have just introduced: the fluidity of matter, the elasticity of bodies, and the 'spring' or *ressort* internal to these bodies. In the previous chapter we briefly introduced the curved, non-uniform motion of bodies in order to get a sense of the urgency behind Leibniz's mathematical discoveries. By returning to this discussion in more detail we'll see how Deleuze now relies on an account of *folding* to understand a key part of Leibniz's philosophy – his law of continuity. We thus have our first instance of a familiar and important point of influence on Deleuze returning in order to be brought under the auspices of his new concern for the concept of the fold.

When isolated, or considered in abstraction, the motion of any body will be straight and uniform. There is nothing about a body taken in isolation that would cause its movement to curve. However, in reality, the motion of a body is always influenced by its surrounding environment, and is compelled to respond to this influence. We saw this in the last chapter (section 4.1), where we quoted Leibniz's preface to his *New Essays on Human Understanding* (a text which Deleuze cites often in *The Fold*, but never in *Difference and Repetition* or *Logic of Sense*). There, Leibniz refers to 'the jumble of effects of the surrounding infinity' which always provides an exception to uniform motion (1996: 57).

Thus, each part of matter is open to constant influence from an environment from which it is never completely isolated or separated, and it is this that accounts for the necessarily curved or non-uniform motion of bodies. The curvature which is evident within matter corresponds to the first of the material traits of the Baroque which Deleuze takes from Wölfflin – the idea that Baroque forms are always curved and show a resistance to straight edges. We can also describe this jumble of effects from the surrounding environment as a type of pressure exerted on a body, and thus draw an additional correspondence to Wölfflin's second trait – the idea that Baroque forms are subject to a kind of weight or pressure. Matter is compressed by its surrounding environment, and it is this which gives it a curvilinear movement. The effect of the surrounding environment is evident enough in most cases: the uniform motion of the cannonball rolling down the hill is interrupted because the rough ground constantly affects its course. But Leibniz insists that *no* part of matter can ever be isolated, thanks to the nature of matter itself. Matter is infinitely divisible, and this entails a continuity between each of its parts, and a corresponding susceptibility to influence. Leibniz summarises this continuity with a well-known phrase: 'nature never makes leaps'. For a body to be isolated it would have to remain indifferent to, or disconnected from, the matter that surrounds it. But for Leibniz such a discontinuity between the parts of matter is impossible: the 'gap' between any two parts of matter we consider always contains a third part that exists between them. As a result, even the space where two bodies 'touch' is not really a point of discontinuity because the division between the two becomes blurred as each divides infinitely into further parts. And if discontinuity is impossible then it follows that no part of matter can be isolated, or rendered indifferent to an influence from its environment. We've already seen that the 'blurring' of the division between bodies or forms is what Wölfflin calls the most important feature of the Baroque. As well as in architecture, it appears again in Wölfflin's distinction between the 'linear' style of painting characteristic of the Renaissance and the 'painterly' style of the Baroque: 'The earlier [Renaissance] style is entirely linear: every object has a sharp unbroken outline and the main expressive element is the contour. The later [Baroque] style works with broad, vague masses, the contours barely indicated; the lines are tentative and repetitive strokes, or do not exist at all' (1964: 31). It is this characteristic of matter as continuous and infinitely divisible which is called the 'fluidity' of matter, Deleuze's first 'fundamental notion' in Leibniz's theory of matter.

To describe matter as fluid can mean one of two things. Deleuze uses the term to designate this continuous influence that extends between the parts of matter. The fluidity of matter means that each of its parts is constantly open to its environment, and each part therefore has a curved motion as it moves in response to the effects of this environment. In this sense, matter is fluid in the same sense as a pond of water, in which any disturbance eventually reverberates throughout the whole pond. This is why Deleuze quotes the following line from Leibniz: 'The whole world is like a pond of matter in which there are different currents and waves' (LP 7). Leibniz himself used the term fluidity in a slightly different, although closely connected, sense: to designate the indifference of matter to its own division. The 'more fluid' a matter is, the easier it may be divided, and matter that is 'absolutely fluid' can be divided continuously at any point. This would be opposed to, for example, the atomist theory of indivisible parts of matter that are absolutely 'hard'. Given that Leibniz is committed to the infinite division of matter, it would seem to follow that he is also committed to the absolute fluidity of matter: matter that can be infinitely divided can surely be divided at any point. In fact, however, Leibniz does not think that matter is absolutely fluid, and distinguishes his theory from, for example, Descartes' theory of absolutely fluid matter. According to Descartes' theory, matter is absolutely fluid because the parts of matter are always *separable*: they can always exist independently of one another. However, Leibniz relegates this theory to the same category as uniform motion: both remain useful as abstractions, but absent from reality.

> I think that perfect fluidity is appropriate only to primary matter – i.e. matter in the abstract, considered as an original quality like motionlessness. But it does not fit secondary matter – i.e. matter as it actually occurs, invested with its derivative qualities – for I believe that no mass is ultimately rarefied and that there is some degree of bonding everywhere. (Leibniz 1996: 222)

In opposition to Descartes, then, Leibniz claims that matter is not absolutely fluid because there is always 'some degree of bonding' or an element of inseparability between the parts of matter. This is the first place in *The Fold* where Deleuze mentions a tendency for Leibniz's philosophy to break the connection between separability and *real distinction*: while two parts of matter are inseparable, they may nevertheless be really distinct (LP 8). This theory is an important part of Deleuze's reading of Leibniz in *The Fold*, and we'll see the claim that 'real distinction does not imply separability' return in its most important form in the question of the separability of soul and body. But how can we reconcile the inseparability that exists between parts of matter with infinite division? The answer, Deleuze thinks, is the inorganic fold. First though, let's look at this idea of inseparability in more detail.

We have already seen a weak sense in which parts of matter may be said to be inseparable: each is open to an environment which determines its particular curved movement. Matter is inseparable from the influence of this environment, unless we consider it in abstraction. But this sense of inseparability does nothing to explain

Material Folds

the resistance to division which prevents matter from being absolutely fluid in the Leibnizian sense. This requires a stronger sense of inseparability, which designates the *coherence* or *cohesion* of the parts of matter. Matter can only be 'absolutely fluid', Deleuze writes, if it completely lacks coherence. Parts of matter in a relationship of coherence thus attain at least some degree of 'hardness' or resistance to division. In this state, they are called masses, aggregates or bodies. The fact that all bodies maintain a degree of hardness (the coherence or inseparability of their parts) is thus why matter cannot be absolutely fluid. Leibniz writes:

> We should think of space as full of matter which is inherently fluid, capable of every sort of division and indeed actually divided and subdivided to infinity; but with this difference, that how it is divisible and divided varies from place to place, because of variations in the extent to which the movements in it run the same way. That is what brings it about that matter has everywhere some degree of rigidity as well as of fluidity, and that no body is either hard or fluid in the ultimate degree – we find in it no invincibly hard atoms and no mass which is entirely unresistant to division. The order of nature, and in particular the law of continuity, equally pull down both alternatives. (Leibniz 1996: 59)

This feature of bodies, that they have 'some degree of rigidity as well of fluidity', we can call the *elasticity* of bodies, the second fundamental notion or material trait Deleuze finds in Leibniz. This leaves us with two questions. First, how can we make sense of infinite division, if some parts of matter are inseparable from each other? Second, what is it that determines the relationships of coherence between the various parts of matter and allows them to form masses, aggregates and bodies?

According to Descartes' theory, when matter is continuously divided it dissolves into a series of non-extended points that are entirely separable from one another. An infinite number of these independent points constitutes the continuum of matter. Above, this fluid matter was opposed to the atomist theory of absolutely hard atoms. In fact, however, these theories are similar in so far as they both posit some kind of *separable minima*: whether finite bodies in the case of the atomists, or an infinite number of non-extended points in the case of Descartes.[3] Leibniz, however, opposes this idea of separable minima in each case because he thinks, as we've just seen, that there is 'some degree of bonding everywhere'.

Central to Deleuze's reading of Leibniz is thus the rejection of the idea of 'minimal elements' that can stand independently of each other:

the division of matter does not leave us with atoms or points. Instead, infinite division is reconciled with the continued coherence of matter by replacing these separable minimal elements with an infinite number of inseparable *folds*. Thus, Deleuze writes: 'The unit of matter, the smallest element of the labyrinth [the continuum of matter], is the fold, not the point' (LP 9). With this, Deleuze makes the concept of the fold a crucial part of how we understand Leibniz's material continuum. By extension, as we'll see, it becomes a crucial part of a new understanding of the first feature of Deleuze's Leibnizian structure: the differential continuum that lies at the base of the 'world' prior to its envelopment in expressive subjects. The image of the fold illustrates that when we divide a mass or aggregate we are not left with individual, isolated parts, but rather with an infinity of smaller and smaller masses, each of which retains some measure of coherence, or a relationship with other parts of matter. A single 'fold' is a relationship between two or more parts of matter: they are folded into or over each other in such a way that they become inseparable. At no point, therefore, do we reach an independent single atom of matter or a Cartesian point, but always parts that are already related to or folded over one another in order to form an aggregate or a mass. In other words, matter is always *composite*, and never *simple*. 'The fold is always between two folds, and this between-two-folds seems to happen everywhere' (LP 19).

With the introduction of this new idea of folding, the way we think of the infinite divisibility of matter needs to be adjusted. Traditionally we might imagine a process of breaking things apart, like the image of cutting something in half over and over again. Folding, however, gives us a different image. Opposed to Descartes, the 'labyrinth of the continuum' or the continuous nature of matter should not be understood as a straight line which dissolves into independent points, but like an infinitely folded piece of fabric or a sheet of paper. This image, which is crucial to Deleuze's account of the fold, comes straight from Leibniz himself: 'The division of the continuous must not be taken as of sand dividing into grains, but as that of a sheet of paper or a folded tunic, in such a way that an infinite number of folds can be produced, some smaller than others, but without the body ever dissolving into points or minima' (Leibniz 1903: 614–15).

However, we can imagine a folded sheet of paper or tunic in two different ways. The folds could be neat and orderly: carefully folded in half in order to fit into an envelope or drawer. Or they could be far less orderly: the paper could be scrunched into a ball and the tunic stuffed into a box. Again, then, we find an opposition between

Material Folds

straight, uniform lines and curved, non-uniform lines. Deleuze criticises Descartes for searching for the 'secret of the continuous' in rectilinear paths, ignorant of the 'curvature of matter'. Leibniz's folds of matter, by contrast, are curved, Baroque folds, like the draping cloths that characterise Baroque sculpture, or the tunic which has been stuffed into a box. Matter is like one of these pieces of cloth: it is folded, but not folded neatly over itself; rather it is furled, crumpled and creased as if compressed and squeezed. If we 'zoom in' on one of the creased folds, we do not find a smooth section of fabric, but always another fold. The fabric is already folded at every point, just as matter is already folded into coherent masses at every point.

This leaves us with a second question: why is the smooth cloth of matter disturbed and forced to crumple? Or in other words, what causes the coherence or folding of matter in the first place? The tunic in the box is folded because it is compressed and squeezed by the sides of the box. Similarly, the folding of matter is caused by the influence of 'compressive forces' that act on every piece of matter. Here we return to the second material trait of the Baroque: weight or pressure. Baroque architectural forms are 'almost crushed by pressure', and now we can say the same thing of Leibniz's material bodies. In fact, we have already introduced this concept of compressive force, but above we referred to it as the 'influence of a surrounding environment'. There, this influence explained the curved movement of bodies: it is the pressure of the environment which 'boxes in' a body and forces it to move in a non-uniform way. But this compressive force of the environment also plays a second role: its pressure is what forces the parts of matter to fold over each other and form relationships of coherence. The parts of matter thus form masses thanks to compressive force, like metamorphic rocks formed by the pressure of the earth. But what exactly constitutes this compressive force? When it comes to curved movement, the 'surrounding environment' can refer simply to other bodies: the rolling cannonball's movement responds to rocks, the grass, the air and so on. But this is not enough to explain the pressure which applies to every part of the universe. A force acting on any single part of matter can be explained by its surroundings, but there must also be a compressive force acting on the *totality* of matter. This is a much more complex issue, and refers to the state of the world itself. Just like the bodies that populate it, we can say that the world must have a unique curvature or 'bent': The box that contains the fabric of matter has its own curved shape. In his 1986 lecture Deleuze says: 'With Leibniz the world is fundamentally affected by a curve, [...] a curvature of the universe' (16/12/1986). We will not address this yet, but the shape of this box, or the curvature of the world, is the result of the principle of perfection, or in other words of God's choice to realise the most perfect possible world. And the reason the world *must* be curved, Deleuze will argue, is ultimately so that it can be enveloped within the monads which come to express it.

This universal compressive force is not enough to explain folding on its own, however. Or rather, it is not enough to explain the complex folded structure of matter. If an unrestricted compressive force were to relentlessly push 'inwards', then matter would be crushed into a single point. In fact, however, there is a counteracting force, or something within matter which pushes 'outwards' just as compressive force pushes inwards. This resistance comes from a spring-like force within matter itself, pushing back against the pressure of its surroundings. The French word Deleuze uses is *ressort*, which suggests not just spring, but a kind of motivating spirit. Deleuze borrows the term from Gueroult, who describes the *ressort* of bodies in Leibniz's metaphysics. For now, we can take this term in its most literal sense, as if matter really were like a spring that pushes outwards unless it is compressed by an external force. Again, we recall Wölfflin's identification of a tendency for Baroque artistic forms to 'overflow' or 'burst' out of their frames (or at least to try). It is as if our analogical piece of cloth had a springy, spongy texture – it pushes against the sides of the box that holds it, and if it weren't for the pressure of the box it would spring out and all of its creases would unfold. The result is a matter which is 'cavernous' or porous. It is not dense, but 'spongy', containing endless interior spaces, pierced with passages and surrounded and penetrated by the subtle fluid of matter. Hence Deleuze's reference to the use in Baroque architecture of travertine, which results in 'spongy, cavernous forms'. Gueroult writes: 'How can we conceive of "the spring" ["*le ressort*"] if we do not suppose that the body is composite, and thus that it can shrink by flushing [*chassant*] from its pores the subtle particles of matter which penetrate it, and that in turn this more subtle matter can expel from its pores another more subtle matter, etc. to infinity?' (Gueroult 1967: 32). Matter is thus subject to two opposing forces: endlessly pushing outwards as a result of its own spring-like nature, and endlessly pushed inwards by the compressive force of the universe. And the result is an endless folding of matter into and over itself.

Material Folds

But perhaps the most important point of all this for Deleuze is that it is not a static tension: the folds of inorganic matter remain constantly animated, full of endless turbulence and vortices. This is our third Baroque material trait: the dynamism of 'quivering' transitions and 'generous whorls'. In effect, then, this is the return of the 'restlessness of the infinitely small' that we found so important in the last chapter. The word Deleuze uses for the folds of inorganic matter is *repli*. But this word carries with it a crucial secondary meaning. The *replis* of matter refer not just to folds, but to the infinite *retreat* or *withdrawal* of matter in the face of our attempts to give it a clear contour, or a static form. Each time we think we have found a sharp boundary, it turns out to 'quiver', become blurred, and refer us endlessly to deeper and deeper folds. In his lecture on *The Fold*, Deleuze describes matter as 'a power which never stops folding / withdrawing [*replier*]' (16/12/1986).

The inorganic fold thus has two defining characteristics. First, it implies the *inseparability* of whatever is folded. In this case it's the parts of matter; below it will be the mind and the body, the spiritual and the material, the intelligible and the sensible (again, however, this inseparability does not necessarily entail that we cannot make a real distinction between the two). Second, what is folded is folded *to infinity*: each fold dissolves into further folds, and with this comes the restlessness of the infinite nesting of differences which forms such a crucial part of Deleuze's reading of Leibniz. With this image of folding we are better placed to understand the importance of folding not just for Deleuze's reading of Leibniz, but for his characterisation of the Baroque as a whole. On the first page of *The Fold*, Deleuze is clear that it is not just a general idea of folding that defines the Baroque, but specifically the fold which 'goes to infinity': 'the Baroque curves and bends folds, pushes them to infinity, fold upon fold, fold within fold. The Baroque trait is the fold that goes to infinity.' Finally, we note that when taken together, these two characteristics (inseparability and infinity) imply something else: an inability to clearly distinguish the boundary between two things. Here we were only concerned with the boundaries between the parts of matter, but the same idea will return with greater force in Deleuze's claim that 'we cannot tell where the sensible ends and the intelligible begins' (LP 88).

We've seen that matter is folded into inorganic masses or aggregates. While the parts of these aggregates are coherent, this coherence is forced upon them by the compressive force of the world that surrounds them. In this sense, inorganic folds are determined externally, or from the outside: the individual part of matter plays no role in determining how it is bent and buffeted around by the pressures of its environment. For this reason, Deleuze gives these inorganic folds an additional name: 'exogenous folds'. But there is another type of fold operating within the material lower level of the Baroque house – an 'endogenous folding' particular to organisms and organic matter. With this, Deleuze's account of Leibniz begins to emphasise themes of enfolding and envelopment, which will culminate in an account of souls themselves.

5.4 Baroque Biology and the Organic Fold

For Deleuze, the relationship between inorganic matter and organisms in Leibniz's philosophy is one more instance of the kind of relationship we encounter repeatedly throughout *The Fold* and which we first saw in the last section. On the one hand, the two are *distinct*: organisms behave very differently, and are subject to different kinds of forces and laws, than the masses or aggregates of inorganic matter we have just been discussing. But on the other hand, the two are implicated with and folded into each other, in such a way that they become *inseparable*. 'Distinct but inseparable' is one of the defining characteristics of the fold as a concept, and *The Fold* as a book.

We saw above that inorganic matter is best described as made up of folds rather than independent points or atoms. The result is a matter which always retains some level of coherence, cohesion or complexity. Because of this complexity, Deleuze claims, there is 'an affinity of matter with life, with the organism' (LP 9). The complexity already inherent in matter provides a propensity for the development of life. If organisms are defined in part by the complex relation of their parts, then their formation would remain an 'improbable mystery' or even a miracle if matter simply dissolved into independent points without any cohesion. Life becomes increasingly likely, however, given the 'infinity of intermediary states' already present in the folds of matter. Deleuze gives the analogy of trying to form a coherent word or phrase by randomly assembling individual letters. This process is far more likely to result in a recognisable word or phrase if, instead of individual *letters*, we begin with already-formed *syllables*. Deleuze also references Leibniz's *Protogaea* to support this point. The *Protogaea* is a lesser-known text in which Leibniz speculates about the history of the Earth. In it, he argues that God's creation of the structure of the Earth echoes the structure of animals or plants: 'There is no doubt that *something like* the formation of plant or animal occurred when the creator wove the first fabric of the tender earth' (Leibniz 2008: 25. My emphasis.).

However, Deleuze's reading simultaneously maintains a fundamental difference between the inorganic and the organic; namely, that the organism is endowed with some degree of *interiority*. Unlike the 'exogenous folds' of inorganic matter, the organism has an interior determination, and is thus characterised by its own 'endogenous' or interior folds. With this, we are introduced to the second type of fold at work in *The Fold*: folding as an *envelopment*. Our first image of folding (the crumpled piece of fabric) is no longer adequate to grasp this second type of folding. A new image is needed: the enveloping fold is more suitably represented by a piece of paper that is neatly folded over itself towards its centre, reducing in size each time, in order to form an *envelope*. It is the fact that the organic fold envelops something that creates the interiority that defines organisms. Organisms are enveloped (folded) and developed (unfolded) in order to attain their own measure of internal determination. But what exactly is it that is enveloped? We'll find the answer in Deleuze's claim that Leibniz's commitment to a theory of *preformationism* (sometimes just *preformism*) makes organisms into a type of 'baroque machine'.

Leibniz argues at various points that organisms are a kind of machine, albeit of a very different kind than the mechanical, man-made machines we are used to. While we can construct complex mechanical machines that contain a vast number of parts, an organism is 'infinitely machined' because each of its *parts* is also a machine (and each of the parts of this machine is a machine, and so on). Discussing the differences between 'the mechanisms of the Divine Wisdom' (organisms) and the 'greatest masterpieces of the craft of a finite mind' (mechanical machines) Leibniz writes: 'A machine made by human art is not a machine in all of its parts [. . .] But the machines of nature, living bodies, are still machines in their smallest parts, into infinity' (PPL 649).[4] We might at first assume that the 'machines' that make up the parts of an organism refers simply to its various cells and organs. But Leibniz's claim is much bolder: they are other complete organisms. Leibniz writes: 'If matter is arranged by divine wisdom, it must be essentially *organised* throughout and there must thus be machines in the parts of the natural machine into infinity, so many enveloping structures and so many organic bodies enveloped . . .' (PPL 589). Thus, each organism envelops an infinite number of other organisms, which themselves envelop yet more organisms, and so on. Deleuze adopts one of Leibniz's favourite metaphors: it is as if every part of every organism harbours within its interior a pond that is full of fish. And each of these fish itself contains an infinite number of ponds with an infinite number of other fish, and so on. It is easy to see the influence on Leibniz of the seventeenth century's first microscopes, with their revelation that even the smallest drop of water is teeming with life. The organic fold thus refers first of all to this process of envelopment in which organisms are infinitely 'nested' one within the other.

But the organic fold also refers to the state in which each one of these enveloped organisms exists: as enveloped, it is 'folded' in on itself, like a tiny seed. What's more, each of these enveloped organisms has the potential to be *un*folded, or *de*veloped. The unfolding of an organism is its transformation from a completely folded, seed-like state, into a developed state. Above, where we looked at the inorganic fold, unfolding was a relatively unimportant operation: to unfold one of the inorganic, exogenous folds that makes up the fabric of matter leaves us with just another set of folds. But the unfolding or development of organic, endogenous folds refers to the actual growth or development of an individual organism. According to Leibniz, an organism does not *create* other organisms. Rather, its progeny develop or unfold from within, where they had already existed in an enveloped or folded state as one of the infinite number of organisms that occupy its interior. This is Leibniz's theory of 'preformationism': organisms are always already completely formed, but they lie dormant within another organism until the time comes for them to be developed. He writes: 'The formation of organic animate bodies appears explicable in the order of nature only when one assumes a preformation already organic, I have thence inferred that what we call generation of an animal is only a transformation and augmentation' (Leibniz 1985: section 90). An organism is therefore not *born*; but rather developed: 'Animals and all other organised substances do not at all begin when we believe them to and their apparent generation is merely a development' (PPL 455). In other words, not every fish is forever confined to its pond; some emerge into higher waters.

Deleuze emphasises Leibniz's preformationism precisely because he so often describes it as a process of folding and unfolding. Thus, Leibniz writes that an organism is 'transformed through the different foldings which it undergoes' (PPL 455) and that 'there is no transmigration of souls but only a transformation of the same animal,

Material Folds

as its organs are differently folded and are more or less developed' (PPL 456). The terms envelopment and development return us to the concepts of folding and unfolding. And so do two other terms: involution and evolution. These words refer not to the various folds of an individual organism, but to the *species* as a whole. The evolution of a species is understood as the same type of unfolding. Deleuze writes: 'The first fly contains all the flies to come, each being called in turn to unfold its own parts, when the time comes' (LP 13). Each organism in a species is infinitely and instantaneously folded at the creation of the world, but the species itself unfolds finitely and slowly, as the universe itself unfolds.

Leibniz's theory of preformationism, of course, strikes us as far-fetched. The idea of tiny animals being nested within each other is bizarre. Indeed, the preformationist theories of Leibniz and his successors did not survive their encounter with newer, opposing theories of *epigenesis*. Epigenesis maintains that the early development of organisms, their morphogenesis, is a process of progressive differentiation: the initially homogeneous, undifferentiated interior of an egg gradually develops into cells and organs. Here, the organism is not preformed, and it does not refer back to a specific pre-existing organism; it refers instead to a general outline that provides guidelines and tendencies for its development. And unlike preformationism, this development is not just a matter of growth or augmentation, but a process of moving from the general to the increasingly specific.

Deleuze tries, however, to hint at a number of ways in which certain aspects of Leibniz's preformationism may be redeemed. The theory of preformationism, Deleuze claims, is perhaps how the Baroque period conceived of the same 'truth' that epigenesis refers to today; and this truth is to 'conceive of the organism as a fold, an originary folding or bending' (LP 15). Given this fundamental similarity, therefore, the only real difference between Leibniz's preformationism and modern epigenetics lies in their different conception of folding. And here, Deleuze thinks, maybe preformationism even has an advantage. If the process of epigenesis is a process of folding, then it is a process which *produces* or hollows out folds from an initially *non-folded*, smooth field. The folds of epigenesis are 'pushed up from a relatively spread out and unified surface' (LP 15). By contrast, the fold of preformationism always ensues from another fold: every fold originates in the interior of a similarly folded organism. Abstractly, then, Deleuze claims that the fold of epigenesis is a 'differentiation of an undifferentiated', while the fold of preformationism, by contrast, is a 'difference which is differentiated', or a differentiation of the already differentiated. Deleuze here makes interesting (perhaps questionable) use of some Heideggerian terms: the fold of epigenesis is an *Einfalt*, or a 'fold-of-one', whereas the fold of preformationism is a *Zwiefalt*, a 'fold-of-two', or a fold between two. When viewed in this way, Deleuze thinks, it is less certain that preformationism is obsolete. With this idea of the *Zwiefalt* or fold-between-two, we are returned to the key characteristics of Baroque folding as such. And this final discussion makes it clear that the endogenous fold shares the same key feature as the exogenous fold: it continues to infinity. Here it is not an infinite inseparability, but an infinite internal envelopment.

5.5 The Fold-between-the-two

Matter is thus folded twice, once under compressive or elastic forces, and once again under 'plastic' (LP 15) organic forces: the inorganic fold and the organic fold. The inorganic and the organic, Deleuze writes, are like two vectors whose tendency is to move in opposite directions. The inorganic tends towards larger and larger masses, forced together by compressive force and operating purely mechanically. The organic, as it folds inwards, tends towards smaller and smaller masses, where an 'individuating machinery' operates. We can make two points about this. First, despite the way they have been introduced, the inorganic fold is not primary; it is not the foundation from which the organic arises. Organisms themselves do not simply spring out of inorganic matter: there is never a point in time where we transition from an inorganic mass to an organism, as if the inorganic was transformed into the organic. Rather, the emergence of an organism always refers back to another, already formed organism from which it unfolds. An animal does not emerge spontaneously from the earth; it is born. And the seed that grows into a tree has always come from another tree. Second, the universe is not a giant organism. Organisms envelop other organisms in their 'interior milieu', but it is not the case that all organisms are enveloped in the interior milieu of a universal organism. While organic folding continues infinitely in an 'inwards' direction, in the sense that every organism contains other organisms, it does not continue 'outwards', in the sense that not every organism is contained within a higher level organism. The organism is infinitely folded, but not infinitely unfolded.

A particular picture therefore begins to emerge. The two sorts

Material Folds

of forces, the two sorts of folds, masses and organisms, are 'strictly coextensive'. There are no fewer organisms than parts of inorganic matter. Leibniz writes: 'There is no part of matter which is not actually divided and does not contain organic bodies' (PPL 590). We can explain this by returning to the image of the fishpond. 'Each part of matter', Leibniz writes, 'can be thought of as a pond full of fish' (PPL 650). Organisms are therefore everywhere, even while the pond itself is inorganic: 'One cannot say that every portion of matter is animated, any more than we should say that a pond full of fish is an animated body, although the fish are' (PPL 586). The interior milieu of an organism is therefore made up of 'parts' which are inorganic, although these parts, like ponds, always contain more organisms. In turn, the 'parts' of these organisms themselves are more inorganic masses. While an organism might seem distinct from the inorganic, then, when we 'zoom in' on an organism all we find is a particular arrangement of inorganic masses (the ponds): masses that have been organised. How then is the organism distinct from these inorganic masses? If the fish is nothing more than an organisation of inorganic masses, what does its existence consist of? The answer is that the organism *just is* precisely this particular organisation, enveloped under a *unity*. The organism is a collection of inorganic masses that has been given a boundary, but it is not a mass itself. Instead of a mass, which is a being by aggregation, the organism is a true unity. In so far as an organism is a particular organisation of masses, everything can be explained in terms of mechanical, material plastic forces. Everything, that is, except the unity which an organism possesses. To explain this unity requires introducing the concept of the soul.

Deleuze ends the first chapter of *The Fold* with the claim that the unity of an organism is explained only by reference to a soul. We should not let the use of this term conjure up religious themes just yet, however. For now at least, the souls in question are animal souls. In fact, we can just as well call them 'principles of life', and below we will even call them 'active forces'. An animal soul provides a unity around which plastic forces can perform the synthesis of the organism, or the organisation of inorganic masses. The unity of every organism thus refers to the unity of the animal soul that 'inhabits' it:

> I perceived that it is impossible to find the principles of a true unity in matter alone or in what is merely passive, since everything in it is but a collection or aggregation of parts to infinity. Now a multitude can derive its reality only from the true unities, which have some other origin and are entirely different from points, for it is certain that the continuum cannot

be compounded of points. To find these real unities, therefore, I was forced to have recourse to a formal atom, since a material being cannot be at the same time material and perfectly indivisible, or endowed with true unity. (PPL 454)

We can think of this habitation almost literally: the animal soul, or the 'formal atom' is localised in the organism (or perhaps, as we will see just below, 'projected' in the organism). This means that however the organism is transformed, and even when it 'dies' (which, as we have seen, is just as much a re-folding or diminishment), it contains the same soul. But we have also seen how, as part of the theory of preformationism, every organism has always existed, albeit largely in a folded, seed-like state. This means that the organism's animal soul, as well, must have always existed along with it. When the time comes for an organism to develop, it unfolds, and as it does so its soul is opened up to its material surroundings ('a theatre', writes Deleuze) and perceives and feels in accordance with the degree of unity that it brings to its organic body. Not only, therefore, is the organic body inseparable from the soul which is the basis for its unity, but the soul is inseparable from its body, which it relies on for its particular point of view.

This leads to a strange picture, however. What happens to organisms that are folded like seeds in the body of Adam, and that are destined to eventually become human bodies? Human souls, we'll see, are reasonable souls, and as such are clearly distinguished from animal souls. But when a human body is still folded away somewhere deep inside Adam, is its soul nevertheless a 'reasonable' soul? Leibniz thinks not. Even a seed that is destined to become human only has an animal soul until it unfolds and reaches a degree of organic development suitable for man, which means, according to Deleuze, a state of development in which it can form 'cerebral folds'. It is only then that its animal soul 'becomes reasonable'. The human soul therefore has a complex relationship with its body. On the one hand it is inseparable from its body, and always contains an element of 'animality' that entangles it with the folds of matter. But on the other hand it is able to achieve a degree of development which allows its elevation to a world of reason, so that it rises above all other folds. A tension exists between the body's crushing, gravitational materiality and the soul's metaphysical elevation. This is another instance of the generalised tendencies, one heavy and one weightless, which characterise the Baroque. The reasonable soul's elevation moves it to a different realm, a different level or stage: 'the theatre of matter has been replaced by that of minds, or of God' (LP 17). With the introduction of the soul, therefore, our discussion moves to the 'upper', metaphysical level of the Baroque house. But if the soul is above, and its body is below, how are they related? The answer lies somewhere in the claim that, just like the parts of inorganic matter, the soul and the body are 'really distinct but nevertheless inseparable'. Once again Deleuze is making use of this key Leibnizian doctrine. The two levels of the Baroque house are distinguished as part of 'one sole and same world': two floors of the same house. Despite this, with the introduction of this upper level, we must think of the 'localisation' of the soul in the body in its own particular terms. The soul is not *contained* in the body; it is rather a projection, from above to below – from the upper level to the lower level. This is in conformity, Deleuze notes, with the projective geometry discovered by Desargues, a Baroque mathematician.

The upper level of the Baroque house is introduced to accommodate elevated, reasonable souls. But in fact we must go back and reinterpret animal souls in light of what we have just seen. Although Deleuze's account compels us to move our attention to the metaphysical level of the Baroque house only with the introduction of reasonable souls, in fact it turns out that the more primitive animal souls introduced above also reside on this upper level. The reasonable soul and its body are really distinct, in so far as they belong to two different levels, but they are nevertheless inseparable. Similarly, Deleuze thinks that just as animal souls are inseparable from the organism they unify, so too are they really distinct. The way Deleuze reads back and refigures his earlier discussion of animals souls in light of his introduction of reasonable souls is typical of his exegetical style in *The Fold*. An initial, tentative introduction of a set of concepts is gradually rendered more complex until it folds back on itself and reinterprets what came before in light of new developments.[5]

Like reasonable souls, then, the location of an animal soul in the body is a matter of 'projection'. Below, everything happens mechanically, in a machine-like fashion. Plastic forces are called 'derivative forces', and are defined purely in relation to the inorganic masses that they organise. They generate an interiority, but this is only an 'interiority of space, not yet of the notion' (LP 12). They enclose on the inside what was previously purely outside or exogenous; but they must refer to 'true interiorities which are elsewhere'. These are souls which, by contrast with derivative forces, are 'primitive forces', or 'immaterial principles of life' – they refer to the inside of an organism, and are defined 'by analogy with the mind'.

But Deleuze doesn't stop there. Not just organisms, but even inorganic masses refer to 'souls' on the upper level. What could this mean? A body (as an inorganic mass), as we have seen, follows a 'curved' movement purely under the impulsion of the first kind of force we looked at: compressive forces. We may now also call these 'derivative' forces that operate purely on the lower, material level: they determine the curve of the body through the mechanical action of other bodies, which act as obstacles in its environment. Without these other bodies in the way, a body left all alone would move in a straight line. But the same situation arises as with plastic forces and organisms above. Derivative, compressive forces explain everything about the movement of a body except its unity. The unity of a curved, variable and irregular movement is 'always an affair of the soul' (LP 12). It refers to a 'superior unity', which exists on the upper level. But this unity pertains to the inside of the body, no longer its external determination which is the realm of compressive forces. It contains the 'law of curving', or the law of folds and of changes in direction. In 1702 Leibniz writes: 'I have frequently shown with regard to bodies themselves that although there are mechanical reasons for the details of phenomena, the final analysis of the laws of mechanics and the nature of substances compels us to resort to active indivisible principles' (PPL 578).

Deleuze relies on Gueroult (1967: 204–5) to explain this complex point. While we can explain a straight movement in terms of an internal spontaneity, we cannot explain why this movement would ever change, or why it would ever become curved. But Gueroult makes the point that this is simply because a scientific grasp of the body is always partial. It is because some element of the 'spontaneity' of bodies escapes us that we must resort to a science of interactions and collisions in order to explain curved movement. But, from the perspective of the whole universe, this curved movement is explained internally, because the body's future state is predetermined within it. From the perspective of the 'Whole', the body's curved movement results from its internal spontaneity, not from its compression by an environment. Only from the abstract perspective of physics is the body's curved movement explained in terms of interaction with other bodies.[6]

The same movement, therefore, is simultaneously determined from the outside, by the shocks and collisions of the environment, related

Material Folds

to derivative force, and also from the inside, where it is unified by primitive force. When viewed in terms of the outside determination, the curve is always accidental: it is a deviation from the straight line which is the body's natural inclination. But when viewed from the inside determination, or in Gueroult's terms the view of the Whole, it is primary. The motive force which causes movement is therefore understood by the physicist mechanically in terms of a surrounding environment, and by the metaphysician from inside, metaphysically, in terms of the harmony of the body with the whole universe. As far as the physicist is concerned, the body is a mass or a being by aggregation, while for the metaphysician it is a unified substance. We must never lose sight of the fact that the relationship between the soul and the body is never directly causal. It takes place 'from the point of view of pure unity or of union, independently of all causal action' (LP 16). Leibniz writes: 'There is no need to say that the soul changes the impulses of the body, and we can readily conclude also that it is just as unnecessary to assume that the material mass sends thoughts to the soul' (PPL 578). Rather, there is a 'non-causal correspondence' at play, or a kind of parallelism, not dissimilar from the one we introduced in Part I.

The point of this is that if we want to *explain* movement, we must turn to the soul, or principle, which unifies it, and in particular we must explain the soul's *own* curvature. The soul has its own curve, and Deleuze also calls this a fold. It's not the same as the curved movement of bodies, but Deleuze will apply the model of folding here as well: there are 'folds in the soul' just as there are folds in matter. This curve explains why each soul is unique, and why it behaves how it behaves. It is the principle of its individuality.

Here, we can step back and see the return of some ideas that were introduced as far back as *Expressionism in Philosophy: Spinoza*, and which we discussed in section 1.6. There, we saw how Leibniz's critique of Descartes involved supplementing mechanism with a theory of active forces, positing an 'inner nature' of bodies which unifies their movements. Now, however, we are in a position to go further, and ask where the soul's own curve or fold comes from. The perspective of the 'Whole' returns us to the question of the *world* in which each body resides. To explain why each soul has the particular curve that it has, requires explaining the structure of the world. Here, we are not in wholly unfamiliar territory: this 'world' is an ideal space, just as in Part II, and what characterised this ideal space there was its particular *distribution of singularities*, determined by a process of vice-diction. It was these singularities which defined monads; they were the events included within a monad that constituted its concept or notion. They were, in effect, what individuated each monad and made it unique. We find exactly the same process at work in *The Fold*. Just as singularities determined monads in the last chapter, there is something equivalent in *The Fold* that will determine the unique curve or fold of each soul. Deleuze introduces it in the opening sentence of the second chapter: 'The ideal genetic element of the variable curve, or the fold, is inflection' (LP 20). It will soon become clear that the 'point of inflection' corresponds to what Deleuze had in *Difference and Repetition* and *Logic of Sense* called a *singularity*. Turning to the point of inflection thus marks the return of the singularity, the second key feature of Deleuze's Leibnizianism.

Notes

1. Does a more unified reading of Leibniz also mean a more scholarly one? We find varying opposed positions. For instance, Adam Wilkins argues that Deleuze's interpretations of Leibniz 'tend to involve a sort of systematic reconstruction that is not too tightly tied to the text under discussion' (Wilkins 2008: 134), whereas Dosse quotes the Leibniz specialist Michel Fichant: 'In rereading *The Fold*, I've realized that Deleuze is far more faithful to Leibniz than we might have thought' (Dosse 2013: 451).
2. This is a good moment to explain why I will rely on references to the French edition of *The Fold* over the next two chapters. The crucial thesis that two things can be really distinct while remaining inseparable is first mentioned at LP 17, where Deleuze writes: 'L'âme et le corps ont beau être inséparables, ils n'en sont pas moins réellement distincts.' Even though the soul and body are inseparable, they are nevertheless really distinct. However, the current English edition of *The Fold* translates this sentence as: 'The body and soul have no point in being inseparable, for they are not in the least really distinct' (Deleuze 2006: 13). According to the current translation, then, the body and soul are not inseparable, and they are not really distinct. This is a reversal of Deleuze's claim and, if we were to rely on it, it would make his overall argument concerning the relation between the upper and lower levels of the Baroque universe much harder to understand.
3. 'The atomist hypothesis of an absolute hardness and the Cartesian hypothesis of an absolute fluidity are joined all the more by sharing the same error, by posing separable minima, whether under the form of finite bodies, or whether as infinity under the form of points' (LP 9). I argue in this section that the 'form of finite bodies' refers to the atomists, while the 'form of points' refers to Descartes. Niamh McDonnell and Birgit

Kaiser both instead suggest that the 'form of finite bodies' should be attributed to Descartes (McDonnell 2010: 66, and Kaiser 2010: 212).
4. See also, *Principles of Nature and Grace*, section 3: 'And this body is organic when it forms a kind of Automaton or Machine of Nature, which is a machine not only as a whole but also in the smallest parts that can be noticed' (PPL 637).
5. This style is not exclusive to *The Fold*. We often find Deleuze using phrases like 'We were too hasty when we said ...', or 'It turns out that ...', as he returns to and reinterprets his own earlier accounts. It also adds to the difficulty of understanding any of Deleuze's work unless each train of thought is carried through to its conclusion.
6. Gueroult relies on the following key passage from one of Leibniz's letters to De Volder: 'All change comes not from outside, on the contrary, there is in all finite substance an internal tendency of change, and the change could not be born naturally elsewhere in the monads. But in the phenomena or aggregates, all new change derives from a contest of shocks, conforming to laws derived, in part from metaphysics, in part from geometry; because the abstractions are indispensable for the scientific explanation of things. After this, we consider in the mass, the singular parts as incomplete and assume that each only receives partial action, and it is only in the concurrent action of all that the whole is achieved. So we think that each body tends itself towards the tangent, but that, by the continual action of other bodies, its real movement is produced following a curve. But in the substance itself that is complete per se and envelops all things, is contained and expressed the construction of the curved line itself, because all the future is predetermined in the present state of the substance. Between the substance and the mass, there is thus as big a difference as that between complete things as they are as such and incomplete things such as are received by us, by abstraction. These incomplete representations allow us to determine in phenomena which action must be assigned to such part of matter, and to distinguish and explain all things by reasons: which necessarily postulates abstractions' (Leibniz 1880: Vol. II, 252–3. My translation. For an alternative translation see PPL 528).

6

Spiritual Folds and the Upper Level of the Baroque House

Deleuze uses the upper level of his metaphorical Baroque house to reintroduce the ideal space of singularities which we described in detail in Chapter 4. It returns in *The Fold* couched in a new language of folds and points of inflection, but most of its elements remain familiar. We can introduce points of inflection by considering a simple curved line, like an 'S' shape. Just as in previous chapters, we treat this curve purely as a geometrical figure, regardless of what it represents. On this curve, as we saw in Chapter 4, there is a certain point that stands out from the others as remarkable or singular. There we called it a singularity; here in *The Fold*, Deleuze calls it a 'point of inflection'. We can identify it precisely by calling it the point on the curve where the curve changes direction. Mathematically, we say that the curvature of the curve changes sign, from negative curvature to positive curvature. Imagine the curve is the path taken by a car: the point of inflection, halfway through the journey, is the moment when the steering wheel switches from left to right, or vice versa. Initially, however, Deleuze turns to art, rather than mathematics, to explain points of inflection, and in particular to the theory of Paul Klee.

Just like in chapter 1 of *The Fold*, Deleuze initially approaches the central issue of the chapter from an angle, through a more-or-less analogical discussion of art. Unlike chapter 1, however, we're no longer dealing with Baroque architecture, but with an expressionist painter. This is important for two reasons. First, there is the obvious fact that Paul Klee is not a Baroque artist. Above, our comparisons between Baroque architecture and Leibniz's conception of inorganic matter were justified by appealing to universal traits, expressed by, but by no means limited to, Baroque architecture. Now, for the first time, we are confronted with the possibility that Baroque traits are not even limited to the Baroque period itself. Deleuze writes that Klee's emphasis on the point of inflection in any given line or curve demonstrates his 'affinity with the Baroque and with Leibniz' (LP 20). The third chapter of *The Fold* and the question it poses ('What is Baroque?') tries to show how Baroque traits are easily identifiable

Spiritual Folds

in artistic and philosophical works produced outside of the narrow period of history that the Baroque strictly refers to. This means that Deleuze's references to later figures (and Klee is only the first) should not just be read as notable yet ultimately inconsequential instances of Leibniz's lasting influence. Instead, as legitimate expressions of the Baroque in their own right, these surrounding figures can help us interpret Leibniz's philosophy, just as certain features of Baroque architecture help us understand Leibniz's conception of matter. Second, we wonder if there is some significance to the fact that in this chapter Deleuze draws on painting rather than architecture. Architecture was ideally suited for a comparison with Leibniz's theory of matter: both are described in a language of masses, spaces and weight. But now that we've begun to ascend away from the material and towards the spiritual side of Leibniz's philosophy, Klee's abstract painting seems more appropriate.

6.1 Klee, Cache and Points of Inflection

Deleuze places Klee in opposition to his colleague, Wassily Kandinsky, and draws a parallel between this and the opposition between Leibniz and Descartes. Both Klee and Kandinsky identify the 'point' and the 'line' as the two initial core elements of painting. But Kandinsky is Cartesian, Deleuze claims, because his points are not a mathematical abstraction; they have extension, colour, density and so on. They are 'hard'. Such a point becomes a line only when it is impelled to move by an external force, and by default it moves in a straight line unless acted on by more than one force. Even when it does change direction, its angles are also 'hard': the change in direction is sudden, leaving us with a sharp corner. Deleuze contrasts this to Klee's Leibnizianism. For Klee, the point is always a point of inflection, like those we introduced above. The point of inflection is like the 'cusp' of a curve, or the point where a line changes direction. Here, Deleuze calls it a 'point-fold', indicating that the point of inflection is also the point where a line is folded. To distinguish Klee's point-folds from Kandinsky's hard points, Deleuze takes as his model the first three figures of the 'active line taking a stroll' which opens Klee's *Pedagogical Sketchbook*, reproduced on page 21 of *The Fold* (Klee 1968: 16).

The first of Klee's figures is a simple curved line, with its points of inflection. The second figure shows us that this curved line is never isolated. Rather, it is always mixed and intermingled with other curves, even in its smallest parts. The line is therefore not a figure with a 'hard', precise or clear outline. Here Deleuze detects an affinity with Leibniz's rejection of isolated straight lines and separable bodies, which we looked at in detail above. Leibniz writes: 'we can never assign to a body a certain precise surface, as we can do if there are atoms' (Leibniz 1880: Vol. II, 119).

The third figure 'marks the shadow of the convex side' of the curve at each point. This highlights the concave side, or the side facing the centre of curvature around which the line curves. Each segment of a curved line has an 'inner-facing' (concave) and 'outer-facing' (convex) side. Which side is concave and which is convex is defined by the location of the locus of the curve, or the point around which the line is curving. But these sides swap at every point of inflection. Another way of defining points of inflection, then, is as those points where the side of the line which was facing outwards becomes the side which is facing inwards towards the centre of the curve.

But this third figure is also significant because it highlights for the first time the importance of 'centres of curvature'. Later in chapter 2, Deleuze draws his own rough sketch of Klee's curved line, this time with the centres of curvature explicitly marked (LP 27). These centres of curvature constitute a new kind of point, not found on the curve itself, but rather a kind of *perspective* on a certain section of the curve. These centres of curvature will return below as the 'site' or point of view which eventually comes to be occupied by a soul or monad.

Besides Klee, Deleuze finds another opportunity for an explanation of inflection, this time borrowing terms from Bernard Cache's architectural work *Earth Moves*.[1] Deleuze turns to it here in order to provide a bridge between the artistic presentation of inflection we have just seen in Klee, and the more traditional mathematical presentation found in Leibniz. From Cache, Deleuze extracts four key properties of the point of inflection. First, the inflections of a curve are *intrinsic singularities*. These are opposed to extrinsic singularities, which would be the 'extrema', or in other words the maximum and minimum, or the peaks and troughs, of a curve. Unlike extrinsic singularities, intrinsic singularities do not refer to coordinates: they are indifferent to the values of the axes of the coordinate system within which the curve is embedded (Cache 1995: 16). Second, points of inflection correspond to what Leibniz calls an *ambiguous sign*. Deleuze makes much of this term in Leibniz, but for now we

Spiritual Folds

will restrict ourselves to its mathematical definition. In mathematical terms, points of inflection are points where the curvature changes sign. If we were to assign the movement of our car a positive number every time we are moving to the left, and a negative number every time we are moving to the right, then the point of inflection is where the value of our movement changes from a positive to a negative number, or vice versa. The inflection is like the point at which the steering wheel is completely straight. At that moment it is neither left nor right, and its sign is therefore 'ambiguous'. The law of continuity prevents us from simply saying the value of the curve is zero at this point, as we will see just below. Third, points of inflection are *weightless*, writes Deleuze: there is not a 'vector of gravity' or an external impulsion to move in a certain direction. Finally, the inflection is the *ideal Event* of the line, where something 'happens' to it. As the ideal event or the virtual singularity, the point of inflection provides the 'commencement' of this world, or as Klee writes in a different text, it is the 'locus of cosmogenesis' (Klee 1998: 56). The point of inflection is the condition for the reality (not just the possibility) of a precise curve, whose form it determines.

In our discussion of points of inflection so far we've only been considering a very simple curve, the 'S' shape of Klee's first figure. However, as Deleuze's discussion of Cache continues, we see that the point of inflection is actually located on 'an infinitely variable curve'. What does this mean? For an initial definition Deleuze references Helge von Koch, who defined one of the first 'fractal' curves. Koch calls this 'a continuous curve without tangent' (Koch 2004: 25), thus conforming to the Baroque requirement of 'rounded' angles. We are already familiar with the themes of continuity and irreducible complexity that are bound up with our theory of curves. Just as we can never isolate a single part of matter, so we can never isolate a single point on a curve. However far we 'zoom in', we always find a deeper level of intermingling and complexity. The curve varies infinitely, or is infinitely variable, at every point. This kind of curve, Deleuze writes, is 'more than a line and less than a surface', and it envelops an infinitely 'spongy or cavernous' world (LP 23). The model provided by Koch's curve is inadequate, however, precisely because as fractal it is defined by a law of similarity. Each additional level of the curve's complexity is determined by its self-similarity, and the only thing that distinguishes each part from any other is its particular size in relation to the rest. But this all changes, Deleuze claims, when we consider variation in terms of 'fluctuation' instead of internal similarity. Limited to similarity, infinite variability referred to the fact that between any two points we can discover a new point, no matter how close they are. In other words we can always descend to, or zoom in on, a part of the fractal curve between two copies and find a new copy. By contrast, fluctuation means that any interval between two points contains the potential (or 'latitude') to 'add a detour' or to be the site of a new folding. Whenever we think we have identified a contour, or a straight edge (a tangent), it dissolves or fades in front of our eyes and is replaced by 'formal powers of the material' which 'rise to the surface' and present us with 'detours and supplementary refolds' (LP 23).

What becomes of the point of inflection when it is located on an infinitely variable curve characterised by fluctuation? Each point of inflection itself harbours a new detour. The point of inflection is thus, Deleuze thinks, 'vortical'. It operates through a perpetual 'delaying' of itself, or a postponing of the change in direction of the curve. The curved line ends up being endlessly folded into a spiral, never reaching the point of inflection. This spiralling, vortical, turbulent line perpetually defers the point of inflection. At the same time, the line itself has a 'fractal mode of constitution'. Here, however, the term fractal does not refer to a similarity of form, but to an infinite nesting of vortices themselves. Repeating the third element of Wölfflin's architectural analysis which we looked at in the last chapter, Deleuze writes that each turbulence is fed by further turbulences, and because we never find a straight contour, it only ends like the 'froth of a wave or a horse's mane'. It is, as Cache writes, 'a universal lapping of waves that cannot be represented by a straight line or even a swirl, but only by a surface of variable curvature that is perpetually out of phase' (Cache 1995: 38). In *The Fold*, therefore, the singularity or point of inflection itself becomes vortical.

6.2 Inclusion

The point of inflection is thus a singular point that sits on the curve itself. It is a singularity-event – one of many that together will determine the form of individual curves and thus serve as the 'locus of cosmogenesis', thereby defining the structure of a world.

But we also saw just above that there is another kind of point, which does not touch the line itself, but which is nevertheless defined in relation to it. This is the 'centre of curvature', or the meeting place, on the side of concavity, of all the 'curved tangents' which define the

Spiritual Folds

curve (LP 27). It is the point around which the line curves, and we saw above how Deleuze supplements Klee's diagrams of the curved line with his own diagram which explicitly marks these centres of curvature.

Deleuze claims that this centre of curvature is the 'point of view' that represents the variation of the curve or its inflection. The determination of points of view such as these lies at the foundation of Leibniz's perspectivism, Deleuze believes. Crucially, however, this point of view is not a point of view that belongs to an already-defined subject. Rather, the subject itself is formed by or dwells within the point of view. With this, we see Deleuze returning to one of his most important Leibnizian themes, which in *Difference and Repetition* he called vice-diction and in *Logic of Sense* he called static ontological genesis. The individual subject comes *after* the pre-individual singularities or points of inflection that define a point of view. Here in *The Fold*, Deleuze makes use of a new term taken from Whitehead: the subject is no longer a sub-ject, in the sense of an underlying or standing underneath. Instead it is a 'superject', or something which *arises* out of the point of view.

To explain the concept of the point of view Deleuze turns to a new set of geometrical terms. The point of view is like the tip of a cone, he thinks.[2] If we cut away a 'slice' or a section of this cone, then we are left with particular figures: 'the circle, the ellipse, the parabola, the hyperbola, and even the right angle and the point' (LP 29). All these sections, with the individual figures which result, are the variants of the point of view. These variations are *folded* or enveloped within the point of view, and don't exist outside of it. It is, Deleuze writes, an 'involution'.[3]

Deleuze relies on Michel Serres' comprehensive *Le système de Leibniz et ses modèles mathématiques* to delineate the main consequences of this new theory of conic sections. The key point for Deleuze is the importance of the point of view. For any given domain it is the point of view which establishes truth. It is by assigning a point of view that we 'classify the variation' or 'determine the case'. Thus, in every area of Leibniz's philosophy, physics and mathematics, Deleuze thinks, it is the point of view which serves as the point of jurisprudence or the site of the art of judging. It is always a matter of finding the right point of view, or rather the best point of view, without which there would be disorder or chaos. It is the point of view, in other words, which allows for the determination of the indeterminate.

Deleuze's reading of Leibniz thus takes him from the continuous variable curve with its points of inflection to the points of view on this curve, or from folding to envelopment. This is a move from inflection to inclusion. The course of Deleuze's argument follows what, in the introduction of the last chapter, we saw Deleuze call the 'non-philosophical reading' of a philosopher. In this case, the sensible intuition Deleuze relies on arises from the question 'why is something folded?' His answer is that something is folded only so that it can be put inside something else: 'Things are only folded to be enveloped; things are folded to be included, to be put inside' (16/12/1986). We have seen that points of inflection are folds that define the structure of a whole world of individual curves. Now Deleuze claims that this world is curved or folded in order to be enveloped or included in something. This envelopment no longer refers to enveloping coherence or cohesion, like the egg which envelops organic parts, but to an envelopment of 'inherence' or 'inhesion'. The folded world is virtual, and exists actually only in an envelopment, or in that which envelops it.

A point of view thus serves as the basis for a process of inclusion which envelops a world defined by points of inflection or singularities. But it is not the point of view itself which includes or envelops this world. Instead, the point of view is occupied by a soul or subject, and it is this subject which includes the world. A soul includes that which it grasps, seizes, or apprehends from its particular point of view. Or in other words it includes the points of inflection on which it is a point of view. And these points of inflection and the world they define remain a virtuality which exists only within the subjects which include them: 'Inflection is an ideality or virtuality which only exists actually in the soul which envelops it' (LP 31). The move from inflection to inclusion is thus, for Deleuze, a movement from the virtual to the actual. Inflection defines virtual folds, while inclusion defines the soul or subject which envelops these folds. Deleuze writes: 'The infinite series of curves or inflections is the world, and the entire world is included in the soul under a point of view' (LP 34).

Before looking at enveloping subjects in more detail, we can at this stage distinguish three types of point, or three types of singularity, in Deleuze's reading of Leibniz in *The Fold*. The first is the 'physical' point (LP 32), or the point of inflection of the variable curve. As we have seen, this is not an atom or a Cartesian point. It is a 'point-fold', fractal and vortical – somewhere between a line and a surface. Second, there is the 'mathematical' point, or the point of view. This is the centre of curvature: the place, foyer or site of the conjunction of curved vectors. The third point is the 'metaphysical' point, or the soul or the subject, which occupies a point of view, or is projected into a point of view. The soul is a superior point, of another nature, which corresponds to the point of view.

Subjects or souls are thus a kind of metaphysical point, and Leibniz calls these 'monads'. He takes the term monad from the neo-Platonists, for whom it referred to a unity which envelops a multiplicity. When Leibniz discusses monads as points of view, he often uses the metaphor of a single town, which is viewed from many different angles by different points of view. But this doesn't mean that, for instance, a certain street corresponds to each point of view. Rather, each point of view encompasses the whole town. The point of view thus does not grasp a particular determined street, but rather the variety of all the possible routes or journeys along all streets, from one to another. The town is thus like a labyrinth, but it can be *ordered* by a particular point of view. Similarly, a monad grasps or encompasses the entire series of all curves and inflections, under a certain order. We saw in Chapter 4 that for Deleuze's Leibniz the 'world' is an infinite collection of series which converge with one another. In *The Fold* Deleuze makes this same point slightly differently: the world is the infinite curve which touches at an infinity of points on an infinity of other curves. It is itself the convergent series of all the series (LP 35).

Why, if the world exhibits such universal convergence and harmony, is a single universal point of view impossible? Why does Leibniz insist on an infinity of irreducible points of view and souls rather than a single 'universal spirit' which would occupy a universal point of view and grasp the entire series at once? Although we understand the world as the sum total of all its possible variations and orders, at each moment we must privilege a particular 'partial sequence', like a particular slice of a cone. The partial sequence is like a street belonging to the town, but it is related to the entire town. Each monad includes the entire series, and thus expresses the entire world, but it always expresses more *clearly* a certain small region of the world – a 'department' or quarter, or a finite sequence. Two souls or monads do not have the same sequence, or the same clarified region. While each soul includes the same infinite series, or the same world, it does so according to a particular order following its quarter, department, or region of clear expression.

We mentioned briefly at the end of Chapter 4 the importance of two pairs of terms for Deleuze's reading of Leibniz: clear-obscure and distinct-confused. Leibniz breaks the traditional correspondences between these terms, arguing that clarity is found in confusion, while the distinct remains obscure. Here in *The Fold*, Deleuze returns to these terms to describe how monads come to clearly express a certain portion of an otherwise obscure world. To understand the details of this process requires confronting one of the most confusing aspects of Deleuze's account: how do souls come to include the world, if the world exists only within the subjects which include it? Deleuze formulates the problem in the terms of one of his favourite of Leibniz's arguments, found in his letters to Arnauld. There, Leibniz reconciles two positions: On the one hand, the world in which Adam sins only exists within Adam the sinner and within the other subjects which compose this world. But on the other hand, God doesn't create Adam directly, but the world in which Adam sins.

We've seen Deleuze refer to this point often, as far back as *Expressionism in Philosophy: Spinoza*. But this time he characterises it in a new way: the world may be *in* the subject, he writes, but the subject is *for* the world. God produces the world 'before' he creates souls, because he creates souls for the world that he includes in them. The soul is a product or a result – it results from the world which God has chosen. The move from the world to the subject thus leads us to a 'torsion', or a convoluted position where the world only actually exists in subjects, but all subjects relate to this world as to the virtuality which they actualise. This is the difference, Deleuze thinks, between a being for the world and a Heideggerian being *in* the world. Closure is a condition of being for the world, and is what allows the subject to 'represent infinity finitely' (LP 35). The world needs to be put in the subject, so that the subject can be for the world. This 'torsion' constitutes the fold between the world and the soul. In *The Fold*, Deleuze interprets expression in these terms. Expression is a process with two sides: the soul is the expression of the world (actuality), but only because the world is the expressed of the soul (virtuality). Thus God creates expressive souls because he creates the world which they express by including.

One of the key aspects of Leibniz's metaphysics, and one which Deleuze heavily emphasises, is the definition of monads we've just introduced: they are completely 'closed'. Monads, Leibniz writes, 'have no windows through which anything could enter or depart' (PPL 643). But monads, we have seen, are also souls which clearly express a certain region of the world. Deleuze opens chapter 3 of

Spiritual Folds

The Fold with a discussion of the closed nature of monads. This discussion reintroduces the idea of a dark or obscure background against which a monad draws its clear region of expression. We introduced this idea at the end of Chapter 2 (section 2.3) with the image of the boat cutting through the water. Here, Deleuze refers instead to the closed-off, isolated chambers which occupy the upper level of the Baroque house, which serve as an elaborate metaphor for the closed interiority of monads.

Deleuze's account begins with another turn to art. A traditional painting, Deleuze writes, always has an exterior model, and in this sense it is a window: it represents something that is let in from the outside. Deleuze draws on the analysis by art historian Leo Steinberg, who writes in his *Other Criteria* of 'the conception of the picture as representing a world, some sort of worldspace which reads on the picture plane in correspondence with the erect human posture' (Steinberg 2007: 82). A shift takes place, however, when painting begins to invoke images that do not have an exterior model. Steinberg thinks this has been the trend in modern painting since Robert Rauschenberg: 'The pictures of the last fifteen to twenty years insist on a radically new orientation, in which the painted surface is no longer the analogue of a visual experience of nature but of operational processes' (Steinberg 2007: 84). Deleuze thinks that in the case of Rauschenberg, the surface of the painting is no longer a window onto the world, but instead an 'opaque table of information on which is inscribed the encrypted line' (LP 38). The painting is no longer a window onto an outside, but an internal table where lines, numbers and changing characters are inscribed.

Leibniz's monads should be interpreted in a similar way, Deleuze claims. If monads are the closed rooms or private chambers of the upper level of the Baroque house, then they have no window onto an outside world. And yet Leibniz garnishes the interior walls of these rooms with 'linear and numeric tables'. On the interior walls of the monad, windows onto the outside are replaced by internal folds. The Leibnizian monad is a room whose walls are entirely covered with lines of variable inflection. The walls are like stretched canvases which ripple with 'moving, living folds'. Nothing comes in from the outside, and nothing goes out. Rather, everything is drawn from the monad's own interior dark background. Everything that is visible in the monad is purely internal.[4] Regardless of how complicated the 'decoration' of the interior is, however, it is always ordered by the monad's point of view. The infinite curves or folds which move across the interior walls of the monad are grasped or ordered by a particular point of view.

At the end of the third chapter, Deleuze returns to this theme, this time in the context of the use of light and colour in Baroque painting. The difference between light and darkness is a useful metaphor for Deleuze because it is not a straightforward opposition between two strictly divided things or extremes. Rather, there is a mixture of light and darkness at play on each level. The dark background of the interior of monads corresponds, Deleuze thinks, to a development in Baroque painting (LP 44). With Tintoretto and Caravaggio, the white canvas or the white background is replaced by a dark background. This changes the status of the canvas. Things now 'emerge' from this dark background, and are defined by being covered or uncovered, or by gradually coming out from the shadows, rather than by their sharp contours. Colour is now a matter of different levels of shadow.

Monads don't have slots or windows by which light enters. They do, however, have their own internal, 'sealed' light. This light is illuminated when the monad or soul is elevated to the level of a reasonable soul, and produces an area of white light. This white area is the clear region of the monad, or the region of the world which the monad expresses clearly. But this region 'degrades' towards the dark background. From this dark background, 'things' emerge as shadows cast on the white area, shadows which can be more or less sharp, strong or well formed. With this, Deleuze is trying to emphasise two things. First, the monad has its own internal light which generates a clear region, but the contents of this clear region always arise from the obscured dark background which surrounds it. Second, there is no clear opposition between the light and the darkness: light is 'progressive' and 'transmitted by degrees', or in other words there is a continuous and gradual change from light to dark as the edges of the clear region dissolve into the shadows. The clear and the obscure become inseparable, and the idea of a sharp contour becomes impossible.

We are thus faced with the new Baroque concept of *chiaroscuro*, or the clear-obscure. The inseparability of the clear and the obscure, combined in the notion of chiaroscuro, extends beyond painting and can be placed in opposition to Descartes in two senses, which mark him as a 'man of the Renaissance' rather than of the Baroque. First, from the point of view of the physics of light: for Descartes light is characterised by sharp contours and a clear distinction between light and darkness. Secondly, and more importantly, from the point of

Spiritual Folds

view of the 'logic of the idea' itself, where the terms clear and obscure suddenly become more significant. We will return to this below, but the point is that this ambiguity between clarity and obscurity undermines Descartes' sharp division between ideas which are 'clear and distinct' and ideas which are 'obscure and confused'. The chiaroscuro model of light fills the monad as a continuous series which we can follow in two directions. The two extremes of this series are the completely obscured, dark background and the clear, white light. But between these extremes lies the world which is expressed by the monad. The clear region of the monad is illuminated by white light, and gets increasingly darker or shaded towards its edges, eventually giving way to shadows as it spreads towards the dark background of the monad.

The impossibility of pinpointing a clear divide between the clear and the obscure, the light and the dark, reminds us of many of our earlier discussions: matter cannot be isolated because the discontinuity between masses 'dissolves' as matter is divided; while the curve is never a straight line because each point once again dissolves into further points as we 'zoom in'. It is the 'labyrinth of the continuum', a constant theme throughout all of Deleuze's readings of Leibniz. But there is something new going on in *The Fold*, which we haven't seen before. The blurred edges and retreating restlessness of the continuum are extended into the domain of ideas themselves. The confusion is no longer between two points on a line, but between the conceptual and the representational itself: the 'readable' and the 'visible'.

6.3 The Fold of the Baroque World

It's clear that a key to Deleuze's interpretation of Leibniz's monads is this autonomy of their interior – the windowless, doorless monad remains closed off from any exterior. In fact, Deleuze claims, the upper level of the Baroque house is an interior *without* an exterior. At the same time, the lower level of the Baroque house is the opposite: an exterior without an interior. One of the characteristics of Baroque architecture is a new scission between a building's façade and its inside: the independence of the exterior and autonomy of the interior. On this point Deleuze again cites Wölfflin: 'it is precisely the contrast between the exacerbated language of the façade and the serene peace of the interior which constitutes one of the more powerful effects that Baroque art exercises on us' (Wölfflin 1964: 45). We thus have a new set of terms through which the upper and lower levels of the Baroque house are distinguished. The façade, unlike the private chamber of the monad, is 'full of holes': it has doors and windows everywhere. But these doors and windows only open from the outside onto the outside – they never access an interior. The organisms which exist on this lower level do, however, 'sketch out' an interiorisation, Deleuze writes, even if it is 'always in progress and never achieved' (LP 39). A fold passes through the living organism and designates at once the absolute interiority of the monad as the metaphysical principle of unity and closure, and infinite exteriority as the physical law of matter. These are two irreconcilable infinite milieus, Deleuze claims, and relies again on an argument from Michel Serres. Serres writes: 'the domain of the physical, the natural, the phenomenal and the contingent is entirely immersed into the infinite iteration of *open* chains: in this, it is non-metaphysical. The domain of metaphysics is beyond, and *closes* the iteration: it fixes it' (Serres 2001: 762, my emphasis). The monad is thus the fixed point which escapes the labyrinth of continuous matter and 'closes infinitely divisible space' (2001: 762).

If these two infinite milieus (the façade and the interior, the material and the metaphysical, the external and the internal) do not 'touch', there must be a new mode of non-causal correspondence between them. Here again we return to an issue that we first introduced in Chapter 2. On the outside is the body, material and determined by physical laws, while the inside is the soul, harbouring its own spiritual spontaneity. In *The Fold*, the harmony between the two relies on the distinction between two levels. The lower level of the Baroque house corresponds to the exterior façade introduced above. Although on this model it is no longer a pure outside, its key characteristic remains: it is full of holes. These holes are determined by the repeated foldings of a 'heavy' matter. Because it is infinitely pierced, the lower level, writes Deleuze, is an 'infinite room of reception or of receptivity' (LP 41). The upper level, by contrast, is closed. It is a pure interior which, in contrast to the heavy matter below, encloses a 'weightlessness', and is upholstered with the spontaneous folds of a soul or a mind. This does not prevent them, however, from composing the two levels of a single house, or a single world: both are distributed or ordered as a function of a single ideal line or curve: the curve of the world. This curve is *realised* on the lower, material level, and *actualised* on the upper, spiritual level. Despite the fact that there is no communication between the two levels, therefore, the fact that they are determined by this single ideal line means that a 'superior' correspondence between the two levels is always maintained.

Spiritual Folds

This ideal curved line is the fold which passes between the two levels of the Baroque house, or between physical matter and metaphysical souls. Central to Deleuze's arguments in *The Fold* is always this distinction and partitioning of two levels as a unique feature of the Baroque, and of Leibniz's philosophy. Deleuze argues that the Platonic tradition gave us a conception of two worlds, while the neo-Platonic tradition gave us a conception of multiple levels, like a staircase which ascends towards the eminence of the One and descends towards the ocean of the multiple (LP 41). But the contribution of the Baroque is the single world with only two levels, separated by a fold whose repercussions on each level follow different regimes, but remain harmonious. Deleuze begins to capitalise the word fold in order to single out this Fold between the two levels of the world from all the other various folds operating on each level. The Fold distinguishes the two levels at the same time as relating them to each other: it is actualised in the folds which are enclosed by the soul on the upper level, and it is realised in the folds formed by matter on the lower level. There always remains a harmony between the two because it is the same unique Fold which is expressed in each. At the end of chapter 3 Deleuze will write that the 'inner song of the soul' and the 'extrinsic fabrication of the material partition' are expressions of the same thing (LP 49). It is, he writes, a 'perfect accord of the scission'. And yet, what is expressed does not exist outside of these expressions.

The Fold is thus the infinitely variable curve, the ideal line, or the Leibnizian world. As that which is actualised or expressed in individual subjects, it corresponds to the Leibnizian world as an 'ideal continuum' which we looked at in *Difference and Repetition* and *Logic of Sense*. There, however, we only looked at one side or level of this world: the individual subjects or monads which actualise a world through static ontological genesis or vice-diction. But here in *The Fold* we see how this world is also *realised* in material bodies. Thus, whereas in Part II we opposed the actualisation of the world to a theory of possibility in which the world is realised, we now see how *The Fold* reconciles and incorporates both as the two levels of a single Baroque world.

In Part II, we argued that Deleuze develops a particular account of Leibniz's philosophy in order to make use of it in a core part of his own system: vice-diction or static ontological genesis, or the process through which individuals are determined by a pre-individual, sub-representational structure. In other words, Leibniz was brought in to fill a particular role within a broader philosophical system. *The Fold*, however, immerses us in an entirely Leibnizian system. Deleuze's construction of this system, by relying on the fold which 'goes to infinity', emphasises more than ever the lively, Dionysian side of Leibniz's philosophy. The result is an account which begins to look more and more like one more expression of Deleuze's own philosophy. We will see just below that there remains, even in *The Fold*, a point at which Deleuze distances himself from Leibniz. But here, there is nothing which would allow us to immediately determine just how attached Deleuze is to this idea of an infinitely variable Fold which is determined twice: actualised in souls and realised in bodies.

This question is especially interesting because Deleuze turns this discussion of the Fold of the world into an explicit engagement with Heidegger's philosophy, which are rare in Deleuze's work (LP 42). The ideal Fold is a *Zwiefalt*, or two-fold, Deleuze claims. We mentioned this term in relation to preformism when we discussed the unfolding of an organism in section 5.4. There it was used to refer to the differentiation of something which was already differentiated (organisms from organisms). Here in chapter 3 of *The Fold*, the *Zwiefalt* is a Fold which 'differentiates and is differentiated'. On the one hand it distinguishes the two levels of the world, or differentiates between them. On the other hand the Fold itself is differentiated as part of the process by which the two levels are determined: the fold's realisation in matter below, and its actualisation in souls above. Deleuze again claims that the key characteristic of the *Zwiefalt* is that differentiation does not refer to a prior undifferentiated, but refers instead to a difference with two sides, which unfold in relation to one another. In Heideggerian terms, there is a coextension of the unconcealing and concealing of Being, and of the presence and withdrawal of beings. The key point for Deleuze is always that the fold distinguishes two sides, but also relates them to each other. They are really distinct but inseparable, and there is some kind of tension between the two that forces them to stretch into each other, or fold over each other.

6.4 Mallarmé: The Visible and the Readable

As chapter 3 progresses, Deleuze begins to describe the difference between the lower level of realised material bodies and the upper level of actualised metaphysical souls as a difference between the *sensible* and the *intelligible*. For the first time in *The Fold* he turns to literature. Deleuze claims that Mallarmé's understanding of the fold as an operation or 'operatory act' marks him as a great Baroque poet (LP 43). Along with Klee, this is another instance of Deleuze taking the term Baroque and applying it to someone or something outside of the traditional 'Baroque period'. To warrant the Baroque label for Deleuze requires a particular application of the concept of the fold, and Mallarmé's work (Deleuze references *Hérodiade* in particular) is one example. The 'fold of the world' in *Hérodiade* is like a fan, writes Deleuze. When the fan is open it makes the grains or the ash of matter rise and fall and swirl around. We perceive what is visible through this veil of dust, which is full of holes or little gaps caused by the foldings of matter. We are reminded here of our earlier definition of matter as 'cavernous' or 'spongy', and as infinitely divisible. These folds reveal to us a view of the 'town', or an appearance of the world (recall Leibniz's favoured image of perspectivism as a view on a town). But simultaneously they obscure the town, or make its continuous withdrawal apparent, because the hole-ridden dust of matter resists being grasped completely. The 'conglomerate of dust' forms 'collectives of hollows'. In other words, inorganic matter forms masses or assemblages. Deleuze calls them 'hallucinatory armies and assemblies'. The term army is a reference to one of Leibniz's favourite examples of a 'mass' or being by aggregation. They are 'hallucinatory' precisely because they are not true unities, but only masses. They are formed by the foldings of matter, but risk being dissolved if we examine them too closely because they contain nothing more than the 'dust' of infinitely divisible matter. This dust belongs to the sensible side of the fan (or the sensible side of the fold of the world), writes Deleuze. The sensible 'arouses' the dust of matter through which we view everything.

But there is another side of the fan, or rather there is a closed fan. The image of the open fan we just looked at evidently corresponds to the 'open' or external lower level of matter, while the closed fan will correspond to the closed or interior upper level of souls. When the fan is open, as we have just seen, it blows on the dust of matter, and corresponds to matter's own complete openness (cavernous, full of holes and infinitely divisible, or in Serres' terms, composed of 'open chains'). But when the fan is closed, it no longer 'pulverises' matter (making it into dust or ash), but rather folds itself up (like an envelopment): the 'thick layers' of the fan constitute an inclusion which is the 'tiny tomb of the soul'. The closed fan is thus folded like the closed interiority of the monad. The open fan corresponds to the folds of matter through which we see. It is the side of the sensible, or the observable. By contrast the closed fan corresponds to the folds of the soul in which we read. We *see* on the lower level, but we *read* on the upper level. The monad, for Deleuze, is like Mallarmé's concept of the Book. The contents of this Total Book can be rearranged to express every possible relation between things, and similarly, the monad contains every fold, because its 'pages' or 'sheets' can be combined infinitely.

On one side, then, we find the refolds of matter, according to which things are visible. Here we find 'collectives' or aggregates, things like armies or herds of animals, which are 'inanities or fictions' in so far as they are not true unities. These collectives are part of the 'dust of matter', which they themselves are endlessly stirring up. This dust is swarming with holes which 'feed our inquietude, our ennui or our dizziness' (LP 43). In the first chapter of *The Fold*, Deleuze calls matter 'cavernous' and 'spongy'. In the third chapter, the same point is made when he points out that the exterior or the façade is 'full of holes'. But with this comes the sense of frantic activity which Deleuze insists accompanies these characterisations of matter: every cavern contains a vortex; and matter isn't just full of holes, it is *swarming* with holes. The continuous nature of matter doesn't just mean that we must resign ourselves to the impossibility of isolating a particular part of the world and grasping it completely. The swarming of matter confronts us whenever we face the world: it makes us dizzy, or fills us with 'inquietude'.

On the other side, or on the upper level, we find the folds of the soul, where 'we no longer see, we read' (LP 43). What exactly does it mean to read the soul? Leibniz uses the word in section 61 of the *Monadology* to refer to the act of determining what happens to a body. While a monad can 'read' only its own clear region, God can read the entire monad: 'A soul can read in itself only that which is represented distinctly there' (PPL 649). The closed chamber of the monad is thus the enclosed 'reading room' within which the Book of the world is read. We are assured that the two levels of the world are part of the same world, Deleuze argues, precisely because what is visible can also be read, and what is read has its own visible 'theatre'. The Baroque, Deleuze thinks, provides a new type of correspondence or mutual expression between the visible and the readable, the sensible and the intelligible: a new kind of harmony.

6.5 The Neo-Baroque

Ultimately, in *The Fold*, Deleuze once again distances himself from Leibniz. It happens initially in chapter 5, where Deleuze turns to Leibniz's theory of compossibility. His account repeats most of the key points we looked at in Part II: Deleuze insists that incompossibility is not reducible to contradiction, and instead functions according to a theory of convergent and divergent series. And once again, the difference between Deleuze and Leibniz concerns what happens when series diverge.

There is a relation of contradiction between the Adam who sins and the Adam who does not sin; they exclude one another. But there is also another type of relation, not between the two Adams, but between Adam the non-sinner and the world in which Adam sinned. We know that the world in which Adam sinned is included or enveloped within Adam the sinner. It is also included in the infinity of other monads which exist alongside Adam the sinner and which express this same world. There must, Deleuze claims, be a relation of exclusion between this world and Adam the non-sinner – Adam the non-sinner contains an entirely different world (the world in which Adam did not sin). While the relation between Adam the sinner and Adam the non-sinner is one of contradiction, the relation between the two worlds which they include is not. Instead, it is a relation of incompossibility. In a footnote, Deleuze again makes the same claim we are familiar with from Part II: 'It seems to us that the incompossible is in Leibniz an original relation irreducible to any form of contradiction. It is a difference and not a negation. It is why we propose in the following an interpretation that rests only on the divergence or the convergence of series: which has the advantage of being "Leibnizian"' (LP 79).

Just like in his earlier books, then, Deleuze argues that relations of compossibility and incompossibility should be understood in terms of the convergence and divergence of series. The only difference here is Deleuze's new emphasis on series as *curves*. A series is a curved line formed around singular points, and these singular points allow curves to be prolonged into each other. The world is comprised of an infinite number of these series, which are called convergent because they can be prolonged into each other. Again, then, compossibility is grounded in a kind of continuity between series.

Conversely, incompossibility depends on a divergence of series: 'another world appears when the obtained series diverge in the neighbourhood of singularities' (LP 80). A point of discontinuity between two series marks the boundary between two exclusive, disconnected possible worlds. The totality of convergent and 'prolongable' series which constitute a world are all compossible with each other. By contrast, the series which diverge are incompossible, and therefore 'pertain to two possible worlds'.

As we've now seen a number of times, there is a strange relation of priority between monads and the world. Monads are antecedent in so far as the world does not exist outside of the monads which express it. But Deleuze is adamant that, according to Leibniz, God directly creates the world in which Adam sins, and then includes it within individual monads. On Deleuze's reading, the world that God creates is a unique series of points of inflection, events or singularities. The world, Deleuze writes, is a 'pure emission of singularities'. He gives three examples of singularities or events that would be enveloped by Adam: 'to be the first man, to live in a garden of pleasure, and to have a woman emerge from one's own rib' (LP 81). But the choice between a fourth singularity 'to sin', or 'to resist temptation', marks a bifurcation between two incompossible worlds. We thus say that Adam the non-sinner is incompossible with our world because he 'implies a singularity' (or includes a singularity-event) which diverges from those of this world.

But Deleuze also calls the relation between the two worlds a *vice-diction*. Deleuze only uses the word vice-diction twice in *The Fold*, each time as a name for the incompossibility between possible worlds. This is a slight deviation from its use in *Difference and Repetition*. There, as we saw in Chapter 4, vice-diction referred to the establishment of relations between singularities, as well as to the envelopment of singularities within individuals. This definition was broad enough that Deleuze could make use of the term in a later context (as the establishment of 'adjunct fields' and the 'condensation of singularities') while rejecting the exclusive nature of divergence that in Leibniz leads to a theory of possible worlds. Here, though, Deleuze remains strictly within a Leibnizian context, where vice-diction is a process which, by establishing an incompossibility between singularities, simultaneously establishes an incompossibility between possible worlds.

Vice-diction operates, and incompossibility is established, as part the 'divine game' which Leibniz's God plays at the origin of the world. We can again list all the key features of this game. First, the game 'emits' singularities. Second, it prolongs or stretches infinite series

Spiritual Folds

which extend from each of these singularities to all the others. Third, it instantiates rules of convergence or divergence which organise these series into possible worlds. Finally, it includes or envelops the singularities of each possible world within the monads or individuals which come to express that world.[5]

In Part II, we explained how this divine game was criticised in *Difference and Repetition* as one more symptom of Leibniz's remaining subject to the requirements of representation. Here in *The Fold*, however, Deleuze singles out Leibniz's divine game as the first attempt to escape some of these requirements. It is not unusual among great philosophers, Deleuze claims, to posit some kind of calculus or divine game which takes place at the origin of the world (LP 82). But all too often, he thinks, these games function according to a 'too human' set of rules. Deleuze is thus criticising, once again, philosophical models which assume a resemblance between condition and what is conditioned: we abstract from our representation of the world and conceive of the ground of the world in the same terms. In Part II we saw how this same criticism lies at the basis of both Deleuze's critique of anthropology in his review of Hyppolite and his critique of representation in *Difference and Repetition*.

But Leibniz's divine game avoids being 'too human', Deleuze thinks, precisely because it is a calculus of infinite series ruled by convergences and divergences, rather than through a logic of contradiction. This calculus, and the relations of compossibility and incompossibility which it establishes, operate on pre-individual singularities in an ideal continuum which escapes the structure of representation and its rules of identity, analogy, opposition and resemblance.[6] But, as we'll now see, for Deleuze, Leibniz's divine game nevertheless remains, at best, a point of transition. The strict partitioning and exclusion of possible worlds in Leibniz's philosophy prohibits the kind of affirmation of divergence which characterises Deleuze's own philosophy.

Deleuze finds the ideal example of this partitioning of possible worlds in the elaborate metaphor that Leibniz constructs in the final three sections of *Theodicy*. There, Leibniz attempts to rewrite Lorenzo Valla's dialogue on free will. He describes a dream that Theodorus has about the fate of Sextus Tarquinius. We are asked to imagine a vast pyramid, which has a summit, but does not have a base, or whose base is lost in mist. Each brick of this pyramid is like its own 'apartment', and each of these apartments is a possible world. The brick that sits at the summit of the pyramid is the best possible world. The pyramid thus represents a hierarchy of the value ('bestness') of worlds. The pyramid does not have a base because the lower worlds are 'lost in the fog': there is no final or last world which we can say is the worst. In each apartment there is a Sextus, who acts out his life as if in a theatre. Next to each Sextus is a large book. One of the pages of this book describes the life of this Sextus in more detail (Sextus' 'clear region' of this world), while the other pages describe all the other events of this world. Once again, there is a combination of that which we see and that which we read which Deleuze think is a trait of the Baroque: in each apartment we see a Sextus, but we also read the book which contains his life and every other event. The apartments of the pyramid differ according to the singularities or events they contain. In one, Sextus goes to Corinth and becomes a famous man, in another he goes to Thrace and becomes king, and so on. In the best apartment, or the one at the summit, Sextus returns to Rome and rapes Lucretia (the event which triggers the downfall of the last king of Rome and the beginning of the Roman republic). Each of these singularities or events diverge from each other, and thus each Sextus is possible, but part of an incompossible world: each apartment is incompossible with every other, and completely closed off from every other.

Following his description of Leibniz's pyramid, Deleuze turns to two other pieces of literature (LP 83). The first is a short story by Borges, 'The Garden of Forking Paths'. There, Borges invokes an imaginary Chinese philosopher-architect called Ts'ui Pen, who invents the image of the 'garden of bifurcating paths', a labyrinthine landscape where every possible moment of decision is mapped. It forms a 'frame' which embraces all possibilities. The second is Maurice Leblanc's *La Vie extravagante de Balthazar*. In Leblanc's novel, Balthazar's quest to find his father armed with three clues leads to a series of encounters with various men, all of whom claim him as their son. Each of these claims appears to be supported by the clues, and we are left with various versions of Balthazar's history, each incompatible with the others but all nevertheless coexisting in the same world.

At first glance, these two stories appear similar to Leibniz's pyramid, in so far as we are presented with a series of possible worlds. But for Deleuze there is a fundamental difference: the literary examples demonstrate an intermingling or entanglement of divergent or incompossible histories. Within the garden of forking paths, every possibility is present at the same time; and while in any given world

Spiritual Folds

Balthazar can only be the son of one of the men, his various histories nevertheless 'develop simultaneously'. Deleuze's references to Borges and Leblanc, with their mutually incompatible but coexisting histories, are thus the first indication in *The Fold* of the return of the fundamental point of divergence between Deleuze and Leibniz: Deleuze affirms the coexistence and communication of divergent series in a way which Leibniz cannot. Leibniz's position is clear: the idea of incompossible events or divergent series coexisting is absurd, and a choice must always be made (or rather, the choice always has already been made) which ensures that only the best is realised.

In Part II, we saw that this necessary choice was criticised by Deleuze in various related ways. In *Difference and Repetition* it was connected to the critique of representation, while in *Logic of Sense* it remained the result of 'theological exigencies'. In *The Fold* we again find a slightly different explanation. Deleuze thinks Leibniz is keen to maintain a vitally important characteristic of God: God does not deceive us. If God allowed incompossible events to exist then he would be a lying, cheating, deceiving God (like the tramp in the Leblanc novel whose lies turn out to be the cause of the intermingling of incompatible events). For Leblanc and Borges, the 'game' of worldly origins has no rules: every possibility exists. By contrast, Leibniz's God gives rules to the game, which state that possible worlds cannot pass into existence if they are incompossible with the world which God has chosen.

Leibniz's Baroque philosophy, claims Deleuze, is positioned precisely at the point of a crisis in 'theological reason'. The Baroque position tries desperately to save the theological ideal, even while it is attacked on all sides by a world which threatens to 'lose all its principles' (LP 90). Thus, by the time of Nietzsche and Mallarmé we get a very different 'game of the world'. Theirs is a game, Deleuze thinks, based on the model of a dice-throw. The difference is that this game refers to a 'world without principle', and the dice-throw is thus an affirmation of chance. The result is that Nietzsche and Mallarmé, like Borges and Leblanc, 'make incompossibility enter into the same fragmented world' (LP 90).

Notes

1. Cache's work had not yet been published, so Deleuze cites its original working title, *L'ameublement du territoire*. Cache attended many of Deleuze's seminars, which inspired the philosophy behind his own work.

Dosse writes: 'Bernard Cache, a young, recent graduate in architecture from the Lausanne Polytechnical School, came to Vincennes during the 1979–1980 academic year, when Deleuze was starting to discuss Leibniz. "I thought, 'This is it! This is exactly what I'm looking for. I still don't know what it is, but this is it.'" He decided to study philosophy and chose Deleuze as his thesis director. A long dialogue began between them that lasted until Deleuze's death in 1995' (Dosse 2013: 452).
2. For a comprehensive account of Deleuze's references to 'conic sections', cf. Somers-Hall 2012a: 187.
3. Deleuze borrows the term involution from the seventeenth-century mathematician Desargues. For a reasonably non-technical account see Field 1997: 200–6.
4. Deleuze finds parallels for this in Baroque architecture with its cells, sacristies and crypts, where 'what is seen is on the inside' (LP 39).
5. Deleuze thinks that by positing an infinity of possible worlds Leibniz avoids the duality of, for instance, Platonism, which makes our world a reflection of a 'deeper', absolute world. Instead, Leibniz makes our world the only existing world, which rejects or 'repulses' all other possible worlds on the basis that it is the best. Thus, just as Deleuze insists that the two levels of the Baroque house are two expressions of a single world, the theory of possible worlds similarly lends weight to the 'single world' as an important motif in Leibniz's philosophy for Deleuze.
6. Sjoerd van Tuinen aptly summarises this point: 'Events insist and subsist in an ante-predicative modality, in constant communication only with other events and with possible worlds. Precisely insofar as they are considered independently, they make up what Deleuze terms the impersonal and pre-individual transcendental field' (Tuinen 2010: 161).

Conclusion: The New Discord

The depth of Deleuze's reading of Leibniz in *The Fold* allows us to determine the consequences of treating Deleuze's philosophy as a neo-Baroque, neo-Leibnizian philosophy. Such a philosophy still operates within a Leibnizian space of infinite depths, singular events, foldings and envelopments. But the Leibnizian principles governing this space have been overturned.

In Chapter 3, we saw how Deleuze's reversal of Platonism begins with the concept of the simulacrum. Simulacra were the untamed differences that could not be brought within the orderly structure of representation. In Platonism, this meant that they were *excluded*, and it was the role of the Ideas to provide the rules for this exclusion and thereby distinguish between well-founded copies and mere simulacra. With the overturning of Platonism, this regulative role of the Ideas is removed. Instead of being excluded, the dynamic, untamed simulacra serve as the ground for the production of a world of representation.

Deleuze's overturning of Leibnizianism does the same thing. God is no longer present to ensure that the divergent series which are produced by the infinite depths of difference are excluded from one another, and partitioned into possible worlds according to rules of order and harmony. Instead, the divergences produced by difference are allowed to coexist, resonate and communicate within a single world. This reversal thus has two key features, which we've seen at various points in *Difference and Repetition*, *Logic of Sense* and *The Fold*.

First, Leibniz's once-and-for-all divine game is replaced by a perpetual 'ideal game'. This game no longer relies on God as the foundation and origin of the world: 'God ceases to be a Being who compares and choses the richest compossible world; he becomes Process, a process which affirms simultaneously incompossibilities, and passes through them. The game of the world has singularly changed, since it becomes the game which diverges' (LP 111). Crucially for Deleuze, while this game accounts for the genesis and production of representation it is itself 'impossible to deal with in the world of representation' (DR 283).

Second, freed from the requirements of representation and the oversight of a just God, an overturned Leibnizianism becomes, above all, an affirmation of divergence:

> Each series tells a story: not different points of view on the same story, like the different points of view on the town we find in Leibniz, but completely distinct stories which unfold simultaneously. The basic series are divergent: not relatively, in the sense that one could retrace one's path and find a point of convergence, but absolutely divergent in the sense that the point or horizon of convergence lies in a chaos or is constantly displaced within that chaos. This chaos is itself the most positive, just as the divergence is the object of affirmation. (DR 123)

It is only here that Leibniz's philosophical resources begin to run dry, and Deleuze instead takes inspiration from other figures. First from Nietzsche: 'This is the point at which the ultimate origin is overturned into an absence of origin (in the always displaced circle of the eternal return). We oppose this displaced circle to the convergent circle of Leibniz' (DR 283). But above all, from art and literature. In *Cinema 2*, which was written a few years before *The Fold*, the defining trait of the 'crystal image of time' is that it allows the coexistence and communication of incompatible events. This is why Deleuze spends so much time discussing films like *Last Year at Marienbad*, which feature multiple, incompatible versions of the same event or story. The crystal image of time is the image which affirms the divergence of series. In *The Fold*, Deleuze writes that 'divergent series trace in a same chaotic world always-bifurcating trails – it is a "chaosmos", like we find in Joyce, but also in Maurice Leblanc, Borges or Gombrowicz' (LP 111). In a footnote Deleuze makes 'special reference' to Gombrowicz's novel *Cosmos*. This is not the only time Deleuze turns to Gombrowicz in order to find the affirmation of divergence that Leibniz could never allow. In *Difference and Repetition* (123) and *Logic of Sense* (47) Gombrowicz's work is similarly referenced as an example of communication between divergent or 'heterogeneous' series.

The Fold is Deleuze's final and ultimate attempt to put Leibniz's philosophy to use in order to articulate one of his central philosophical concerns. This continues a trend which was initiated by *Expressionism in Philosophy: Spinoza*, and properly underway in *Difference and Repetition* and *Logic of Sense*. Deleuze emphasises some parts of Leibniz's philosophy which, in general, other scholars of Leibniz have treated with the most scepticism. Thus, where ideas such as pre-established harmony, the best possible world, or the

Conclusion: The New Discord

monad 'without doors and windows' are often sidelined by Leibniz's much more respectable discoveries in logic, in Deleuze's hands they become the concepts which, when properly formulated, best express the hidden force of Leibniz's philosophy. The inevitable result of this reading is a version of Leibniz's philosophy which emphasises the tendencies to which Deleuze is most sympathetic: Deleuze presents us with his best of all possible Leibnizes. This is taken to such an extreme in *The Fold* that a Baroque blurring of lines begins to contaminate Deleuze's own reading: situated in a world of infinite depths populated by singular events, it is hard to tell where Leibniz's philosophy ends and Deleuze's begins.

In this sense, then, we would wish to grant Leibniz his rightful place among Deleuze's important historical influences. But Leibniz has a unique status, which assures a more ambiguous relationship than the one Deleuze has to figures like Spinoza, Nietzsche and Bergson. In *Anti-Oedipus*, Deleuze cites his own lineage of 'minor' philosophical figures. But a central part of what unites these figures is their resistance to (or 'falling outside of') major, 'State' philosophy. By contrast, Leibniz stands firmly on the side of State philosophy, as someone motivated above all by the desire to maintain order and harmony. With Leibniz, then, we are perhaps faced with a kind of suppressed presence of the minor within the major.

This helps explains, perhaps, why relatively little has so far been written on Deleuze's reading of Leibniz. If the tendency of Deleuze scholarship is to draw a sharp divide between Deleuze's sweeping criticisms of philosophers like Plato and Hegel and his sympathetic readings of Spinoza, Nietzsche, Bergson and so on, then we must ask: on which side of such a division would Leibniz fall? Deleuze's relationship with Leibniz is never entirely critical or entirely sympathetic, making him hard to place in one of these two camps. As a result, we find little consensus within Deleuze scholarship on how exactly Leibniz's role should be interpreted. Smith lists Leibniz as one of Deleuze's 'canonical philosophers' alongside Nietzsche, Bergson and Spinoza (Smith 2012: 21). Stengers insists that Leibniz 'was never venerated as a Great Man' (Stengers 2009: 29). Williams is more typical, and refers to Leibniz as 'unfinished business' until *The Fold* (Williams 2012: 47).

To resolve definitively this ambiguity would require, I think, a portrait of Deleuze's philosophy that is necessarily broad in its strokes. We could try, as others have, to condense Deleuze's various readings of the history of philosophy into a collection of rejected positions, and another collection of endorsements. But the difficulty in tracing a consistent thread across all of Deleuze's works would force us to resort to over-generalisations. The risk is always that the concepts through which we grasp and classify Deleuze's philosophy remain vague and abstract, cast a net whose holes are too large, and fail to capture what is specific to each of his texts taken in isolation. The result is an understanding of Deleuze's philosophy that itself remains vague and abstract. An overly general and abstract interpretation of Deleuze's philosophy risks, perhaps, implying that at its core there resides a hidden *essence*, which stands behind or above its particular instantiations in various books.[1]

The same view risks implying that Deleuze's work in the history of philosophy lacks importance. If Deleuze is saying the same thing over and over, the argument might run, then his works on historical philosophers are nothing more than a kind of 'ventriloquism' (Hughes 2012: 6). He is speaking through, rather than about, a certain philosopher. If this is the case, then Deleuze's historical works lose much of their significance – their contents either a standard piece of historical doctrine, or a piece of Deleuzian philosophy that is probably better explained elsewhere.

To avoid these dangers of abstraction and external reconstruction requires an *immanent* reading of the individual books in question. When it comes to Deleuze's books on the history of philosophy, this presents its own challenges. It would be too hasty to reduce these historical figures to the status of puppets which are animated only by Deleuze's ventriloquism. But it is also clear these engagements are more than just a scholastic exercise. There is a temptation when discussing Deleuze's reading of Leibniz to treat Leibniz's philosophy as an already-established, orthodox system, indifferent to Deleuze's reading. Such a reading presents us with a 'Deleuze' on the one hand, and a 'Leibniz' on the other, but fail to recognise a third, more elusive figure, whose presence I hope I have begun to make clear in the course of this book: a 'Deleuze's Leibniz', or a new, novel Leibnizian system which Deleuze constructs as a result of his own creative reading.

We've traced a tension between two opposed characterisations of Leibniz in Deleuze's work. On the one hand Deleuze admires this malleability of Leibniz's philosophical system (and the 'slipperiness' of its concepts), but on the other hand he condemns the apparent cowardice in Leibniz's motivation: his commitment to 'never offend established sensibilities'. In chapter 3 of *The Fold*, Deleuze gives his own, final explanation of this tension in Leibniz's philosophy

Conclusion: The New Discord

(LP 46). It is an explanation that requires, once again, properly situating Leibniz as the philosopher of the Baroque. Any 'portrait of Leibniz' is marked by the tension between an 'open façade' and a 'closed interiority', especially concerning how he chooses to present his philosophy. Here, the façade is no longer just a feature of architecture, but a feature of Leibniz's own character – he 'hides behind a façade'. Deleuze takes to heart a passage from Nietzsche: 'Leibniz is more interesting than Kant – typically German: good-humoured, full of noble words, sly, supple, pliant, a mediator, incredibly daring for himself, hidden behind a mask' (cited by Bertram 2010: 153). Deleuze refers to Leibniz's ability to present his philosophy from a particular point of view, 'in this or that mirror', depending on the opinions and the apparent intelligence of his audience. By following this strategy Leibniz is constructing a façade for himself, behind or above which his real system remains hidden, 'turning about itself, and losing absolutely nothing to compromises below' (LP 46). By emphasising certain themes in Leibniz's philosophy, Deleuze is trying to express this 'real' system, which Leibniz himself was careful to keep confined in the chamber with closed doors and sealed windows, lest it disrupt the delicate harmony of the Baroque world.

But we've also seen how, in one key respect, Leibniz always remains distanced from Deleuze, such that there is no question that they belong to two distinct, irreconcilable philosophical epochs. Deleuze develops a theory of disjunctive synthesis, or a communication between divergent series. But this is a position which Leibniz cannot be made to endorse. As the Baroque philosopher *par excellence*, Leibniz stands at the moment before the world loses its principles: 'the splendid moment where we maintain Something rather than nothing' (LP 92). However far Deleuze carries Leibniz in *The Fold*, this still remains the point of divergence between them. This is the final expression of the same general point Deleuze returns to each time he approaches Leibniz. In *Expressionism in Philosophy: Spinoza*, Leibniz was the lesser half of the Spinoza-Leibniz anti-Cartesian reaction because he was too concerned with preserving the glory of God. In *Difference and Repetition*, instead of saving God, it was a way of 'taking the principle of identity particularly seriously', and was connected with Deleuze's critique of representation. In *Logic of Sense* it was a case of Leibniz's being 'hindered by theological exigencies'. Perhaps the most general way of characterizing these remarks is to say that Deleuze condemned Leibniz's philosophical conservatism, summed up by his 'shameful declaration' that new concepts should not 'overthrow established sentiments' (LS 133).

But when Deleuze returns to this point in *The Fold*, there is one major difference: the earlier critical tone is now absent. Leibniz's commitment to a principle of harmony and convergence is no longer viewed by Deleuze as a regrettable symptom of too-strongly-held religious views, political cowardice, or remaining subordinate to the structure of representation. Instead, Leibniz's philosophy is completely appropriate to the Baroque world it expresses. Leibniz's philosophy is no longer inadequate on its own terms, it is only inadequate to the new, 'broken' world that Deleuze thinks has come to replace Leibniz's Baroque world. Above, we saw how the unique point of view of a monad was like a particular slice of a cone. Similarly, Somers-Hall accounts for Deleuze's treatment of philosophical systems by comparing them to conic sections. Depending on the angle of the slice, we end up with different sections of the same cone. And just like conic sections, 'Different philosophical systems are in the same manner objective presentations of the world that nonetheless are incommensurate with one another, each presenting a perspective on chaos while leaving open the possibility of other perspectives' (Somers-Hall 2912c: 7). Deleuze can thus maintain that Leibniz's philosophy is completely valid (as in consistent, complete and 'true' in so far as it is a perspective on the chaos), while simultaneously incommensurable with our own perspective.

With this, I think, we can detect in *The Fold* themes which will go on to be developed a few years later in *What is Philosophy?*, Deleuze's last major work. *The Fold* marks a change in the way Deleuze approaches Leibniz. Instead of a limited application of certain ideas, Deleuze creates a whole Leibnizian plane of immanence – a particular 'slice of the chaos' which characterises the Baroque period. And Leibniz as a philosopher has become the conceptual persona who represents this period. Deleuze will go on to conclude that the history of philosophy is 'the coexistence of planes, and not the succession of systems' (Deleuze and Guattari 1994: 59). Leibniz's philosophy is thus no longer an outdated system that can be straightforwardly rejected. Instead of the 'repulsive' or 'shameful' Leibniz found in *Logic of Sense*, in *The Fold* we find, as Stengers writes, 'a philosophical friend belonging to a time no more' (Stengers 2009: 32).

The philosophies of Deleuze and Leibniz are thus two coexisting slices, each adequate to its own world. But, when faced with

Conclusion: The New Discord

this divergence between their philosophical systems, it is no longer a question of choosing the 'best possible', such that one or other must be excluded or succeeded. To make Deleuze's engagement with Leibniz productive requires affirming the divergence between the Leibnizian and Deleuzian series, and allowing them to resonate and communicate.

Note

1. Henry Somers-Hall has emphasised a similar point: 'The change in terminology between Deleuze's texts is not a superficial aspect of his writing, but signifies the attempt to develop new planes of immanence. None of these projects can be anything but provisional, as they open out onto that which cannot be consistently given all at once' (Somers-Hall 2012c: 7). For a different, perhaps opposing, view we can turn to Joe Hughes' *Philosophy After Deleuze*. There, he describes the 'monotony' of Deleuze's texts: 'there are certain concepts that continually reappear so that a family of rats, a pack of wolves, a rhizome, and the transcendental Idea all come to share the same essential predicates. [. . .] This repetition of predicates across various incarnations suggests that there is a more stable concept, somewhere, animating Deleuze's "cases"' (Hughes 2012: 14). Of course, Deleuze *does* repeat the same themes over and over again across the course of his career, but we shouldn't let this excuse a level of abstraction which neglects the detail and immanent development of his individual books.

References

Antonioli, Manoloa (1999) *Deleuze et L'Histoire de la Philosophie*. Paris: Kimé.
Badiou, Alain (1994) 'Review of Gilles Deleuze, *The Fold: Leibniz and the Baroque*', in *Gilles Deleuze and the Theater of Philosophy*, ed. Constantin V. Boundas and Dorothea E. Olkowski. London: Routledge.
Beistegui, Miguel de (2010) *Immanence: Deleuze and Philosophy*. Edinburgh: Edinburgh University Press.
Bertram, Ernst (2010). *Nietzsche: Attempt at a Mythology*. Champaign: University of Illinois Press.
Bowden, Sean (2011) *The Priority of Events: Deleuze's Logic of Sense*. Edinburgh: Edinburgh University Press.
Bukofzer, Manfred F. (2008) *Music in the Baroque Era: From Monteverdi to Bach*. Read Books.
Cache, Bernard (1995) *Earth Moves: The Furnishing of Territories*. Cambridge, MA: MIT Press.
Couturat, Louis (1901) *La logique de Leibniz: d'après des documents inédits*. Hildesheim: Georg Olms Verlag.
DeLanda, Manuel (2002) *Intensive Science and Virtual Philosophy*. London: Continuum.
Deleuze, Gilles (1956) Qu'est-ce que Fonder? webdeleuze.com/textes/218
Deleuze, Gilles (1980) Lectures on Leibniz, webdeleuze.com/groupes/3
Deleuze, Gilles (1981) Lecture on Spinoza, webdeleuze.com/textes/38
Deleuze, Gilles (1986) Lecture on Leibniz, webdeleuze.com/textes/47
Deleuze, Gilles (1988a) *Bergsonism*, trans. Hugh Tomlinson and Barbara Habberjam. Cambridge, MA: MIT Press.
Deleuze, Gilles (1988b) *Le Pli*. Paris: Minuit.
Deleuze, Gilles (1990a) *Expressionism in Philosophy: Spinoza*, trans. Martin Joughin. Cambridge, MA: MIT Press.
Deleuze, Gilles (1990b) *Logic of Sense*, trans. Mark Lester. New York: Columbia University Press.
Deleuze, Gilles (1991) *Empiricism and Subjectivity,* trans. Constantin V. Boundas. New York: Columbia University Press.
Deleuze, Gilles (1994a) *Difference and Repetition*, trans. Paul Patton. New York: Columbia University Press.
Deleuze, Gilles (1994b) 'The Method of Dramatisation', in *Gilles Deleuze*

References

and the Theater of Philosophy, ed. and trans. Constantin V. Boundas and Dorothea E. Olkowski. London: Routledge.

Deleuze, Gilles (1997) Review of Jean Hyppolite's *Logic et Existence*, in Jean Hyppolite, *Logic and Existence*, trans. Leonard Lawlor and Amit Sen. New York: SUNY Press.

Deleuze, Gilles (1998) *Essays Critical and Clinical*, trans. D. W. Smith and M. Greco. London: Verso.

Deleuze, Gilles (2005) *Cinema 2*, trans. Hugh Tomlinson and Robert Galeta. London: Continuum.

Deleuze, Gilles (2006) *The Fold*, trans. Tom Conley. London: Continuum.

Deleuze Gilles and Claire Parnet (2007) *Dialogues II*, trans. Hugh Tomlinson and Barbara Habberjam. New York: Columbia University Press.

Deleuze Gilles and Félix Guattari (1994) *What Is Philosophy?*, trans. Graham Burchell and Hugh Tomlinson. London: Verso.

Dosse, François (2013) *Gilles Deleuze and Félix Guattari: Intersecting Lives*, trans. Deborah Glassman. New York: Columbia University Press.

Duffy, Simon (2006a) *The Logic of Expression: Quality, Quantity, and Intensity in Spinoza, Hegel and Deleuze*. Aldershot: Ashgate Publishing.

Duffy, Simon (2006b) 'The Mathematics of Deleuze's Differential Logic and Metaphysics', in *Virtual Mathematics: The Logic of Difference*, ed. Simon Duffy. Manchester: Clinamen Press.

Duffy, Simon (2010) 'Leibniz, Mathematics and the Monad', in *Deleuze and the Fold: A Critical Reader*, ed. Sjoerd van Tuinen and Niamh McDonnell. Basingstoke: Palgrave Macmillan.

Durie, Robin (2006) 'Problems in the Relation Between Maths and Philosophy', in *Virtual Mathematics: The Logic of Difference*, ed. Simon Duffy. Manchester: Clinamen Press.

Field, Judith Veronica (1997) *The Invention of Infinity: Mathematics and Art in the Renaissance*. Oxford: Oxford University Press.

Gueroult, Martial (1967) *Leibniz: Dynamique Et Métaphysique*. Paris: Aubier-Montaigne.

Hardt, Michael (1993) *Gilles Deleuze: An Apprenticeship in Philosophy*. Minneapolis: University of Minnesota Press.

Hughes, Joe (2012) *Philosophy After Deleuze*. London: Bloomsbury.

Howie, Gillian (2002) *Deleuze and Spinoza: Aura of Expressionism*. Basingstoke: Palgrave Macmillan.

Hyppolite, Jean (1997) *Logic and Existence*. New York: SUNY Press.

Kaiser, Birgit (2010) 'Two Floors of Thinking: Deleuze's Aesthetics of Folds', in *Deleuze and the Fold: A Critical Reader*, ed. Sjoerd van Tuinen and Niamh McDonnell. Basingstoke: Palgrave Macmillan.

Kerslake, Christian (2002) 'The Vertigo of Philosophy: Deleuze and the Problem of Immanence', *Radical Philosophy*, 113 (May/Jun), pp. 10–23.

Kerslake, Christian (2009) *Immanence and the Vertigo of Philosophy: From Kant to Deleuze*. Edinburgh: Edinburgh University Press.

Klee, Paul (1968) *Pedagogical Sketchbook*, trans. Sibyl Moholy-Nagy. London: Faber and Faber.

Klee, Paul (1998) *Théorie de l'art modern*. Paris: Folio essais.

Koch, Helge von (2004) 'On a Continuous Curve without Tangent Constructible from Elementary Geometry', in *Classics on Fractals*. Boulder: Westview Press.

Lærke, Mogens (2010) 'Four Things Deleuze Learned from Leibniz', in *Deleuze and the Fold: A Critical Reader*, ed. Sjoerd van Tuinen and Niamh McDonnell. Basingstoke: Palgrave Macmillan.

Leibniz, G. W. F. (1880) *Die philosophischen Schriften von Gottfried Wilhelm Leibniz*, ed. Gerhardt. Berlin: Weidmann.

Leibniz, G. W. F. (1903) *Opuscules et fragments inedits de Leibniz*, ed. L. Couturat. Paris: Félix Alcan.

Leibniz, G. W. F. (1948) *Textes inedits*, ed. G. Grua. 2 vols. Paris: Presses Universitaires de France.

Leibniz, G. W. F. (1967) *The Leibniz–Arnauld Correspondence*, ed. Haydn T. Mason. New York: Barnes & Noble.

Leibniz, G. W. F. (1985) *Theodicy: Essays on the Goodness of God, the Freedom of Man, and the Origin of Evil*. Chicago: Open Court Publishing.

Leibniz, G. W. F. (1989a) *Philosophical Papers and Letters: A Selection*, vol. 2, ed. Leroy E. Loemker. Dordrecht: Kluwer Academic Publishers.

Leibniz, G. W. F. (1989b) *Philosophical Essays*, ed. and trans. Roger Ariew and Daniel Garber. Indianapolis: Hackett Publishing.

Leibniz, G. W. F. (1996) *New Essays on Human Understanding*. Cambridge: Cambridge University Press.

Leibniz, G. W. F. (2008) *Protogaea*, trans. and ed. Claudine Cohen and Andre Wakefield. Chicago: University of Chicago Press.

McDonnell, Niamh (2010) 'Temporal Interval of the Fold', in *Deleuze and the Fold: A Critical Reader*, ed. Sjoerd van Tuinen and Niamh McDonnell. Basingstoke: Palgrave Macmillan.

Serres, Michel (2001) *Le système de Leibniz et ses modèles mathématiques*. Paris: Presses universitaires de France.

Smith, Daniel (2009) 'Leibniz', in *Deleuze's Philosophical Lineage*, ed. Graham Jones and John Roffe. Edinburgh: Edinburgh University Press.

Smith, Daniel (2012) 'Deleuze and the History of Philosophy', in *The Cambridge Companion to Deleuze*. Cambridge: Cambridge University Press.

Somers-Hall, Henry (2012a) *Deleuze's Difference and Repetition: An Edinburgh Philosophical Guide*. Edinburgh: Edinburgh University Press.

Somers-Hall, Henry (2012b) *Hegel, Deleuze, and the Critique of Representation: Dialectics of Negation and Difference*. New York: SUNY Press.

References

Somers-Hall, Henry (2012c) 'Introduction' to *The Cambridge Companion to Deleuze*. Cambridge: Cambridge University Press.

Steinberg, Leo (2007) *Other Criteria: Confrontations With Twentieth-Century Art*. Chicago: University of Chicago Press.

Stengers, Isabelle (2009) 'Thinking with Deleuze and Whitehead: A Double Test', in *Deleuze, Whitehead, Bergson: Rhizomatic Connections*, ed. Keith Robinson. Basingstoke: Palgrave Macmillan.

Tuinen, Sjoerd van (2010) 'A Transcendental Philosophy of the Event: Deleuze's Non-Phenomenological Reading of Leibniz', in *Deleuze and the Fold: A Critical Reader*, ed. Sjoerd van Tuinen and Niamh McDonnell. Basingstoke: Palgrave Macmillan.

Widder, Nathan (2008) *Reflections on Time and Politics*. Philadelphia: Pennsylvania State University Press.

Wilkins, Adam (2008) *Modes, Monads and Nomads: Individuals in Spinoza, Leibniz and Deleuze*. New York: SUNY Press.

Williams, James (2003) *Difference and Repetition: A Critical Introduction*. Edinburgh: Edinburgh University Press.

Williams, James (2012) 'Difference and Repetition', in *The Cambridge Companion to Deleuze*. Cambridge: Cambridge University Press.

Wölfflin, Heinrich (1964) *Renaissance and Baroque*, trans. Kathrin Simon. New York: Columbia University Press.

Zill, D. G and W. S. Wright (2009) *Calculus: Early Transcendentals*. Sudbury: Jones and Bartlett.

Index

actualisation, 4–5, 41, 51, 54, 62, 102, 108–9, 111–12, 114–15, 156, 158, 162–4
   counter-actualisation, 41, 54, 56
   restituer, 54
adequation, 22–30, 42, 52, 55
analysis, infinite, 4, 88–9, 95–100
anthropology, 3, 64–72, 101, 169
Anti-Oedipus, 175
Antonioli, Manola, 121
Archimedes, 22, 27, 92
architecture, Baroque, 119–20, 122–4, 126–31, 135–6, 152, 161
Aristotle, 75–80
atomism, 34, 132–3, 138, 152

baroque, the, 119–31, 135–9, 141–2, 144–5, 150–1, 153, 160–3, 165–6, 170–1, 178
   neo-baroque, the, 167
Barrell, Stephen, 86, 114
being-for-the-world, 59, 158
Beistegui, Miguel de, 13, 21
Bergson, Henri, 105, 175
Berkeley, George, 93
bifurcation, 6, 104, 168, 170
Borges, Jorge Luis, 170–1, 174
Bowden, Sean, 114
Bukofzer, Manfred, 123

Cache, Bernard, 151–4
Caravaggio, 160
chiaroscuro (clear-obscure), 120, 158, 160–1
clear and distinct ideas, 16, 23–5, 30, 32, 112–13
closure, 107, 124, 158

compossibility, 3–6, 43, 60–1, 63, 88, 95–105, 107–8, 167–9, 173
conceptual persona, 178
contingency, 20, 22, 95–6
continuum, the, 34–5, 50–1, 54–5, 59–61, 84–5, 88–9, 91–2, 95–100, 102–5, 107, 113, 124–5, 128–31, 133–5, 143, 153, 156, 160–3, 165–7, 169
contradiction, 3–4, 9, 61, 64, 66–7, 71–3, 77, 80–4, 96, 99–103, 108, 167, 169
convergence, 4, 6–7, 50, 56, 61, 98–101, 103–5, 107–9, 111, 157, 167–9, 174, 178
correspondence, 36, 44, 46–7, 125, 147, 162, 166
Couturat, Louis, 5
curvature, 89–94, 97, 119, 127–32, 135–7, 146–57, 159, 161–3, 167

DeLanda, Manuel, 114
Desargues, Girard, 145, 172
Descartes, René, 14–18, 22–5, 27, 29–31, 38, 92, 112, 132–5, 151, 160–1
   anti-cartesian reaction, 13–14, 23, 31–2, 35, 37–8, 40–1, 44, 53, 177
dice-throw, 63, 105–6, 171
differential relations, 4, 7, 50, 55, 63, 86, 93–5, 97, 102, 104, 112–13
divergence, 4, 6–7, 61–4, 86, 98–105, 108–11, 167–71, 173–4, 177
divine game, the, 36–7, 61–3, 99, 109–11, 168–9, 173
Dosse, François, 40, 148
Duffy, Simon, 6, 99

Index

Durie, Robin, 114
dynamism, 3, 8, 82, 101, 129, 137

ens perfectissimum, 15–19
envelopment, 86, 103–4, 114, 134, 138–42, 156, 165, 168
Euclid, 22, 27
Events, singular, 6–7, 54, 60–1, 84–5, 96–110, 168–71, 173–5
expression, 4–5, 13–14, 17–18, 21, 23, 26–30, 40–1, 44–55, 59, 61–2, 66, 71–2, 81, 85, 97, 100, 102, 113–14, 134, 149, 157–61, 163, 166–9, 178

Fermat, Pierre de, 92
fluidity of matter, the, 129–33
folds, 10, 102, 114, 119–29, 134–5, 137–51, 154–9, 161–9, 171, 173–8
  endogenous, 138–40, 142
  exogenous, 138–40, 142, 145
  fold-between-the-two, 142
  inorganic, 126–7, 132, 137–8, 140, 142
  organic, 123, 125–6, 138–46, 149, 156, 162, 164
  repli, 137
Foucault, Michel, 75

Gombrowicz, Witold, 174
Gueroult, Martial, 5, 136, 146–7

Hantaï, Simon, 122
harmony, 2, 6–7, 30–1, 34–5, 37, 44, 47, 52–3, 104–5, 123–4, 147, 157, 162–3, 166, 173, 175, 177–8
  pre-established, 5, 36, 49, 174
Hegel, 3–4, 8–9, 64–7, 70–2, 79–80, 82–6, 88, 96, 101–2, 175
Heidegger, 142, 158, 164
Hughes, Joe, 176
Hyppolite, Jean, 64, 66–8, 70–2, 86, 101

identity, 2, 43–4, 46, 56, 61, 69–71, 75–9, 83, 102, 105, 110–11, 169

incompossibility, 3–7, 60–1, 63–4, 88, 96, 98–102, 105, 109, 111, 167–71, 173
infinite divisibility, 34–5, 37, 81, 91, 96, 119, 125, 131, 134, 162, 165
infinitesimal calculus, 2, 4, 88–9, 91–4, 130
inflection, 120, 148, 150–6, 159, 168
involution, 141, 155

Joyce, James, 174

Kandinsky, Wassily, 151
Kant, 66, 69, 101–2
Kerslake, Christian, 10, 38, 66, 86
Klee, Paul, 150–3, 155, 165
Koch, Helge von, 153

Leblanc, Maurice, 170–1, 174

Mallarmé, Stéphane, 122, 164–6, 171
mathematics, Leibniz's, 5–7, 60, 88–92, 99, 103, 129–30, 150–2
matter, infinite divisibility of, 35, 91, 96, 132–4
monads, expression of, 35–7, 45, 47–52, 54, 59–62, 85, 113, 120, 124–6, 157–63, 165–6
  production of, 61, 88, 94–104, 167–8

neo-Platonism, 21, 157, 163
Nietzsche, 76, 109, 171, 174–5, 177
notions, absolute and relative, 19–24, 26–31, 37, 41–2, 50, 53, 85, 95, 119–20

pantheism, 52
parallelism, 44, 147
  non-causal correspondence, 44, 47, 147, 162
perspectivism, 48, 109, 146–7, 152, 155, 165, 178
plastic forces, 142–3, 145–6
Plato, 73–7, 79, 106, 163, 173, 175
Poincaré, Henri, 6
predicates, 42, 75, 77–8, 96, 100, 119–20

preformationism, 139–42, 144
projection, 144–5, 157
Proust, 108

Rauschenberg, Robert, 159
real definition, 15–19, 22, 24, 27, 29, 42, 46, 95, 98
renaissance, the, 119, 123, 127–9, 131, 160
representation, structure of, 29–30, 45, 47, 54, 56, 59, 62–6, 68–9, 72–3, 75–83, 93–4, 100, 102, 105–6, 110–12, 161, 169, 171, 173–4, 178
resemblance, 75, 77–9, 102, 106, 110–11, 169
resonance, 63, 109–11, 125, 173
Rococo, 123

sensation, 102
sense, 54, 66, 67, 70–2, 101–2
sense-events, 54, 102
series, covergent and divergent, 4, 6, 44–5, 50, 61, 63, 98–9, 103–5, 108–11, 156–7, 161, 167–71, 173–4, 177
Serres, Michel, 155, 162, 165
simulacrum, 73–6, 79, 173
singularities, 4–6, 50–1, 54–5, 59–63, 78, 85–6, 88, 95, 97–109, 111–14, 120, 122, 129, 147–50, 152–6, 167–70, 173, 175
  coexistence of, 60, 63, 94, 101, 105, 170–1, 173–4

communication of, 6, 31, 109, 125, 162, 171–2, 174, 177
pre-individual, 60–3, 88, 97–8, 100–2, 155, 163, 169
prolongation of, 50, 98, 108, 167–8
Somers-Hall, Henry, 79, 86, 178
Spinoza, 3–4, 8, 13–15, 18–23, 28, 30–1, 33–5, 41, 44–6, 50–5, 85–6, 175
static ontological genesis, 50, 97, 100, 113, 155, 163
Steinberg, Leo, 159
Stengers, Isabelle, 6, 115, 175, 178
sufficient reason, 2, 9, 14–15, 18, 23, 29–32, 34, 36–7, 40, 42–5, 61–2, 106–7

Tintoretto, 160
Transcendental structure, 4–5, 51, 54–5, 60, 62, 98, 100–2

vice-diction, 61, 62, 63, 64, 67, 73, 82–6, 88–9, 93, 95–7, 100, 103–5, 110, 112–13, 148, 155, 163, 168
virtuality, 5, 51, 54–5, 60, 103, 105, 108–13, 153, 156, 158

Weierstrass, Karl, 6
Whitehead, Alfred North, 155
Williams, James, 115, 175
Wölfflin, Heinrich, 119, 123, 127–31, 136, 154, 161

Zwiefalt, 142, 164

EU representative:
Easy Access System Europe
Mustamäe tee 50, 10621 Tallinn, Estonia
Gpsr.requests@easproject.com

www.ingramcontent.com/pod-product-compliance
Lightning Source LLC
Chambersburg PA
CBHW051118230426
43667CB00014B/2630